# Captive Cities

# Captive Cities

## Studies in the Political Economy of Cities and Regions

*Edited by*

**Michael Harloe**

*Centre for Environmental Studies,*
*London*

Sponsored by the International Sociological Association Research Committee
on the Sociology of Regional and Urban Development

## JOHN WILEY & SONS

Chichester · New York · Brisbane · Toronto

*Library of Congress Cataloging in Publication Data:*

Main entry under title:

Captive cities.

'Sponsored by the International Sociological
Association Research Committee on the Sociology of
Regional and Urban Development.'
    Includes bibliographical references.
    1. Sociology, Urban—Addresses, essays, lectures.
2. Urban economics—Addresses, essays, lectures.
I. Harloe, Michael.  II. International Sociological
Association. Research Committee on the Sociology of
Regional and Urban Development.
HT151.C343        301.36′1        76–44297

ISBN  0 471 99436 7

Photosetting by Thomson Press (India) Limited, New Delhi,
and printed by offset lithography by Unwin Brothers Limited,
The Gresham Press, Old Woking, Surrey.

# Contributors

JORDI BORJA

Centro Estudos Urbanos, Calle Santa Anna 11, Barcelona 2.

ANTONELLA CAMMAROTA

Facolta di Scienze Politiche, Universita di Messina, Messina.

MANUEL CASTELLS

Centre d'Etudes Des Mouvements Sociaux, 54 Boulevard Raspail, 75270 Paris.

NELLA GINATEMPO

Facolta di Scienze Politiche, Universita di Messina, Messina.

MICHAEL HARLOE

Centre for Environmental Studies, 62 Chandos Place, London WC2.

DAVID HARVEY

Department of Geography and Environmental Engineering, Johns Hopkins University, Baltimore, Maryland.

GYÖRGY KONRAD

formerly Academy of Sciences, Budapest.

ELIZABETH LEBAS

formerly Department of Planning, The Polytechnic of Central London, 35 Marylebone Road, London NW1.

JEAN LOJKINE

Centre d'Etudes Des Mouvements Sociaux, 54 Boulevard Raspail, 75270 Paris.

ENZO MINGIONE

Facolta di Scienze Politiche, Universita di Messina, Messina.

RAY PAHL

University of Kent, Canterbury, Kent.

CHRIS PICKVANCE

Centre for Research in Social Sciences, Beverley Farm, University of Kent, Canterbury, Kent.

IVAN SZELENYI

School of Social Sciences, Flinders University, Bedford Park, South Australia 5042.

# Acknowledgements

The principal debt of gratitude must be to the contributors to this book. Without their ready cooperation the complex task of assembling, translating and editing an international collection would have been much more difficult.

Thanks are also due to the translators, Chris Pickvance (the second part of Chapter 2 and Chapter 7), Gray Standen (part of Chapter 4 and the whole of Chapter 5) and Nanneke Redclift (Chapter 10), and also to my secretary, Alison Carling, who typed the manuscript.

Finally, I wish to acknowledge the particular comments and help received in writing the introduction from Ray Pahl, Manuel Castells, Doreen Massey, Chris Pickvance and Enzo Mingione.

M. H.

# Contents

# Introduction

*Michael Harloe*

## 1. New Trends in Urban Sociology; Weberian and Marxist Approaches

In the half-century or so since urban sociology first gained recognition as a distinctive branch of sociology, its state of health has rarely been robust. Indeed, if it was not for the obvious existence of social problems which are located in cities (hence popularly referred to as 'urban problems'), public concern about them and therefore some demand for policies to deal with them, urban sociology might no longer exist as a specific branch of the discipline. However, the growth of the 'urban problem' on a world-wide scale and of state intervention has resulted in a dramatic increase in urban research. Geographers, economists, political scientists, sociologists and others have all sought to make their contributions towards solving their own particular versions of the problem, and governments of every political persuasion have financed them to do so.[1]

It is doubtful whether all this effort has produced much which is of practical or theoretical value. The situation varies to a degree according to the particular discipline involved, and urban sociology has had some impact, especially on town planners and architects. However, very little of this work has been of much value for the development of broader theory, without which any scientific study of society is impossible. If urban sociology has to be sustained on the basis of its ability to predict the room in which members of a particular socio-economic group like to eat their dinner, it becomes, as Rex[2] has pointed out, little more than market research.

In the past few years the ideological nature of much sociology and the uncritical role of the sociologist in the developed societies has been challenged. Many sociologists adopted new theoretical and political positions and some of those who were concerned with urban studies started to reevaluate their branch of the discipline. This activity began in a number of different countries and was carried out by sociologists with widely differing approaches, but a number of them came together at the Seventh World Congress of Sociology at Varna in 1970 to start a discussion of their work and an exchange of ideas and experiences. A new Research Committee of the International Sociological Association was established, the Research Committee on the Sociology of Urban and Regional Development. This book contains revised versions of a series of papers, most of which were presented to sessions of the Committee held between 1970 and 1974, although this introduction contains some references to material which has been published more recently.

The Research Committee's initial position paper stated in a general way the criticisms that it shared with others of much existing urban sociology and contained proposals for a reorientation of the field of study:

'Urban sociologists have been too frequently turned into the handmaidens of those practical professions concerned with making physical changes to the built environment. As a result many urban sociologists have become more concerned with the human relations of the city rather than the sociology of the city: it is as if industrial sociologists had turned themselves into personnel officers.

We believe that urban sociology cannot advance when it has abandoned the central issues which have formed the central focus of the subject: only by a return to these issues can we see a possibility of moving forward in an intellectually fruitful way. It is our task to study society—its distribution of power and other resources, the structural limitations on life chances and the patterns and processes of conflict inherent in the nature of society. We, of course, in this Research Committee are limited to the manifestation of social processes as they occur in a spatial context....'[3]

This was not a new position; sixteen years earlier Ruth Glass had written that the city appeared to be 'the mirror of abstract, impersonal forces—of history, class structure and culture ... [it] represents the reality of both conflict and unity resulting from such abstract, impersonal forces',[4] but her review of current urban sociology which accompanied these comments showed that the significance of this approach was hardly being realized in actual research.[5] However, the Research Committee's more recent statement both reflected and has helped to stimulate the growth of new approaches in urban sociology which, at the same time as they challenge even the subdiscipline to which they claim to belong, do reconnect urban social studies with the central problems and theories of society.

There is a diversity of approaches manifested in the work which has fallen within the broad perspective outlined above. Three of the signatories of the Research Committee's statement, Pahl, Mingione and Szelenyi, have contributed to this volume; some of the substantial differences which exist between their theoretical positions will be discussed below. The papers by Castells, Harvey and Lojkine in particular also display a similar diversity. This introduction will attempt to highlight some of the major aspects of these varied approaches, to compare them and to refer to a number of the problems which they raise. Some of the broader implications of this new development in urban sociology will also be mentioned.

The most useful starting point, because it is the one on which there is a wide measure of agreement among the contributors to this volume, is a critique of 'traditional' urban sociology. The most comprehensive and rigorous (although not unproblematic)[6] version of such a critique has been provided by Castells. He argues that many of the theories and findings of previous urban sociology, particularly the work influenced by the dominant Chicago school, have been heavily and successfully criticized, but usually on empirical grounds.[7] However, few of these critics have been able to put much that is new in the place of the work that they have shown to be inadequate as they have not presented a *theoretical* critique of this work and consequently been able to develop alternative theories. This therefore is the purpose of Castells' major theoretical work to date, *La Question Urbaine*. The first part of the book is mainly critical; Castells reviews a wide range of studies, most of which are American or are dominated by this influence, and shows their inadequacy. The nature of this criticism can be seen in the first section of his paper in this volume. He suggests that much urban sociology, reflecting the conditions of its growth referred to in the first paragraphs of this introduction, is ideology rather than science.

Castells' own comments reflect an Althusserian reading of Marx, but acceptance of his general critique does not depend on this.[8] He suggests that a scientific discipline must have a *scientific* (or *theoretical*) *object* ('a certain conceptual cutting up of reality') or a *real object* ('a specific field of observation'). The study of social mobility is an example of the former type of discipline and industrial sociology of the latter. Urban sociology cannot claim to be founded on either of these types of object. In *La Question Urbaine* he shows that urban sociology can be subdivided into several branches. It has, in principle at least, been concerned, as Park suggested, with 'every social phenomenon occurring in the urban context'. Castells points out that many of these sub-branches do indeed have specific theoretical and real objects, but that these are only called 'urban' because they happen to be studied, sometimes, in cities.

Furthermore, this loose association between the 'urban', i.e. a certain type of space, and a certain type of society has had important consequences. Using Wirth's classic formulation as his example, Castells suggests that urbanism was defined as a specific cultural system 'which was in fact that of the liberal capitalist society in its then current state of historical development in America'. The defining qualities of this urbanism were spatial (size, density and heterogenity); social relations were determined by physical characteristics. The relationship of such a naturalistic urban sociology to the requirements of ruling groups in society is not difficult to see, as Castells remarks: 'urban planning by technocrats replaces the political debates between social groups'. The parasitic relationship of such an ideological urban sociology to the growth of state intervention in urban problems is clear. However, when the nature of the social problems (mainly concerned with social integration and the acculturation of migrants) which formed the original focus of these efforts changed as society developed, this naturalistic sociology was unable to adapt. Therefore it must now be abandoned if progress is to be made.

Castells' own answer to the necessity for a new approach will be referred to below. As already mentioned, it is greatly influenced by a particular type of Marxist theory which is itself challenged by other Marxists (see the contributions here by Mingione, Lebas and Lojkine, for example) and by non-Marxists (of which Pahl's contribution is the main example in this book). Pahl, in rejecting the inadequacies of previous urban sociology referred to above, drew on some of the central concerns and methods of Weberian sociology, such as the role of bureaucracy, the distribution of 'life-chances' and the use of a broad comparative approach, to propose an urban sociology which was based on the recognition that (*a*) there are fundamental spatial constraints on access to resources and

(*b*) there are fundamental social constraints on such access as well.

The combination, in ways which were not theoretically developed by Pahl, of these two factors formed a socio-spatial or socio-ecological system.[10] 'Urban managers' controlled the workings of this system and hence the allocation of life-chances. They were therefore the 'independent variables' of the new urban sociology and the life-chances of the urban populations the 'dependent variables'. This approach, and the more explicitly Weberian but related work by Rex and Moore,[11] has stimulated a major growth of studies which focus on the 'urban managers', but it has also been much criticized.[12] One result of this approach has been the emergence of a type of 'radical' urban sociology which directs its critical attention to the malpractices and incompetence of local bureaucracies.[13] Pahl himself has been increasingly doubtful about the validity of this approach. He has been conscious (quoting Gouldner) of the danger of directing all the attention at the shortcomings of the 'middledogs' while ignoring the far more powerful and important role of the 'topdogs'.[14] In this volume and elsewhere he has now revised his theory.

However, it is useful to refer to some of the problems raised by Pahl's initial formulation, certain aspects of which, as will be seen later, still exist in his current work. In focusing attention on the operations of bureaucrats, in themselves an important element in the study of urban development of course, Pahl failed to relate their activities to any broader consideration of political and social relationships as a whole. Urban sociology was to be concerned with the allocation of 'urban' resources, housing, transport, amenities, and so on. The fact that these were scarce resources was taken for granted, almost as a naturally occurring phenomenon, by Pahl. In fact this scarcity depends on a particular set of social and political arrangements in society as a whole as well as factors which relate more directly to the urban situation. A necessary consequence of this narrow focus was the lack of attention paid to the urban topdogs, which has already been mentioned, and a failure to recognize the importance of conflict between the urban population and the urban controllers over access to resources. (It is interesting to note that Rex, who developed a perhaps more distinctively Weberian approach in comparison with Pahl's early work, paid for more careful attention to the role of conflict in his theory of 'housing classes', but even he focused on conflict *between* these classes in the city rather than considering the origins of the situation in which different groups were forced to enter into competition with one another.)

Pahl's definition of urban sociology seemed to offer the possibility that the discipline would be reduced to a branch of managerial science; better, more sensitive and efficient bureaucracies or (echoing Weber) more politically accountable officials would lead to a solution, or at least an alleviation, of urban problems. Such a conclusion was well suited to the governmental concern with institutional reform which has existed for the last decade or so and the new emphasis in research found some support from these sources. However, as the problems with which they were supposed to deal persisted and even worsened, researchers began to move towards a rediscovery of the importance of more fundamental social, economic and political factors in society as a whole and trace the connections between these factors and the traditional subject matter of urban studies.

Pahl's treatment of space was also problematic. As Castells showed, the Chicago school derived social characteristics from 'natural' factors. Pahl rejected this naturalism but failed satisfactorily to integrate the spatial factor into his analysis. Following an established conception of the factory as a 'socio-technical' system, i.e. a *combination* of social and technical factors (considered therefore as factors which could be separately identified with a distinct and independent existence), he proposed an analogous combination in his concept of the socio-spatial system.[15] From this there follows the conclusion, mentioned above, that urban problems might be alleviated by more efficient bureaucracies, because if space enters as a 'non-social' variable into the determination of patterns of access and inequality, it follows that some inequalities are likely to exist in cities regardless of their social and political arrangements. Pahl still holds to this latter view, as may be seen in his contributions here and elsewhere, but the initial formulation on which it is based lacks precision or theoretical rigour, because the way in which the 'combination' is achieved remains unspecified.

In fact spatial relationships themselves can only really enter the subject matter of urban sociology if it is recognized that they are socially determined (and also, of course, have certain effects as 'socio-spatial' factors). In reality Pahl's identification of certain independent spatially determined urban problems, e.g. those related to the inequalities of access in the concentric urban settlements common to Eastern and Western European cities in an advanced stage of economic development, ignores the fact that such spatial forms are not an essential feature of any such society but are a consequence of a particular organization of economic life, i.e. social factors.[16] Interestingly Pahl now admits that the separation between 'social' and 'technical' that inspired his formulation is doubtful and that technology is not independent of society, but he still suggests that space and society are so separated.[17]

Although these latter considerations still divide Pahl from some other contributors to this volume, the need to base urban sociology on theory which effectively relates urban development to the development of society as a whole is common ground. Anderson[18] has recently summarized the basic elements of this approach suggesting that, although the work now being done is diverse, it has in common a rejection as ideological of the concept of an autonomous urban realm. 'Urban and regional' problems are seen as deriving from more fundamental conflicts which relate to economic growth, social development and political control. This concern with relating problems to an analysis of society which conceives it as possessing a central political and economic dynamic has been called, rather loosely, the 'political economy' approach. Urban sociology therefore becomes concerned with understanding the ways in which this dynamic is expressed in spatial terms.

Clearly, at this stage the continued reference to 'urban sociology' rather than the 'sociology of space' is misleading and apt to invest the term urban with more significance than it now has, being little more than a particular spatial frame of reference which *may* or *may not* have political, social or economic relevance for any given sociological investigation or may merely be an initial context for research, e.g. on a problem which is commonly identified as an 'urban problem'. In no sense does this new approach seek to limit itself to an urban focus (hence the significance of the main French journal which has published much of the recent work, *Espaces et Sociétiés*[19]). This consequence has certain implications which will be discussed in greater detail below.

Marxist theory of capitalist development, which integrates economic, political and ideological factors in the analysis of society (or the social formation), has, unsurprisingly, had a dominant influence on the development of the analysis of the political economy of space.[20] The consequences of this for the existence of a distinctive sociology of space will also be discussed below. Here it is necessary to give an outline of this approach, although this is no easy task beyond a level of generality, given the diversity of distinctive Marxist theories and of their application to the sociology of space. Starting with the central feature of the capitalist mode of production, the fundamental relationship is between those who sell their labour power and produce commodities and those who own the means of production and appropriate the surplus value. This is both an economic *and* a political relationship which is expressed in differing ways in a series of conflicts between the capitalist class and the working class.[21] These conflicts are themselves related in a complex manner but, at base and in ways which require detailed specification, arise from the contradiction which exists between the growing socialization of the productive forces (related to the growth in productivity under the conditions of capitalist competition) and the continued private ownership of capital.

The central relationship is expressed politically in the class struggles which form the historical development of such a society, and in this context the state has a key role in enforcing the dominance of the ruling class and the subordination of the working class, i.e. the reproduction of the capitalist organization of society. This role can in fact only be understood in terms of the class struggle: 'the state . . . should be seen as the condensate of a relation of power between struggling classes'.[22] The consequence is that state actions in any particular situation are not derivable from any abstract propositions about the nature of society in general, or even the capitalist mode of production in particular, although the latter is clearly important. Explanations of such actions can only be given if attention is paid to the specific level of development of political, economic and ideological relations manifested in the class struggle in the situation being examined. Of course various problems arise from this theory, some of which are relevant to the papers in this volume and will be referred to below, but such references must of necessity be partial in an introduction such as this.

Several other features of the Marxist approach are also important. Both the capitalist class and the working class, although they each separately have certain basic unifying interests, are also divided on the basis of their more specific interests and position at a particular moment into different fractions or strata between which conflict can also occur. Furthermore, any given social formation will contain a combination of different modes of production which are complexly related to each other. Thus in capitalist societies, i.e. societies dominated by the capitalist mode of production, other modes of production, e.g. the feudal mode, can exist in a subordinate role together with their distinctive classes and class relations. Once again, the detailed interaction of these elements can only be examined in specific historical situations and the resultant patterns of development are complex. For example, Lenin suggested that up to five different modes of production, in different states of development and in a complex and hierarchical relationship, existed at the beginning of the period of the transition to socialism in Russia.[23] According to Althusser, each mode and each element within each mode develops at a particular rate and is constituted as a series of related contradictions. Such a conclusion seems essential if the observed complexity and path of historical development is to be accounted for. Overall development is therefore uneven and cannot at all be related to the working out of one fundamental (economic or any other) contradiction.

All this has implications for the role of the state, the study of which is central to most of the papers which follow. The various elements in the structure of relations which has been outlined have, as has been implied above, relatively autonomous paths of development. Such developments are only relatively autonomous because they are limited by the 'sum' of the effects that the other elements have on any given element and, in capitalism at least, development (as opposed to revolutionary change) occurs within bounds which permit the continued existence of the basic class relationship of this mode. The state's role is to ensure this continuance, to reproduce capitalism. It follows that state power must itself be relatively autonomous and not permanently identifiable with any one fraction or strata of any of the various groupings in the specific conjuncture. Obviously few Marxists would expect any such identification with the working class anyway. However, this formulation also discounts any long-term action solely in the interests of a single fraction of capital and suggests an explanation of situations in which state power is actually used against particular fractions.[24] To summarize, state power exists to organize the various strata of the ruling class and disorganize the working class in order to ensure the continuance of the capitalist system of domination of the latter class by the former. This political role is manifested in state intervention (or non-intervention) in political, economic and ideological spheres. Because the state is the 'condensate of a relation of power between struggling classes' it is itself split and reflects the contradictions within and between the various elements which have been referred to.

The uneven development of capitalism and its contradictions are expressed spatially—at the global level between countries at different stages of development and in differing relations of dominance and subordination to each other, within countries between different regions and within these regions themselves, e.g. between urban and rural areas and within them.[25] The growing socialization of capitalist production and its concentration in various forms, shapes patterns of urban and regional development. The social contradictions are also manifest in these developments, e.g. between the private ownership of land and the necessity of its appropriation for the purpose of the development of socialized production (for housing, roads, etc.). As the contradictions in capitalism develop, state power is increasingly necessary in order to maintain the system as a whole, and the scope and range of state intervention increases (hence the growth of the state apparatus, the legal system, etc.) and is present in every aspect of social life. The role of the state in urban and regional development, the provision of housing, roads and amenities, the regulation of industrial location, pollution and land use generally, is of increasing importance and is a principal concern of the papers presented here, as are the objectives and struggles of the various classes and fractions which are concerned with these developments, such as industrial and finance capital, land owners, industrial workers, professional groups and rural workers.

Even this broad outline, which can only try to sketch out a Marxist approach, suffers from many omissions and is open to much criticism, but further reference to the large and varied literature which exists on this topic is beyond the scope of this introduction. Furthermore, some aspects of this outline (particularly those which are influenced by the work of Althusser and Poulantzas[26]) would not be accepted by all the contributors to this volume. These points are better taken up with specific reference to their papers below.

It will now be useful briefly to summarize some of the elements which appear to determine the Weberian approach to the sociology of space. This is not so clearly articulated in the literature as the Marxist approach, but Pahl's work supplies the major source in this book. Weber's own direct analysis of the city formed a part of his comparative historical examination of the origins of modern industrialized society (which he largely equated with Western capitalism) in *Economy and Society*.[27] The development of cities independent from a central power and their alliance in the face of that power was a cause and a consequence of the emergence of the bourgeois class and hence of modern society. Weber maintained a distinction (contrary to Marx) between the economic and the political (and the legal) aspects of society; although developments in each sphere had an influence on the others, they were autonomous rather than relatively autonomous. Accordingly Weber could state that he was concerned to develop a political theory of the city and modern society and not an economic one (which could also be developed) or a theory which combined the two elements. His method was to compare political arrangements in a variety of Oriental and Occidental cities in ancient and modern times. (In fact his focus was not nineteenth century urbanism but the first emergence of such cities in mediaeval times.) This apparently historical method, because it only abstracted certain elements of the political organization from their context, in fact approached a fairly advanced level of formal abstraction. Thus, despite certain interesting references to the dominant role played by economic interests in modern cities, Weber could remark (with reference to the similarities in the political organization of mediaeval Italian and early Roman cities) that these occurred because there is only a limited variety of different administrative techniques for effecting compromise between status groups within the city. Therefore similarities in the form of political administration cannot be interpreted as identical superstructures over identical economic foundations: 'These things obey their own laws.'[28] The comparative method here seems to lead to a potentially misleading isolation of common factors in urban development which are formally similar but the social significance of which, for the specific cases of urban development to which they might then be applied, is uncertain. This is because the very process of abstraction from their historical context has robbed them of any connection with these real situations. Such a method is of course not confined to sociology and is a central point in Marxist criticism of the classical economists.

Bendix[29] has suggested that Weber was not concerned to explain how the modern state evolved (this was a job for the historians), but simply to list the institutional prerequisites. Key factors included rational and bureacratic administration and the influence of certain ideas (the 'Protestant Ethic'), and change was related to industrial innovation. Power was defined in individualistic terms ('the probability of a command being obeyed') and not, as in Marx, as class power. Furthermore, Weber, unlike Marx, did not see any apparent distinction between state apparatus and state power, so power and bureaucratic organization are unproblematically linked. The administrative bureaucracies which form the modern state developed interests of their own and Weber's own political life showed the importance he placed on the emergence of political leaders who could curb this power. This is in clear contrast with Marx's view of the state and its relation to economic interests, according to Gerth and Mills:

'in [Weber's] eyes socialism would merely complete in the economic order what had already happened in the sphere of political means. The feudal estates had been expropriated of their political means and had been displaced by the salaried officialdom of the modern bureaucratic state ... capitalist socialisation of the means of production would merely subject an as yet relatively autonomous economic life to the bureaucratic management of the State.'[30]

Thus economic considerations were not the only basis for conflict in society. Class struggles (which Weber, unlike Marx, defined solely in economic terms and related to individual consumption and production) existed but were just one of the forces which underlay social change and the state had an autonomous existence which could not ultimately be linked to such a source. Weber's overall separation of the political and the economic and his conception of their relationship is highlighted by his comment that Marx failed to distinguish between what was strictly 'economic', what was 'economically determined' and what was merely 'economically relevant'.[31] Some of these points will be taken up in the discussion of Pahl's contribution to this book later.

## 2. Epistemological Differences

Some of the most important differences between Marxist theory and therefore Marxist analyses of urban and regional development and Weberian or indeed other analyses derive from their distinctive epistemological and philosophical bases. Many of the debates which occur between Marxist and non-Marxist urban researchers concern questions which at base relate to what is to count as knowledge and how it is produced and is to be understood. Coherent positions on all these issues seem to be rare, and more discussion and thought about them is needed. If the very conception of theory itself differs, discussions which refer to differences between specific theories but which do not take explicit account of this are apt to be conducted in terms which combine considerations relating to these two (i.e. epistemological and specific theoretical) levels in ways which are illegitimate. The few brief comments of relevance to the papers in this book which follow will merely indicate some of the important differences which exist.

Weber conceives society as consisting of a constant flux of events (actions) which is essentially chaotic. These actions are carried out by individuals and are determined by the subjective meanings they place on the actions of others to whom they are oriented. So the object of cognition is the 'subjective-meaning complex of action'. The analyst imposes his own concepts, which of course relate to his own subjective meanings, on to this flux of events. These are ideal types, abstractions of general concepts from the specific historical realities, which then provide the components of theory. This is of course the approach Weber adopted in his analysis of urban politics referred to above. Marx's starting point was altogether different; he did not see society as a flux of individual actions on which the analyst imposed categories which 'could have been different and so were arbitrary'. His view was that 'Society does not consist of individuals, but expresses the sum of interrelations, the relations within which these individuals stand'.[32] These relations are based ultimately on the relations which constitute productive activity. The task therefore is to analyse the relations of production. Of course these relations are not realities which exist independent of human practice. They are relations, not things, but human practice is not voluntaristic (and therefore chaotic); individuals are the 'bearers' of these relations. As Tristram remarks,

'Marx's theory of the ontological basis of the socio-historical realm points to the relative amount of "order" in reality prior to the application of our categories to it. . . . In analysing periods of history prior to the more developed forms of capitalism, Marx examines how these socio-economic formations. . . have become integral parts of action patterns in the forms of systems of constraint and structures of domination.'[33]

The presence and resolution of contradictions in these formations is the reason for development in history. The 'object of knowledge' in Marx is a theoretically organized system of concepts and categories; it is a construct of thoughts which is 'a product ... of the working up of observation and conception into concepts'.[34] They are therefore rational abstractions from reality. However, these are not thought of outside or above their relation to history in the development of theory, for without history they would be empty abstractions. Regarding the possibility of theories constructed on the basis of such general propositions alone, Marx wrote (referring to production),

'There are characteristics which all stages of production have in common, and which are established as general ones by the mind; but the so-called general *preconditions* of all production are nothing more than these abstract moments with which no real historical stage of production can be grasped.'[35]

However, he thought that such propositions were no more than simple tautologies, and therefore elements which could not in themselves be combined into theories. Thus, although they are useful in identifying certain 'common elements' which will be present in any theory of production, such theories must always be about 'production at a definite stage of social development'.[36]

Tristram suggests that Marx's method of developing historical materialism involves the construction of models (which are an organized selection of particular elements which are to be examined) from the processes of society as they concretely exist. These models enable one to check that the object of knowledge has empirical referents and that it is not just an empty abstraction. Thus:

'Marx's object of knowledge is an "ideal average"[37] of the capitalist mode of production, [but] it still has to be shown to be the "ideal average" of real relations. Moreover Marx thinks that the abstract theory must be shown to be valid or invalid by analysing the "historical relations". In fact, Marx specifically warns against treating his theory as suprahistorical. Such an error can only result from failure to recognise that developments have to be studied within their historical contexts.'[38]

For Marx the object of knowledge refers to an ordered reality and only exists, and can only be shown to be valid, within concrete historical relations; the voluntaristic, essentially 'arbitrary' categories of the Weberian analysts have no place in this approach and nor do theories which claim universal applicability. The type of verification/falsification procedures based on the concepts which philosophers of natural science have discussed[39] and which are often advanced as the suitable model for any scientific social analysis are inadequate. (In fact the inability of this 'logic of scientific discovery' to be what it says it is has been emphasized by Kuhn from within a non-Marxist perspective, but his own approach, which cannot be discussed here, has also been criticized.)

Many of these points need to be borne in mind when considering the papers in this volume. They are not just relevant to a consideration of the differences between non-Marxist and Marxist approaches though, because there are some crucial differences between certain Marxist urban sociologists which also derive from the issues raised above. However, Colletti's comments on Weber may be useful in helping to distinguish between the two main approaches which have been discussed so far. He suggests that, for Weber, history is reduced 'to a history of cultural *phenomena alone*; economic structure itself is reduced to the mere *cultural significance* of the economic structure.... All human practice and activity contracts into *consciousness*, i.e. into *intentional behaviour*; it is not what men do that counts but rather the manner in which they *conceive* what they do'[40]. Colletti suggests that ideal types are utopian; they force the simplification and accentuation of trends to the point where notions, e.g. of 'city economy', no longer bear any resemblance to the historical regimes of production to which they refer. They are thus the empty abstractions already referred to, such notions being then used 'to link together the most disparate phenomena, regardless of the specification of socio-historical regimes (as in Weber's concept of bureacracy, the state, etc.), calmly assimilating elements specific to the present and the past'. Colletti adds that Weber found the essence of capitalism not in its economic anatomy or physiology but ultimately in a variety of mental attitudes and forms of behaviour which consist at base of the notion of calculability characteristic of the running of capitalist enterprise, the attitude of 'rational and systematic pursuit of profit'. Therefore capitalism was more or less identified with rationalization.[41]

A final point, which is relevant to the status of urban sociology as a distinct academic discipline, is that Weber's separation of the economic and other aspects of society in the manner which has been described enables him to distinguish between, for example, the economic theory of the city and the political theory of the city, and this obviously provides a basis for the growth of distinct intellectual specialisms, each therefore imposing its particular frame of reference on the chaos of events that is life. Marx's project cannot be defined and confined in this way. 'Pure' economic relations do not exist; the science of social formations (historical materialism) embodies all those elements which provide a separate basis for the distinct (or sometimes not so distinct) social sciences.[42] This is not to say that the economic, political and ideological aspects of society cannot be analysed in ways which focus particular attention on one of these elements in relation to the others, but neither can they be wholly separated for analysis. As has been explained, in Marx's view the failure of the classical economists was that they abstracted in particular but unconscious ways categories such as 'rent' or 'value' from their historical contexts for use in constructing general theories which were held to represent universally true relations between variables. These theories were false or ideological because they actually transformed the original problem into a different problem, e.g. the question 'what is the value of labour' into 'what is the value of labour power', and presented the theory then constructed as the answer to the originally conceived problem.[43] Therefore the division of the study of society into distinct disciplines with 'pure' economic, political or other subject matter seems to lead to science which is distorted by, in Althusser's words, 'ideology which occupies it, haunts it or lies in wait for it' and 'is merely dealing with a certain given reality that is anyway disputed and torn between several competing sciences'. In referring in a footnote in this context to 'many of the branches of sociology and psychology', Althusser might well have included urban sociology in his list.[44]

A further consequence of the Marxist approach to the study of society is that not only the answers but the questions posed within bourgeois social science are seen to be misconceived because of the implicit shift in the problem referred to above. Thus Marxist analysis will not simply produce different answers to the questions but will redefine the very questions themselves. This is why the Marxist contributions in this volume do not simply produce different explanations, e.g. of 'community action' or 'industrial location', but they also transform the very questions which concern non-Marxist urban sociologists. Marxist theory (or for that matter the criticism of alternative approaches) can only be developed through the conscious process of construction of the 'problematic', the theoretical framework (which is unrecognized and ideological in, for example, the case of the classical economics),

'which puts into relation with one another the basic concepts, determines the nature of each concept by its place and function in the system of relationships, and thus confers on each concept its particular significance.... So construed the problematic of a science (or an ideology) governs not merely the solutions it is capable of providing but the very problems it can pose and the form in which they must be posed. It is a "system of questions".'[45]

In fact argument and criticism between Marxist and non-Marxist theories, which often remains overtly at the level of argument over particular theoretical explanations which are assumed to be comparable, sometimes ignores the fact that the questions which each side seeks to answer are also different. Many of the most penetrating criticisms of Marxist theories tend to come from those who apply the same approach, as will be seen from this collection, or from those who attack its philosphical foundations. The new work presented here marks a transformation not only in the theory and content of what has been taken to be urban sociology but question the very terms within which such an activity is constituted—its problematic. The contributions also imply a more consciously active role for theorists in society than approaches which do not redefine the subject matter of study as it is proposed within, and as it is determined by, that society.[46]

## 3. Review of Contributions to the Volume

Pahl's paper restates the rejection, common to all the contributors to this volume, of the ideological urban sociology of the past and aims, by criticizing both the Weberian theory of urban management as it was developed in Britain (particularly by Pahl himself) and French Marxist analyses of the role of the state in urban and regional development, to propose new directions for work.[47] Some of the criticisms of the former approach have been referred to above, but it is Pahl's critique of the latter body of work which needs further examination. In his discussion of the role of the state in Castells' work, Pahl draws conclusions from Castells' remarks about this role, formulated in terms of the latter's Marxist theory, in order to incorporate them in his own distinct theory. The problem may be caused by Pahl's failure to specify the two theories and therefore provide a clear basis for discussion; the illegitimate merging of two distinct problematics seems to result. For example, a reference by Castells to the growth of the state's role in the form of urban planning leads Pahl to conclude that 'there is no doubt that it has developed *its own* (my italics—MH) momentum and capacity for expansion', as if Castells shares this conclusion. Reference to the discussion of Weberian and Marxist approaches above makes it clear that this is not so. Pahl's Weberian state is autonomous; as a consequence he can suggest that the state may move 'from a position where it aids and supports to one where it dominates and controls'. This is a reference to some of Pahl's work which suggests that Britain is changing from a capitalist to a corporatist society. This work, which Pahl has only recently begun explicitly to integrate with his urban social theory, focuses on an analysis of the manner of state intervention in Britain, especially the growth of its role in the economy and its management. The conclusion drawn is that the (autonomous) state is becoming the possessor of a 'third interest', neither that of capital nor labour but of some bureaucratically defined national interest.[48] For Pahl the expansion of the modern state is simply a manifestation of Weber's growth of bureacratic power; the suppression of sections of capitalism is a necessity for national unity rather than the unity of a dominant class, even if the original aim might have been to serve such an interest. Some of these important differences between Pahl and Castells, however, remain implicit in this part the former's paper. In fact Pahl's explicit critique of Castells in this section only appears to consist of a questioning reference to the latter's belief that the 'basic' economic and political issues relate to the contradictions inherent in monopoly capitalism and to a mention of the difficulty of the style in which he writes.

In the next part of his paper Pahl confronts the Poulantzas theory of the state, which Castells also adopts, particularly the question of the relative autonomy of the state. However, this is done not to dismiss it but, rather confusingly perhaps, simply to relate this autonomy to the 'crucial *mediating role*' of urban managers and technical experts between the state and the private sector and between the state and the population. It is difficult to be clear about Pahl's analysis here. Is the distinction between managers and experts important? Are they a part of 'the state' or not? If they are, how can they mediate? Does the reference to the central state authority imply a distinction solely within the state apparatus or power? The difficulties are compounded by a definition, produced at this stage, which suggests that research should be concerned with 'the relationship between "market" distributive systems and "rational" distributive systems, seeing the urban managers as essential mediators between manipulators of the two systems'.

Thus the exact location of Pahl's urban managers remains unclear, but he now moves on to a discussion of the two distributive systems. One deduces from his account that the private sector (capitalism) is dominated by market distribution and the state imposes its own distinct redistributive system. We are clearly in the presence of two ideal types here which actually interact or combine in 'mixed economies'. Once again the only explicit critique of Marxist approaches in this section is a reference to Giddens' dismissal of the state as promoter of the hegemony of monopoly capital.[49] Giddens' argument on this point and the empirical material he uses to support it are not in fact fatal to the Poulantzas theory of the state, in particular the existence of conflict between state and industry being an insufficient basis for dismissing the state's role as it is conceived in this theory.

The last main section of Pahl's paper proposes that the newly defined subject matter of urban sociology should be developed by application of the ideal types referred to above to comparative studies of the state's role in urban and regional development in Eastern and Western Europe. The first difficulty is that this is stated as a comparison between 'rational redistribution' and 'price regulating', i.e. (presumably) market systems. In fact this seems misleading for, as Pahl himself recognizes in his discussion, both ideal types are present in the East and the West alike. Therefore the conclusion that, as urban policies result in disadvantage in both blocs, both systems are exploitative (at least in a Marxist sense, see below) is hardly proven. However, once again, definite conclusions are not possible as the exact nature of the two redistributive systems is nowhere defined. Thus, is the '*socio-political process*' which largely determines allocation not a reflection of a 'price-regulating' situation in which professional labour power merely earns a higher 'social' if not money wage (and often this as well, or course)? Moreover, Pahl's adoption of Giddens' definition of 'exploitation' in terms of life-chances simply underlines the fact that, for a Marxist and a Weberian, these are two completely different concepts which relate to different problematics. For Marx, exploitation is present in a relationship which, in all its complexity, is economic, political and ideological, whereas there are individual sources of exploitation in the alternative approach; only the label is identical. 'Life-chances' are descriptive categories related to power. This in turn is defined by Weber as an individual's ability to have a command obeyed, whereas there is no such individualistic definition of (class) power in Marx.[50]

Pahl's proposals for the subject matter of urban sociology and the questions he wishes to examine are not those of the Marxist approach, and his assumption that he has identified a programme of urban and regional research for Marxist and non-Marxist alike, because it is defined in terms which imply a prior acceptance of one of these approaches on the part of the analyst, probably cannot be sustained, at least as proposed in his paper. Pahl's political economy refers to certain formal characteristics of allocative systems (compare Weber's treatment of the political organization of cities) and the work by Castells and others to which he refers has, for the reasons already discussed, a wholly different focus, even if, at the most basic empirical level, it is analysing the same reality, e.g. indices of housing disadvantage. Given these problems, it must be doubted whether Pahl's contention of an agreement between the two approaches on some of the issues that he outlines in his conclusion is correct. If this is so, it is also doubtful whether the type of comparative test of the two approaches that he outlines is possible. Discussing these issues recently, Castells is reported as suggesting that, from his perspective, 'comparative analysis is mainly valuable for the analysis of defined variables (i.e. not broad abstractions—MH), and within the same type of system, rather than for analysis between two differing systems,'[51] for him much of the social behaviour in the socialist countries is simply not explicable in terms which derive from Pahl's theoretical orientation.

Castells' paper very briefly outlines his critique of urban sociology, which has already been referred to above, summarizes some of the key points of his own approach and gives an outline of the manner of its application to the analysis, by himself and Godard, of the development of the Port of Dunkerque.[52] Lebas' paper contains a critique of some of the theoretical and methodological aspects of Castells' work. This work was originally influenced by the Marxist writings of Althusser but more closely by the development of Althusser's work (concerned with Marxist philosophy, i.e. dialectical materialism) by Poulantzas and his group. These writers are concerned with the Marxist study of history, i.e. historical materialism, the science of social formations, in its various branches. Althusser has been heavily criticized (and has indeed reacted to some extent to this) and as Poulantzas' work has developed his initial differences with Althusser have widened.[53] Castells' own work has taken place during, and in the context of, these changes, but his basic theoretical work to date, *La Question Urbaine*, arose from his work in the late sixties (it was published in 1972), before some of the more recent changes in Poulantzas' theory. As a consequence, some of the problems that stemmed from Castells' initial formulation and are discussed in Lebas' paper and this introduction would probably now be recognized by him.[54]

A full outline of Althusser's approach cannot be attempted here, but a central element is his account of the relationship between the economic and the other 'instances or levels' (i.e. political and ideological elements) of a social formation. This relationship consists of a complex but unified 'structural whole' in which these levels 'are distinct and "relatively autonomous", and coexist within this complex structural unity, articulated with one another according to specific determinations, fixed in the last instance by the level or instance of the economy'.[55] Each element can develop at different rates and the contradictions between and within elements are determined not by a single simple factor, e.g. economics, but by the complex effects of the structured whole. He refers to them as 'overdetermined' or 'complexly-structurally-determined.'[56] In any given historical period one instance will be dominant, but which it is will vary according to the overdetermination of the contradictions. The economic is determinant in the last instance in that it 'determines which of the instances in the social structure occupies the determinant place',[57] including itself. Relative autonomy therefore involves a special conception of autonomy, a variation within invariant limits. The relationship between structures and individual men is a key element in this theory:

'the structure of the relations of production determines the *places* and *functions* occupied and adopted by the agents of production (i.e. individuals—MH). . . . The true subjects (in the sense of constitutive subjects of the process) are. . . the relations of production (and political and ideological social relations). . . . [These] are irreducable to any anthropological inter-subjectivity—since they only combine agents and objects in a specific structure of the distribution of relations, places and functions, occupied and "supported" by objects and agents of production.'[58]

Castells, in an outline of his approach in *La Question Urbaine*,[59] closely follows Althusser. Castells states that all society, and therefore all social forms such as space, are founded on the historical articulation of several modes of production. A mode of production is a particular combination of the instances or 'systems of practices'. The economic level determines 'in the last instance' this particular combination. The combination between, and the transformation of, the different systems and elements of the structure occur through social practice, i.e. actions of individuals determined by their particular location in the different places of the structure already defined. These actions, which are contradictory (because of the contradictory nature of the structure) react on the structure and produce new effects. These effects do not arise from the consciousness of individuals but from a specific combination of the practices which is determined by the structure. This capacity for modification only exists within structural bounds although it can effect the pace of the structure's historical development and so modify it considerably.

Turning now to the analysis of space as 'an expression of the social structure', Castells suggests that it is necessary to study how space is created by the elements of the economic, political and ideological systems, by their combinations and the social practices from which they proceed. He then develops this analysis at length. Basically he seeks to break down the three instances into a series of subelements at different levels which form the overall complexly articulated structure. The various empirical objects, institutions and processes of urban research can all be classified according to this extensive list of subelements. Thus, for example, the economic instance is divided into production, consumption and exchange, and then production, to take just one example, into elements internal to the work process (e.g. factories and raw materials), the relations between the work process and the economic instance as a whole (e.g. the industrial environment) and the relations between the work process and other instances (e.g. administration, information). Further distinctions enable the position of the 'support agents' in whose practices the various structural contradictions are manifest to be specified. Thus housing, which is an element subsumed under consumption, is further subdivided according to certain levels (luxury houses, slums, etc.) and roles (lodger, owner, etc.).

Castells summarizes his method thus:

'the relationships which the different sub-elements of the urban system, their roles and levels, have among themselves and with the social structure define the conjuncture of the urban system. The insertion of the support agents in the structural backcloth thus constituted, will define urban social practices, the only significant realities for our research.'

Castells proposes to apply the urban system outlined which 'is only a concept' to 'clarify social practices, concrete historical situations, both to understand them and to uncover the laws governing them'. What has to be added for a full analysis is 'a theoretical conception of the practices through which the structural laws are realised'. The connection between the structural analysis, social classes and politics is made by 'the analysis at one and the same time of interventions of the institutional system and its challenge by social movements'. As no social structure exists without contradictions, i.e. class struggle, the analysis of the urban system leads necessarily to the study of urban politics.[60] In the subsequent sections of his book Castells divides this, for purposes of analysis, into an examination of urban planning (the intervention of the political instance on the urban system to ensure the reproduction of the dominant mode of production) and urban social movements ('systems of practices' effecting structural change in the urban system, or substantial modification of the balance of forces in the class struggle). The first approach starts with structures and the second with practices, but, as Pickvance says, 'they are two sides of the same coin'. Thus urban social movements are a realization of contradictions in the urban system and the force of an urban social movement will be the greater the more contradictions are realized in its existence.[61]

Castell's separates structures and practices for analytical purposes, although he states that in reality structures and practices are not separable. A large part of the book consists of a rather abstract series of taxonomies of the 'urban structure', breaking down the three main instances in the way referred to above. The analysis of urban planning proceeds along similar lines, but the concluding analysis of 'urban social movements' is far closer to the type of historical analysis which is more usual from Marxist writers. It is the former type of approach which Pahl is objecting to in his paper when he refers to the 'almost functional analysis' of Castells. This comment (which is based on Parkin's critique of Althusser[62]) is more polemical than accurate but it does highlight some of the problems in *La Question Urbaine* and in the work of Althusser and, to a lesser degree perhaps, Poulantzas.

Garnier has criticized Castells' approach in *La Question Urbaine*[63]. The core of his objection is that the 'structuralism' on which it is based is unable to integrate the contradictions of social practice with its explanatory schemes (based on the analysis of 'urban structure'). All Castells can do is to link the structural field he has traced to the problematic of social relations and the class struggle. Garnier believes that this adoption of one of the fundamental bases of Poulantzas' approach is inadequate and the distinction between the two types of material in the book already referred to is symptomatic. The dynamics of urban transformation are not explained by the *a posteriori* introduction of social relations and political class practices as these latter *embody* the relations between certain structural elements. New rules which emerge in the interaction of these practices derive therefore from the contradictory nature of the structural ensemble of which they constitute the effects. The social contradictions which define the class struggle are not therefore exterior to the structural logic.

Of course Castells agrees in theory that structures are realized only in practices. However, in his writings he seems to separate them in the way described, except in some of his specific studies of urban situations. The result, as Garnier concludes, is that Castells oscillates between Althusserian theoreticism and concrete studies which, in departing considerably from this framework, do genuinely develop the Marxist analysis of urban problems. Interestingly, although unsurprisingly, Laclau has recently criticized Poulantzas in ways which are very similar, suggesting that his theory is formalist (i.e. form predominates over content), that his approach when faced with a complex reality is to react with 'taxonomic fury' to create a theory which is so abstract that all contact with reality is eventually lost, that the various basic elements of the 'structuralist' approach which are assumed to exist (why are there only three instances, for example?) are established in a purely descriptive way and that the relations between them are simply names not theoretical concepts. On the other hand, Laclau thinks that some of Poulantzas' specific historical analyses are very interesting, but 'this result has been achieved despite, not because of his method'.[64]

Many of Laclau's points have been touched upon in other critiques of the 'structuralist' approach.[65] The basic problem highlighted by all these commentaries is the relation between the real object and the object of knowledge in Althusser's original work. Althusser often refers to four basic practices rather than the familiar three already referred to; the fourth is 'theoretical practice'. No real justification for this is given, nor for the claim that each of the basic practices is an act of production whose general structure is identical to that of material production. This view then enables Althusser to explain that theory advances by taking raw material (concepts and abstractions existing entirely in thought) and applying the means of theoretical production (the problematic) to produce the product, theory. So the production of theory takes place entirely in thought, despite the label theoretical *practice* and the analogy (for that is all it is) with material production. Althusser would therefore reject Tristram's suggestion that Marx did relate thought and reality in his work via models.[66] It is principally this treatment of the real/thought distinction which leads to the faults which Laclau and others have found in the work of Althusser and Poulantzas and which seems to be present in the more theoretical writing of Castells as well. It seems impossible to incorporate structures/ practices as a totality in such an approach, and the difficulty of connecting the theoretical framework with concrete historical analysis which exists in much of the work results. Glucksmann has aptly described this as an 'authorless theatre'.

In fact Althusser has reacted to these criticisms to some extent, if perhaps rather unsatisfactorily (now he relates theoretical structure to political practice)[67]. More importantly, Poulantzas has made plain his break with the epistemological position outlined above, pointing out fairly enough that it was conditioned by a reaction to historicism and economism. He now agrees that his earlier writing suffered from a certain 'theoreticism' and 'formalism'.[68] Castells would probably accept a similar charge against his own major theoretical work which he has always regarded as a preliminary rather than a final statement. However, Poulantzas at least seems to think that only relatively minor changes in his approach are necessary, e.g. more concrete analyses and greater attention to the presentation of these analyses, making it clear that they are not just 'illustrations' imported into a wholly theoretical discourse. To the present writer at least, this still seems to leave begging the major question of exactly how the link between concrete realities and theory is made in this approach. Poulantzas and Castells would deny their original Althusserian solution, but what is put in its place? Can the 'structuralist' approach and method of procedure of *La Question Urbaine* be maintained or is this something which ultimately obstructs the analysis of real situations rather than aiding it?

Lebas's paper, which reports on an attempt to come to grips with Castells' approach in a research situation, illustrates some of the difficulties involved and underlines the danger of a reversion to mere juxtaposition of facts and theories in the application of such an approach together with a displacement of the study of the specific nature of the class struggle in its historical context from the centre to the periphery of analysis. Her comments are mainly directed at Castells and Godard's major work on Dunkerque, *Monopolville*, which is selectively summarized in the second part of Castells' paper in this collection. The reference in this section of his paper to a methodology which consists of trying to show a correspondence between 'the theoretical chain' and a 'chain of observation' by means of *logical connections*, is a purely descriptive explanation and seems to underline the difficulties that Lebas and others have drawn attention to.

A further problem in *La Question Urbaine* which Garnier refers to is Castells' inability, in his outline of the urban structure, to combine at this level of analysis the consequences of the historical fact, which is accepted, that any actual social formation contains a number of different basic modes of production in complex combination, not just the 'pure' capitalist mode which Castells concentrates on. Two solutions might be offered to this problem. Firstly, that all that is necessary is a further elaboration of the theoretical analysis of the 'structured whole' or, secondly, that such an analysis must deal with each mode separately before using them together to analyse the differing and historically determined ways in which the combination of modes actually appears in reality. However, apart from the difficulty of taking account of the fact that the structured whole can in no way be seen as a simple combination of the different modes because of their effects on each other, the lack of an answer by Castells to this problem casts doubt on the validity and usefulness of the elaboration of the urban system as it is presented, in his work, as a preliminary stage for the examination of urban practices. Garnier suggests that Castells, by isolating the capitalist mode of production from its structural context, is unable to grasp the complexity of real events.

The desire for a neat taxonomy which associates the different elements of a logical system of concepts with particular realities also seems to be a determining factor in Castells' definition of an urban unit and his focus on collective consumption in his analysis of the state's urban role, as referred to in his paper here. Castells remarks that social analysis of space *per se* is impossible because it is a social product and 'is always specified by a clearly defined relation between the different instances of a social structure ... and the conjuncture of social relations which follows them'.[69] This, particularly given Castells' analysis of the 'fetishisation' of space and the ideological concept of 'the urban' in previous work, might seem a sufficient starting point for a definition of the nature of the Marxist study of spatial processes. Paradoxically though, and with little evident justification, Castells still wishes to accept the 'urban' as a special focus of analysis. Pointing out that previous urban sociology has in fact concentrated on relationships to space and 'collective consumption' (e.g. goods and services provided for mass consumption), he proposes to make these his subject matter and proceeds to define an 'urban unit' as a spatial unit of reproduction of labour power, 'production space being regional space and that of reproduction being called "urban space"'.[70]

Clearly such a linkage allows a model of the urban system (or the regional system) to be built and be referrable to empirical data and other factual material. However, in accepting some sort of distinction between 'regional' and 'urban' in this way, Castells separates two processes (production and reproduction) which in reality seemed to be combined in spaces which are defined as urban or regional and, as Ecker[71] has pointed out, he seems to undermine the prime relevance of production and the study of its effects to any Marxist analysis of space. Thus, Castells' subsequent concentration on consumption bears comparison, in some respects, with previous urban sociology and with the Weberian urban sociology which has been discussed above, both of which he has severely criticized. It also partly corresponds to a focus in Harvey's work which will be referred to later.

The manner in which Castells then treats consumption is also interesting. As outlined in his paper here, he suggests that the economies of advanced capitalist countries rests more and more on the process of consumption, i.e. the realization of surplus value or the extension of the market. Also, the growing economic concentration under capitalism results in a growing spatial concentration of the organization and management of collective consumption 'which determines the structure of residential space, and, hence, of urban entities'. The state, through its role in providing and managing these collective facilities, increasingly dominates urban life, and its role results in the politicization of 'the urban question' and the significance of urban social movements which oppose the state's activities. The identification of 'urban entities' in this manner has already been criticized, but Ecker has drawn attention to some other points as well. She suggests that the problem of realization of surplus value is not the main factor in the emergence of the urban phenomena to which Castells refers. The improvement of urban conditions via state provision is more importantly a reaction to the falling rate of profit of capital and hence its inability to provide wages sufficient to ensure the adequate reproduction of the labour force for the purposes of production and/or its inability to finance the cost of other factors entering into production. In other words, it is mainly a problem connected with the generation rather than the realization of surplus value.

Such an approach would certainly seem to fit better with the everyday observation that direct state enterprise (in not only the urban sphere) has often seemed particularly to concentrate on sectors which are unprofitable because of productive conditions and, furthermore, that there have often been pressures which sought to restrict the state's role to such sectors and/or reduce its role in areas where profits could be obtained but where there might have been state involvement, partially at least in response to political pressure from non-capitalist social interests.[72] Moreover, although the increasing role of collective consumption (in itself a concept which requires further analysis—e.g. are all facilities collectively provided also collectively consumed?) and the state in urban life is unarguable, the totality of consumption processes involved in the reproduction of the labour force consists of a variety of activities ranging from wholly 'collective' to wholly 'individual', as Preteceille's recent interesting work has shown.[73] Why therefore separate out one particular part of this totality as the exclusive object of analysis rather than adopt a broader framework which simply regards this element as one important tendency?

To summarize, the separation of consumption from production in Castells' analysis, with the consequent operationalization of the urban/regional distinction, and the focus on collective consumption for the study of the role of state urban policies seems far too narrow a perspective and is misleading. 'Urban' processes and forms cannot be understood without reference to the production of capital *and* the reproduction of the labour force. Collective and individual consumption are both important and are both influenced by state policies and by the practices of capitalist enterpise. All these factors are realized in terms of class practices and hence class conflicts, which are only partially expressed through and in urban planning and urban social movements. To take one example, wage rates (as determined by individual capital) will greatly affect housing conditions regardless of the state's role in this area, and trade union pressure will often be the other main determinant and thus have its own important effect on these conditions. To regard such influences as predetermined factors which then enter into urban studies is to commit an error akin to that which Castells might advance in criticism of Pahl's approach, of abstracting the problem for analysis from its true problematic.

Harvey's paper demonstrates the convergence that is now occurring between the work of those with various disciplinary backgrounds in the analysis of the political economy of space. Pahl's work developed out of his initial concerns as a geographer and Harvey shares this original source. His paper here needs to be seen in the light of the approach he outlines in his major contribution to date, *Social Justice and the City*,[74] although he, like other contributors, has since continued to develop his work. In this book he rejects 'liberal formulations' of the theory necessary for understanding the generation of inequality in the city and associated theories for examining the relationship between social processes and spatial forms. He concludes that such theories avoid coming to terms with the context of the problems they seek to study, capitalism and its key relationships. Thus the first part of his book is similar in aim to the first section of *La Question Urbaine* but while Castells is mainly concerned to criticize urban sociology, Harvey is more concerned with urban economics and geography.

Concentrating on housing, Harvey then develops his own analysis. He regards the market as the origin of inequality and identifies a key role for the state in the management of consumption. Suburban development in America is a deliberate capitalist creation in order to combat the rising tendency to underconsumption in the economy. The creation of debt-encumbered and therefore conservative suburbanites also aids political control; these people have a personal stake in the preservation of the economic *status quo*. Harvey therefore, like Castells, singles out the market—the realization of surplus value and consumption rather than its creation, i.e. production—for attention. He suggests that a growing social, economic and political crisis surrounds this mechanism for controlling underconsumption that is the financial superstructure (which is the 'mediating link' between the urban process and the necessities of the underlying dynamic of capitalism in the United States). His paper analyses some of these factors and their consequences for the changing nature of various neighbourhoods in Baltimore.

Harvey's work derives from Baran and Sweezy's theories of monopoly capital[75] (by which they refer either to a monopoly or, more normally, oligopoly in the conventional definitions), and O'Connor's work, *The Fiscal Crisis of the State*, is also a major influence.[76] Baran and Sweezy suggested that the modern crisis of capitalism was caused, not by the long-term tendency of the rate of profit to fall due to the increasing organic composition of capital, a problem of the generation of surplus value, but rather by the inability to sell the goods produced in the market, i.e. insufficient demand. This view which has factors in common with Keynes' theory of the pre-war depression leads on to an analysis of how underconsumption is combated. Baran and Sweezy suggest two main mechanisms are now effective, unproductive consumption (e.g. the growth of services whose wages are deductions from surplus value) and state expenditures (hence, for example, theories about the 'permanent arms economy'). They even explicitly identify suburbanization as a check to underconsumption just as Harvey does. The extent of this waste is measured by the difference between the actual surplus, measured by reference to national income not currently consumed but invested in expanding productive activity, and the far greater potential surplus if production was 'rational', which has to be estimated. The split of capital into a monopoly sector and a competitive sector, and the domination of the former, able to ensure its retention of the bulk of the gains from increasing productivity for reasons Baran and Sweezy analyse, leads to a tendency for the surplus to rise and therefore for increasing instability.[77]

O'Connor builds on this foundation in setting out his analysis of the growth of state expenditure. His argument has been neatly summarized by Gough.[78] The growing socialization of production (a consequence of capitalism accelerated by monopoly capital) necessitates greater state intervention to ensure private profit, and hence *social capital* expenditure on roads, education, etc. However, this develops further productive capacity, especially in the monopoly sector, but demand rises more slowly and surplus capacity and population occurs. This then leads to a further round of *social expenses* outlays which aim to generate demand but not add to capacity; arms expenditure and welfare relief are two examples of these. This growth of state expenditure tends to create a structural gap between state revenue and expenditure, i.e. the fiscal crisis of the state. The major answer to this problem is inflation. The reform of the fiscal structures (referred to by Harvey in his contribution) is another. Both give rise to further contradictions and Harvey demonstrates in his Baltimore study some of those which arise from fiscal reform.

Gough suggests that O'Connor's theory is based on two factors: firstly, the growth of social capital which is an observable fact and, secondly, two false 'laws', the tendency to working class immiseration and to underconsumption. He suggests that the first of these laws 'is nowhere seriously entertained today' but points out that the second is still commonly held in America because of the influence of Baran and Sweezy's work. However, this thesis in its various forms has been subjected to severe criticism by those who assert that the fall in the rate of profit is still the central phenomenon of capitalism.[79] Gough criticizes those who posit this as a 'law' as well, and he also rejects the view which is at least implicit in O'Connor (and Harvey as well) that the state's role is premised on breakdown theories of the economy. These imply that the economic is an autonomous factor (in the 'Weberian' rather than the 'Marxist' sense) which tends to break down if not assisted by the state which is itself a passive tool in the hands of the bourgeoisie. Gough believes that both types of 'law' give insufficient weight to the role of class struggle in shaping state expenditures, especially social ones.[80] He prefers Poulantzas' analysis of the state which suggests that it has a relative autonomy from the economic system and is constituted as a relationship between conflicting classes. From this point of view, Harvey could be criticized for introducing the class struggle as a factor *consequent* on the structural economic changes analysed in his paper.

Although the role of the capitalist state is not a functional response to falling profits, Gough does believe that lack of profitability is the basic reason for current problems, but that this deficiency is no in-built tendency but a consequence of the 'balance of class forces'. He outlines the major trends in the socio-economic structures of capitalism as the 'accumulation and concentration of capital, proletarianisation and education of the labour force and the population generally and urbanisation' and these are caused by the socialisation of production, 'the inevitable corollary of the development of the capitalist mode of production'. This has resulted in a growing socialization of the costs of production, i.e. growing state expenditures. The sharpening of international competition since the last war, economic growth based on a 'post-war settlement between capital and labour' and the rising expectations of the labour movement form the historical context for this upward movement.

Gough's subsequent analysis of state expenditures (based on O'Connor's own classification) divides them into three types. These are social investment, in order to increase productivity and, other things being equal, the rate of profit; social consumption, to lower the reproduction costs of labour with a similar result; and social expenses, required to maintain harmony. As O'Connor points out, 'nearly every state expenditure is part social investment, part social consumption and part social expense'. So water or transport, for example, are a means of production when utilized by industry and consumption goods when utilized by households. These types of distinction, which have also been discussed in Preteceille's work,[81] suggest yet again that the concept of 'collective consumption' has been rather oversimplified and state policies concerning it cannot be wholly equated with the reproduction of the labour force. Gough also implicitly criticizes the explanation that the state is concerned with unprofitable sectors only, for it not only provides goods but also finances private providers who often make good returns.

In conclusion, Gough's detailed discussion of state expenditure in advanced capitalism and his careful analysis of its structure, based on O'Connor's work in this respect, leads to a doubt about some of the underlying assumptions in Harvey's paper. In general Harvey's emphasis on the role of finance rather than productive capital in cities has been criticized. He does not go quite so far as Levfebvre who sees finance capital, i.e. that concerned with circulation rather than production, becoming the dominant force in society, and urban conflicts, based on the role of such capital in property speculation and land, supplanting work-place conflict—a theory heavily criticized by Castells.[82] However, Harvey distinctly sees this as a possibility,[83] but his critics suggest that finance capital must remain secondary to productive capital because it ultimately has to abstract its wealth from surplus value and so is subordinate to the latter in the last analysis.[84] It is notable that Poulantzas has recently criticized a similar claim, namely that circulation capital rather than productive capital is dominant, in the analyses of imperialism given by Gunder Frank and Emmanuel; these analyses also, of course, focus on the realization rather than the creation of surplus value.[85] It is also interesting to note that Poulantzas (following Lenin) also regards finance capital as being a merger between banking and industrial capital in which the contradictions between the two still exist; furthermore, while banking capital (which may be closest to Harvey's definition of finance capital, but his texts are ambiguous on this point) can apparently be in control, the dominant role still falls to productive capital.[86]

Work previous to that presented here by Lojkine[87] seemed to share some of the assumptions which have just been discussed. As others do, he sees capitalist urban development as a result of the growing socialization of production. Of course cities existed before capitalism, because of the division of labour in previous modes of production, but the capitalist city is characterized above all by collective consumption and the growing concentration of productive activity. Lojkine therefore, unlike Castells, defines the urban agglomeration as 'a spatial combination of the various elements of production and reproduction of capitalist social formations'. Urban problems are related to the contradiction between the technical necessity for socialization and the social necessity for competition which becomes sharper as capitalism develops and the struggle to maintain surplus value continues. Lojkine identifies three aspects of this: firstly, the problem of anarchic capitalist competition leading to uneven development, i.e. regional problems; secondly, the obstacle to urban development caused by individual land ownership which he suggests is declining due to its appropriation by financial monopolies; and, thirdly, the problem of the financing of urban facilities, of the means of collective consumption and of material (transport and communications) and social (banking and commerce) circulation. Lojkine says that most of these are unproductive, i.e. do not give rise to surplus value. Even though they are necessary conditions for the generation of surplus value, they are essentially paid for out of surplus value which arises elsewhere. This 'expenses capital', although necessary, also has an effect similar to that which Marx suggested was produced by constant capital, namely causing the rate of profit to fall. Pickvance, commenting on this, expresses doubt about the argument at this point, referring to the general controversy about the validity of the falling tendency of the rate of profit and also suggesting that it is unclear why the organic composition of capital should increase as expenses capital grows.[88] However, remembering that Lojkine says that this is unproductive but necessary capital, it does not seem difficult to conceive it as somewhat akin to constant capital whose increase gives rise to the effect concerned.

Lojkine's next step is more puzzling. Having explained the effects of this 'devalorized' (unproductive) capital in terms of a falling rate of profit by reference to a rise in the organic composition of capital and suggested that state intervention provides devalorised capital (in the form of urban infrastructure, etc.), he says that this is in fact a way of boosting the profits of capitalism which have declined due to the tendency for overaccumulation, i.e. underconsumption. As Ecker has noted, this apparently confuses the two theories we have already referred to, the first of which concerns the creation of surplus value and the second its realization. She also suggests that state provision of urban facilities is best seen as being primarily related to the former problem, although help in aiding the profitability of capital does of course also strengthen capital's hand in the international competition for markets which is required for the realization of surplus value.[89]

The validity of theories of monopoly capitalism based on underconsumption has already been questioned, but Lojkine's conception of the state's role is also worth examination. He is an important exponent of the theory of state monopoly capitalism, developed particularly by the French Communist Party. This suggests that the dominant role in society is occupied by monopoly (big) capital, and this is in opposition to non-monopoly capital with whom the working class can at least partially form an alliance. According to Poulantzas, who criticizes this theory,[90] it conceives the state's role in the context of an analysis of production which treats the productive forces and the relations of production separately and sees the productive forces as being the prime determining factor in the relations between these two. State intervention is largely neutral and is a technical requirement of the development of the productive forces, but this just happens to serve the purpose of aiding the private accumulation of capital. Lojkine's reference to the technical necessity for socialization and the social necessity for competition would seem to reflect this view. So the state is conceived as a tool in the hands of big capital rather than a political apparatus for the unification of the bourgeoisie, and thus relatively autonomous.

Poulantzas then develops his own analysis of monopoly capital, relating it to the need to concentrate production in order to extract surplus value. The falling rate of profit is not the final cause of this though, it is merely an idex of 'the resistance (i.e. struggle) of the working class against its exploitation'.[91] The argument is similar at this point to that advanced by Gough. Poulantzas then presents an elaborate analysis of the different fractions of capital and their interrelations, in particular defining monopoly capital (also confusingly called 'finance capital') as a merger between industrial and banking capital in the manner already described. Monopoly capital involves a concentration of economic (i.e. effective) ownership which is often initiated by banking interests either directly or indirectly and, secondly, an intensive exploitation of labour (which affects non-monopoly capital as well in fact). However, monopoly capital's domination is not complete; it is resisted by other fractions of capital and the working class and weakened by its own internal conflicts. The outcome of all this will vary according to the particular evolution of individual countries, which must therefore be studied.

Poulantzas claims that, far from seeking to extinguish non-monopoly capital, monopoly capital has certain uses for it, e.g. in order to channel and bring into use unskilled rural workers, to pioneer new types of production and to bear the brunt of working class struggles. This being so, the relationship between the two is one of domination and dependence, rather than antagonism, as suggested by the theory of state monopoly capitalism. Poulantzas claims that the state is still relatively autonomous, acting as the unifier of the different conflicting sectors of monopoly capital and, more generally, as the unifier of monopoly and non-monopoly capital in the overall interests of capital, which in Poulantzas' view, of course, cannot actually be identified with any one specific sector of monopoly capital but rather with a 'long term interest' of capital as a whole.

The theory of state monopoly capital, on the other hand, which, Poulantzas states, presumes 'a fusion of the state and the monopolies in a single mechanism', suggests that these were once independent entities with the state having its own 'power' and that now monopoly capital has 'captured' the state.[92] Apart from pointing out that such a theory is akin to those of writers such as Dahl or Galbraith (it also, of course, has similarities with aspects of the Weberian analysis), Poulantzas points out that state action which favours non-monopoly capital is hard to explain on such a basis.[93] In fact, Poulantzas argues that Lojkine holds confused views on this topic, for, while elsewhere he supports the fusion thesis, in the paper we have been discussing in this introduction so far Lojkine *does* refer to the state as a political organization which serves the whole bourgeoisie and not just monopoly capital.[94] To summarize, Lojkine's previous work seemed to combine elements of several distinctive theories of modern capitalist development and the role of the state. This resulted in certain ambiguities which remain to be resolved. However, in his paper in this collection he explicitly rejects definitions of urban policy which view the state either as a resolver of technical problems or as a regulator of contradictions 'above' classes and accepts that it is an 'active reflection' of the class struggle. (As might be expected he also criticizes Castells implicitly, suggesting that urban policies are not simply concerned with the reproduction of labour power but also with the reproduction of capital itself.) Furthermore, the following analyses do not entirely seem to follow the pattern which Poulantzas' account of Lojkine's basic position would imply. He concentrates on the dominant role of monopoly capital in urban development, even suggesting that it has now overcome the historical obstacle of individual land ownership, contrary to his earlier view, and regards the conflicting requirements of big and small/medium capital as important in analysing such development. However, he also makes it clear (with reference to a case study of Rennes) that state policy is influenced by the resistance of small/medium capital to monopoly and also by working class pressure. Moreover, he suggests that policies are formed in the context of struggles which relate to alliances between monopoly and other fractions of capital. In passing he counterposes this to the 'mechanistic and functional' view of those who 'accord the State a regulative function in relation to regional and urban planning through which it neutralises urban social conflicts to the benefit of the dominant class fraction', even when this is sometimes against the interests of individual agents of the dominant class, provided that the hegemony of the class is preserved. One must presume that this is seen as an account of Poulantzas' views but, if so, it seems to be an inaccurate reduction of his actual theory. Apart from the fact that Poulantzas refers to state action on behalf of 'the power block as a whole' and not just the dominant fraction, he does not believe that the state regulates social contradictions. Furthermore, Poulantzas would not suggest that the state neutralized anything but would agree, with Lojkine, that any 'concessions' are of secondary importance and do not eliminate social contradictions.

On the other hand, sometimes Lojkine's terminology in his contribution here seems to imply that the state is 'external' to class relations, despite his earlier reiteration that it is not. A similar possibility can be seen in his conclusion that some urban policies do not seem to be explicable by any interest currently expressed by the monopoly or other fractions of capital, either singly or in alliance, or by the direct interests of the working class. These *must* therefore be due to an 'anticipation' by the political authorities of the predictable resistance by the dominated class. Apart from the circularity of this argument which seems to impose a rather facile theoretical deduction on an empirical fact, as Pickvance has noted,[95] Lojkine might seem to be suggesting some independent regulative power on the part of the state. The exact nature of his conception of the role of the state bureaucracy is unclear; it is possible that he would agree with Poulantzas' own conclusion on this point, which does suggest that 'in certain specific conjunctures, this social category can function as an effective social force ... intervening in the political field and the class struggle with a weight of its own'.[96] Whether this is a satisfactory answer to the problem Lojkine raises must be doubted though, for Poulantzas, having defined class fractions and strata 'on the basis of differentiations in the economic sphere, and of the role, quite a particular one in these cases, of political and ideological relations', then simply asserts without prior discussion that social categories also exist, defined not it seems with reference to the economic sphere but 'principally by their place in political and ideological relations'.[97] If this is so, it is hard to see how such categories cannot be held to have some 'independent power' and it raises some doubts about whether Poulantzas' overall theory of the *relative* autonomy of the various elements of the social formation, on the one hand, and the determination by the economic in the last instance, on the other, can be fully sustained. Although neither Poulantzas nor Lojkine will accept the existence of an autonomous bureaucracy on the Weberian model as a central factor in the political sphere, they do perhaps seem to imply that it can on occasion function in such a way.

Mingione's paper presents yet another approach to the Marxist analysis of urban and regional development. Although he accepts the general critique of previous urban sociology, he refers to the fact that the response to this critique has been varied and mentions Castells, Harvey and Pahl as representatives of some of these variants. He rejects the identification of the 'urban' with consumption and is concerned about the problem that much Marxist analysis has in relating theory and empirical observation. Mingione places the historical study of particular countries and the class struggle at the centre of his work on urban and regional problems. However, this requires complex analysis, in particular of specific class relationships. Mingione's method is to define the relationship between territory and the dominant productive and class system and then to elaborate this account in more detail. He states that there are three aspects to a definition of territory: firstly, it is 'a map of the social relations of production because it is fundamental to all these relationships'; secondly, it is itself a means of production; and, thirdly, it is a consumer good in short supply. In fact it could be misleading to separate out these factors in such a list because, as Mingione says, the first aspect is 'the most general aspect of the definition and refers to the complex synthesis of the social relations of production in their spatial form, and not, as it might seem, merely a descriptive geographical aspect of socio-territorial relationships'. What Mingione is referring to might more clearly be called 'social space' rather than territory, whereas the next two elements in his definition refer to ways in which land enters into the social relationships of production that form the basis for the first aspect. Thus the way Mingione uses the concept of territory here seems to be unsatisfactory. This varied use of the word pervades the following discussion which relates its first 'aspect' to uneven development caused by exploitative class relations between different areas on a regional, national and international basis. The second aspect is related to the use of land for agriculture and buildings and refers to land ownership and planning as class-based processes. The third aspect is related, in effect, to the reproduction of the labour force, the focus of much old and new urban sociology, especially with reference to housing. Housing problems are also class based; workers get poor houses, rising rents expropriate the wages their struggles have gained them and the control of land by the state and private interests is itself an instrument of class repression.

The way in which Mingione relates his general theory of Marxist historical materialism, as applied to the specific social formations dominated by the capitalist mode of production (his immediate object of analysis), to the social problems of urban and regional development is perhaps not theoretically coherent enough. However, it is a useful way into his discussion of the subject matter of these problems, industrial production, land and the relevant consumer goods. It also avoids a separation between structures and practices. Thus, for example, 'housing' enters the conceptual framework as it arises in the three class-based processes which he has outlined. This enables Mingione to develop his subsequent analysis which aims to substantiate and demonstrate the class-based nature and development of urban and regional problems with reference to the actual process of historical development, mainly as it has occurred in Italy. He does this in a way which seems to relate theory and observation more closely than is evident in some of the other writers he criticizes earlier in his paper.

This method involves extensive and detailed historical, social, political and economic analysis, much of which still has to be developed. In his contribution to this book, for example, Mingione only deals in depth with some aspects of one phase of capitalist development (primitive accumulation) and its consequences for urban and regional development. Even then his starting point is an assertion that Italy's territorial imbalance between the South and the North is the product of the simultaneous occurrence of the main types of accumulation (primitive, capitalist 'in the strict sense' and imperialist), an event specific to Italy. To demonstrate that this is so requires a detailed account of the capitalist and 'territorial' development of Italy and its comparison with, and relation to, development in the other main capitalist countries. Mingione has now presented such an analysis elsewhere and it provides the context for his contribution to this book.[98] In comparison with Germany, for example, where the agrarian class was responsible for national unification and for starting the capitalist revolution, it was the Northern capitalist bourgeoisie that promoted unification in Italy. However, this bourgeoisie faced opposition to development from the Southern feudal land owners who were strongly established. Its only course of action, given that the radical abolition of land ownership was ruled out by the lack of a strong peasant demand for it and that moderate reforms would be opposed by the land owners, was to form an alliance with the Southern aristocracy.

It is in the context of such a pattern of development that Mingione presents his analysis of Italian urban and regional development in this collection, while his colleagues, Nella Ginatempo and Antonella Cammarota, present their more detailed case study of housing in the Southern Italian town of Messina. A consequence of this pattern has been that the Southern economy stayed locked in its stagnant, feudal agricultural state whereas the North developed, although rather slowly due to Italy's lack of raw materials, an inadequate financial structure and the effects of the unmodernized Southern agricultural sector. Italy's consequent domination by other more highly developed countries affected the nature of its development, e.g. placing more emphasis on advanced heavy rather than light industry. The more recent decentralization of some industry to the South has not solved the regional imbalance. Large-scale capital-intensive plants employing little local labour and often noxious, they are no more than industrial islands in a declining agricultural economy which has provided a source of cheap labour and a secondary consumer market for Northern industry. Urban growth continues in the larger Southern cities purely as a consequence of the collapse of agricultural employment, and these towns contain a bourgeoisie which derives much of its wealth from building speculation and a work force which is un- or underemployed in a variety of marginal occupations, or which receives public patronage in the form of government jobs, or which is in the building industry.

Mingione develops brief general analyses of his three class-based 'aspects' of territory in terms of the location of population and economic activity and the changes in economic and political structures, of the role of land ownership and planning and of the housing problem; these are then both related to, and developed via, a discussion of their nature in Southern Italy. This results in the identification of a number of basic causes and types of urban social conflict which are now present in the South. Mingione notes that the complex relationships between different elements of the ruling class and the working class vary from country to country. Thus important differences can be noted in countries where the working class are strongly integrated within the system and therefore have some effect on policy (as in Scandinavia, Great Britain, America and West Germany—in different ways) and countries, such as Italy, where a strong alliance between land owners and capitalists (but not a conflict-free one) means that land-use strategies serve their interests more directly and to the detriment of the working class. Furthermore, the differences between fractions of the working class are particularly acute in countries of the former sort because of the benefits which some of them receive. In such countries Mingione sees the need for the emergence of a strongly organized sector of the working class based on large modern industry to act as a focal point for unified action on urban and regional problems. However, he seems to suggest that in Italy, and possibly in France as well, there is already a more broadly based working class group which plays the major role in such conflicts.

As Mingione stresses, an analysis of the 'social base' of urban protest, i.e. the objective conditions which underly conflict and the various class interests involved in it, is not enough. One needs to understand how a 'social force' arises, i.e. how people become conscious of the objective conditions and their interests and organize in order to achieve the latter. It is symptomatic of Mingione's approach that he does not seek to identify a detailed set of general propositions at this point because he believes that detailed analysis of specific situations is the only real way to answer the questions. Nevertheless, one can identify some broad trends which are likely to govern the nature of urban struggles. Thus, in countries where the working class is highly integrated, such struggles will be fragmentary, locally based, involve heterogeneous social groups, only be concerned with immediate issues and collapse when they are solved, and make little fundamental impact. On the other hand, in countries where a broader class conflict is more evident, urban struggles are more often taken up by major working class political and trade union organizations and are thus seen as a part of a wider conflict.

In conclusion, Mingione's approach to the social analysis of regional and urban development rejects most of the recent attempts to restrict this to some special content, such as that contained in earlier urban sociology or in the diverse attempts of Pahl, Castells and Harvey to reconstruct such a context, whether it be the study of the urban bureaucracy and of the distribution of urban resources, collective consumption or the construction of the social infrastructure. Mingione's work is concerned with all these topics, but is set within the more general framework of an historical analysis of urban and regional development as a consequence of the evolution of the capitalist mode of production; his approach is more a multidisciplinary one than specifically sociological. Indeed, his main attempt to begin providing a conceptual framework (via the use of a definition of 'territory') linking his general theory of society and his specific historical analyses of urban and regional development, i.e. a special context as above, seems to be the least convincing part of his paper.

Szelenyi and Konrad's contribution bears comparison with both Pahl and Mingione's work, in the first case because it, too, focuses on the spatial distribution of unequal access to urban facilities and 'urban management' and seeks to make comparisons between capitalist and more developed socialist societies; in the second case because Szelenyi relates his conclusions to an historical analysis of the mode of production in Hungary, the country with which he is particularly concerned. Also, as in the case of Mingione's paper, Szelenyi and Konard's work can best be understood in the context of the more general considerations Szelenyi has given elsewhere[99] to this historical context.

In this latter work Szelenyi notes the similarity between the recent interests of urban sociologists in Eastern and Western Europe. Much of their work has focused on inequality as indicated by differential access to urban facilities and has tried to formulate policies which might ensure a more just distribution. In East and West the advice of sociologists was increasingly sought by the state which, in market and non-market economies alike, was the principal source of investment in the urban infrastructure. In the West such endeavours were based on the presumption that the state was an essentially neutral apparatus which could be used to bring aid to the underprivileged. In the East the orthodox view was that it was a workers' state. Other contributions to this book show how the neutrality of the capitalist state has been questioned; Szelenyi's work and that of his colleagues led them to a critical examination of the socialist state. The paper reprinted here reports on some of the empirical work which has stimulated this reappraisal.

The paper analyses one of the major causes of social tension in Hungary today. The rapid post-war growth of industry and its concentration in urban areas has not been matched by a comparable expansion of the infrastructure. This phenomenon of 'underurbanization', in conjunction with the system for allocating housing, creates a situation in which only more highly qualified workers can live near their work in the towns and those who have fewer skills are forced to live in the surrounding rural areas, often in poor housing with few services, and commute to work. Thus the division between rural and urban residence is increasingly also a division between lesser and more privileged groups in society as a whole.

This results from a policy of industrial expansion which required heavy investment and a pool of cheap labour. Regional planning sought to curb urban growth so that funds would not be diverted from industry. Also, agricultural prices were depressed in order to subsidize urban wages. Planners sought to justify their antiurban policies in terms of equality or the 'general interest', or by representing decisions as 'technical' matters. The similarity of such ideological explanations to those often given by their counterparts in the West is striking.[100] The authors point out that, as the state was dominated by the interests of industry and as it also controlled urban and regional development, the determination of the latter by the former was firmly established. However, the planners' ideology did not logically lead to the conclusions that it often sought to justify. For example, equality between regions as an ideal contrasted sharply with the reality of industrial concentration and uneven development, and the ideal became an ever more distant objective.

The pattern of development which occurred in Hungary produced unequal access to housing, entertainment, retail services and, perhaps most importantly, education which, in particular, helped to ensure that deprivation (and relative privilege) was transmitted to successive generations. Many rural commuters have to work in the city by day and on domestic smallholdings in the evening in order to supplement low earnings. This is a source of instability because the division of labour between the two activities is sensitive to the economic balance of advantage between them, and industries complain about the volatility of their work force. Therefore underurbanization has contradictory effects for industrial and economic development, for urban and regional planning and for social relations.

Since writing this paper Szelenyi has sought to place his analysis of recent Hungarian urban and regional development in its historical context. He focuses on the nature of the state in Eastern Europe and, drawing on Weber's work, contrasts the growth of the capitalist city based on political autonomy and self-government and having a tradition of conflict between central and local interests with the Asiatic city which lacked autonomy in a society based on a strong central bureaucracy. Szelenyi notes the existence of private ownership and a market in the former type of society and its absence in the latter.

Szelenyi suggests that it is these long-established differences between East and West rather than, in the first instance, changes that have occurred since the last war that underly the current phenomenon of underurbanization. When the Eastern European societies began to modernize, hundreds of years before the socialist revolution, they were already a long way behind the West. For this reason a higher rate of expropriation of surplus and a faster accumulation of capital was needed than could be assured by following the Western path of a gradual introduction of the market and private ownership. There is some evidence that the Russians (and to an extent the Hapsburgs) were aware, because of their contacts with the Mongols and Turks, of the advantages of the Asiatic mode of production and their reforms helped to establish an autocratic state which initiated a distinctive path of economic development based, for example, on serfdom rather than its abolition. Therefore pre-revolutionary, industrializing Hungary was not dominated by the capitalist mode of production, although elements of the market were present together with a 'redistributive' system based on a strong central state. Although Eastern Europe might eventually have been dominated by capitalism, the socialist revolution ensured the ascendancy of the 'redistributive' system.

Szelenyi also suggests that industrial development did not lead to an acceleration of urban growth similar to that which occurred in the West. Furthermore, the power of the central state was such that local reform and bureaucratic administration occurred 'from above'. Szelenyi is conscious of the need for further careful comparisons between countries within each system, because major differences exist, e.g. the centralized French state and the relative weakness of central control in Hungary compared with Russia. However, the broad conclusion is that the nature of the newly emerging system of urban and regional management described in his paper in this book stems from problems which are more 'East European' than socialist. Although there was popular power immediately after the Russian revolution in 1917, the task of building socialism required the swift reassertion of the central power of the communist party and the local soviets became agencies for the extraction of surplus and its transference to the state budget. This pattern was repeated in post-war Eastern Europe; often the organizations and even the personnel of the previous centralized regime were simply taken over. The result is a society with a combination of socialist characteristics, such as the near absence of private ownership and economic growth and wages unregulated by the market, and pre-revolutionary ones, such as the special role of the state in modernization, and elements of the land tenure system and the social structure built on it. However, the system has now evolved in certain respects. Further economic development now requires a high level of infrastructural investment, so urban and regional policy is becoming more concerned with the distribution of expenditure in the most 'rational' manner. Administrative reforms, such as the new system of local government based on larger units, are a consequence, as is the concentration of infrastructural development in relatively few industrializing areas, so leading to greater disparities.

Of course Szelenyi is aware of the increasing role of the state in these matters in the West, too, and the consequent similarities between certain aspects of planning and urban and regional development in the East and the West. However, he adds,

'But from an historical and structural analysis it must be sufficiently clear that despite certain parallels, the socialist redistribution and the contemporary Western regional grant economy were brought about by different socio-economic forces, and because they operate in a different structural context they will produce different contradictions.'

Szelenyi's analysis makes a distinctive contribution to the debate about the comparative study of urban and regional development in Eastern and Western Europe. He rejects Pahl's view that a common commitment to technology and rationality is responsible for similar urban and regional contradictions in both regions. Although urban inequalities exist in both and the range and form of state intervention has some strong similarities (including, at a certain level, 'rationality' and 'technology'), they are based on historically determined differences in the economic and social necessities of the reproductive process. Therefore Szelenyi would agree with Castells' comment (on observed similarities between soviet and capitalist cities) that 'formal analogies between types of behaviour are only meaningful when related to the social structure in which they are found', but would not agree with his assertion that such similarities are probably a consequence of the persistence of certain aspects of the formerly dominant capitalist mode of production in the socialist countries. Nor would Szelenyi agree with those who also assume this previous domination and now assert that capitalism is reestablishing itself in a new 'state-capitalist' guise.[101]

A stronger challenge to Szelenyi's theories may, however, come from those writers who reject the conception of the 'Asiatic' mode of production. Anderson's recent work, in which he criticizes Marx's concept of the Asiatic mode of production as descriptive and inadequate, is an example of this.[102] Anderson would also disagree with the simple distinctions Szelenyi makes between the medieval state in the East and West; both were dominated by feudal absolutism rather than the former by this system and the latter by an autonomous bourgeoisie, even though the presence at least of this latter factor in the west did significantly affect its path of development in ways different from those of the East. However, in Russia for example, by 1917 the social formation was dominated by the capitalist mode even though the state remained a feudal absolutism. Therefore, Anderson concludes, as does Szelenyi, that the revolution was not made against the capitalist state at all,[103] but evidently would not agree that this therefore denoted the absence of domination by the capitalist mode of production.[104] In general, Szelenyi's analysis seems to make little distinction between the nature of the dominant mode of production and the nature of the state, yet neither can be inferred from the other as he seems to suppose. It is to be hoped that sociologists in the East and the West will be able to develop their analyses further, both by detailed studies such as those of Konrad and Szelenyi and by drawing on the more general studies available of the nature of different modes of production and of the transformation from one dominant mode to another.[105]

The last two papers in this collection are both concerned with urban social movements. Pickvance's analysis of recent French work on this topic is an illustration of his own particular stance in the debate between the two main theoretical approaches to the study of urban and regional problems which have been discussed in this introduction, and which he has outlined in his own introduction to a collection of recent Marxist contributions to urban sociology. In his collection Pickvance suggests that other theoretical approaches may be of *complementary* use to explain objects of study ignored by historical materialism. He suggests that

'historical materialist concepts will have most purchase in those fields most closely concerned with the reproduction of social formations, and in respect of those institutions most concerned in this process, and least purchase in those fields and institutions most marginal to it, e.g. interpersonal relations in informal contexts, artistic production, social movements on "moral" issues.'[106]

Furthermore, Pickvance also believes that, within the general framework of an historical materialist analysis, theoretical gaps can be filled by reference to conclusions drawn from other types of sociological analysis, i.e. by *supplementing* historical materialism. His contribution to this volume may be seen as an example of this.

Such an approach bears comparison with Weber's contention that the sociologist imposes his own concepts in analysing events. It is hard to see how a Marxist method which posits a wholly different relation between theory and reality can be compatible with this view. Pickvance implicitly regards historical materialism as a theoretical approach which is applied to a certain content matter, identical to that analysed by alternative approaches. However, as we have seen, this is not so, for it is not just the explanations that Marxist theory gives that are different but the questions and therefore the content matter, also. Colletti has pointed out 'that Marxist method can never be divorced from the particular objective patterns which are reflected in it ... nor can any serious Marxist substitute or integrate the objective material patterns with "objects", as offered him by the procedures of other methodologies'.[107] Thus, in suggesting that historical materialism would be of little value in the analysis of, for example, artistic production Pickvance ignores the fact that important Marxist analyses of art do exist but they differ from other approaches in both the ways already refered to above.[108]

In his contribution to this collection, Pickvance aims to criticize certain omissions in recent French work on urban social movements and to supplement these analyses by reference to other work. In an earlier paper he examined a series of studies which, he argued, concentrated on the role and nature of protest movements and underemphasized the study of local authorities and their effects and other means of obtaining change in the 'urban system'.[109] As he notes, these omissions are not intrinsic to the Marxist approach, but it is less clear that his subsequent conclusion that Marxist analyses might be added to by theories from elsewhere follows. The more obvious conclusion might be that they need further elaboration and amendment from within the same perspective.

Some of the details of Pickvance's discussion of the relationship between social base and social force bear out the contention that, though he draws attention to important weaknesses in some current work on urban social movements and raises considerations which have to be taken into account in any reasonably adequate theory, the *lacunae* he detects do not require resolution in non-Marxist terms. For example, recent studies which have been content to define the social base in purely demographic terms and ignore value orientations are clearly defective, but other Marxist writers are, contrary to the impression given, quite aware of the complex relations between classes and fractions of classes and the importance of differing ideologies. The final comments in Mingione's paper are an illustration of this fact.

The following section of Pickvance's paper, suggests that Rex's work on housing classes[110] provides a useful source for discussion of the role of consciousness and organization in the formation of an urban social movement and makes the accurate observation that the studies he reviews pay little attention to this problem. This is really a criticism which is highlighting the difficulties that arise from the particular distinction between structures and practices made by Althusser and reflected in *La Question Urbaine*, already discussed in this introduction. Pickvance illustrates the significance of this problem by reference to two concepts of consciousness derived from Rex. These are the 'urban value system', a hierarchical ranking of 'ways of life' in different districts/ types of housing which 'overlays' the 'objective' class structure; and 'ethnic identity' which also imposes itself on the basic class division. Of course, as used by Rex, this also assumes a disjunction between structures and practices and it reduces the concept of class quite radically, abstracting certain important aspects of this concept from its definition only to reimpose them on what remains. In fact, as Rex's two concepts of consciousness are used purely for illustration in Pickvance's text, the argument that they are consequences of class relations, which Marxists would claim to be demonstrable, does not arise here.

However, the concluding discussion in Pickvance's paper on the determinants of participation in organizations does seem problematic. Insofar as these determinants are intended to be *independent* explanatory variables rather than consequences of the distinctive situation of a class or fraction of a class, they alter the basic concept of class itself. Of course factors such as the amount of time and its availability are important considerations when analysing organizational participation; however, to admit this point is not necessarily thereby to conclude that such factors are independent of class position, nor that 'terms of entry' can be similarly isolated for analysis. As Pickvance himself points out, such analyses abstract from the 'political conjuncture', i.e. the balance of the forces in the class struggle generally, which Marxists such as Mingione and Borja, whose paper completes this collection, argue cannot be ignored.

Borja's review of the nature and antecedents of urban social movements in Spain is particularly interesting because they have arisen there in a context markedly different to that in the rest of Western Europe, in an authoritarian state in which modern capitalism has been slower to develop than elsewhere in the region. In a nation lacking the usual democratic and trade union rights which exist elsewhere, urban protest can serve as a means of mobilization for wider objectives. On the basis of Castells' definition of urban social movements, these are likely to be more strongly developed in Spain than in the rest of Europe where industrial and political action is less restricted.

Borja's paper first seeks to establish the nature of the economic transformation that is affecting Spain and its urban consequences, concentration of population, creation of an underemployed urban labour force and lack of investment in the infrastructure. Rigid planning controls and property speculation ensue. New peripheral housing areas lack facilities, city centres die due to high land values and the *barrio* or neighbourhood reappears as the unit of social cohesion and collective action. Having established the nature of the various interests which are present in Spanish urban development, Borja analysis how, because of the necessity for the state to intervene in the urban problems that arise, new political structures are required to enable people to participate in the determination and operation of urban policies. However, the general nature of the Spanish political system is not responsive to such needs and it is often impossible to, for example, mobilize enough support from the various urban interests for major redevelopment schemes and more general plans.

Borja identifies the following as the main agents in Spanish urban politics: major property interests linked to finance capital, small owners, the population of settled residential areas (upper, middle and traditional working class) and the population of the deprived areas (some middle and mainly working class). Each has a particular relationship with the government but none of them have a wholly adequate one. His paper shows how the conflict between the various interests led to urban policies which were often impossible to achieve or which were of a contradictory nature. These stimulated the various groups to action in order to increase their influence on the government.

Referring back to Pickvance's paper, it is interesting to compare Borja's detailed and far from purely demographic analysis of the nature of the social base to Spanish urban social movements. Furthermore, the second part of his contribution is initially concerned with the question of the transformation of this social base into a social force. Lack of working or middle class protest until the sixties is related to political and economic factors which made effective action unlikely. Borja therefore connects the rise of an organized protest with the likelihood that some demands are capable of at least partial acceptance, that being 'legitimated' in this way they achieve some success which encourages continuity and development of the movement. The detailed analysis of six different types of urban movement which follows concludes with a series of general observations on the factors (which include a range of economic and political considerations) which affect the success of the movement, such as the type of government agencies involved, the nature and importance of the issue and the type of protest organization. His analysis of the political aspects of urban movements deals with the functions they perform in mobilizing and linking class-based conflict groups and in influencing the more general political struggle for a democratic system. Aspects of this struggle have support from elements of the dominant class as well, when such struggles are in their interests too. However, a key factor for Borja (as for others such as Mingione) in explaining the emergence of an active movement is 'the mediation of those active and dedicated individuals who constitute the most advanced element of the population'.

This concluding paper may lack the degree of theoretical organization present in some of the other studies of urban social movements which Pickvance criticizes. However, its author does not wish to impose an ahistorical abstraction on historical material which reflects the complex economic, political and ideological factors determining the nature and actions of these movements in Spain. Nor, in comparison with some Italian work on the same topic referred to by Mingione in his paper, does Borja take for granted the existence of consciousness in their formation. This, of course, is hardly surprising because, as he notes, public support for such movements is the main guarantee against government reprisals.

## 4. Conclusion

This long introduction has concentrated on a critical analysis of some aspects of the new body of work presented in the papers which follow. A wholly adequate and comprehensive treatment would have consumed even more space, but it is hoped that enough has been discussed to illustrate the broad range of work now being done and its connection with many of the issues which are central to the study of society. Neither of these claims could have been made for the bulk of past urban social research. It is obvious, both from this introduction and from the papers that follow, that the book contains 'work in progress' rather than assured and polished products of some well-established intellectual specialism. All of the authors are developing their theoretical and empirical research and, in many cases, are as aware as their critics of the problems that their provisional conclusions raise. However, little of this work has been collected together in a way which makes comparison possible and fewer still are the criticisms that have been available in print and in English. This book is one step towards broadening the discussion of this new work and the range of those who are able to participate in it.

The movement away from the type of urban research which provides, in Pahl's words, 'new ways of wiping up the drips from a leaky tap',[111] to the more fundamental appraisal denoted by the study of the 'political economy of space', which all the contributors to this book accept, raises interesting questions concerning the relationship of the new types of research (and teaching) which it demands to those who sponsor such activities in society, principally the state. It is Pahl again who raised the issue most clearly when he pointed out that research which demonstrates, for example, how powerless to effect redistribution planners really are, or how complex or misconceived are the subjects of policy, may well make those in government who sponsor such research feel cheated and irritated. Writing in a British context, he has predicted an unpopular future for the urban sociologist and suggests that law or even accountancy are likely to be more popular skills!

On the other hand, it is interesting to note that much of the recent French work discussed in this book is a product of state-sponsored research. It remains to be seen whether this is a general development or one which is specific to a particular period of French history and that society's distinctive intellectual and political tradition. Furthermore, the questions raised by such a situation, for Marxist analysts at least, go deeper still. Pahl, however, is certain that the alternative to critical urban research is little more than the urban ideology which Castells has so effectively identified,

'positivistic research in the social sciences is essentially a means of providing "facts" for interest groups. The government or local authority sponsor research to justify the policies which they later pursue; minority groups use other "research" to justify their opposition to given policies.'[112]

He adds that his own involvement as a government adviser at the public enquiry into the Greater London Development Plan showed him that 'experts could readily be hired to support almost any position with appropriate research and documentation'.[113]

As already mentioned in the context of Marxist work, this new urban research also has its consequences for the position of its practitioners within the traditional disciplinary framework of academic study. Urban and regional development has been the subject of study for sociologists, economists, political scientists, historians, geographers and others, but the boundaries of their concerns as defined by these specialisms have failed to match the complexity and interrelatedness of the concrete phenomena they seek to analyse. This has led a search for an inter- or multidisciplinary approach which has been manifested in various forms, ranging from collections of articles, each written from a distinct specialist viewpoint, to the search for some general unifying perspective, e.g. 'theory of planning'.[114] Such efforts tend to lack conviction. On the one hand, they can find no legitimate way of going beyond self-imposed disciplinary boundaries, leaving the connections to be made in the imagination of the reader; on the other hand, theory tends to be reduced to a collection of vague or tendentious generalities. The established structure of academic teaching has discouraged such attempts anyway and Pahl's recent invitation to a conference[115] to discuss the relationship between the type of research reported in this book and urban sociology courses raises an issue which has yet to be resolved.

*London*
*May 1976*

## Notes

1. For example, in Britain the growth of state-sponsored planning research and education in the sixties has been particularly rapid. Thus Eversley has recently estimated that central government expenditure on planning research has grown from £0.294m in 1966 to £3.583m in 1975 and the total research and development budget for the Department of the Environment (all types of research) stood at over £25m in 1974–1975. (Eversley, D.E.C., *The Growth of Planning Research Since the Early Sixties*, Social Science Research Council, London, 1975.)
2. Rex, J. A., Sociology and planning: a dialogue, *Municipal Review*, 95–96, February 1969.
3. Text of a statement prepared by the Board of the Research Committee on the Sociology of Regional and Urban Development at its meeting in Budapest, 5th and 6th April 1972.
4. Glass, R., Urban sociology in Great Britain (1955). Reprinted in *Readings in Urban Sociology* (Ed. R. E. Pahl), Pergamon, London, 1968, p. 48.
5. Although, in Britain at least, earlier work in the nineteenth and twentieth centuries did display this broader concern. (*Ibid.*, pp. 53–59.)
6. For example, Pickvance has recently argued that Castells' dismissal of certain aspects of the theoretical content of previous urban sociology is unconvincing. (Pickvance, C. G. Historical materialist approaches to urban sociology, in *Urban Sociology: Critical Essays* (Ed. C. G. Pickvance), Tavistock, London, 1976, pp. 3–10 and 30–32.)
7. Castells, M., *La Question Urbaine*, Maspero, Paris, 1972, Parts I and II, pp. 17–149. To be published in English (Arnold, London) shortly. A basic outline of his critique is also contained in, Is there an urban sociology? (1968) and Theory and ideology in urban sociology (1969), in *Urban Sociology: Critical Essays* (Ed. C. G. Pickvance), Tavistock, London, 1976, pp. 33–84.
8. Althusser, L., *For Marx*, Vintage, New York, 1970, and Althusser, L., and Balibar, E., *Reading Capital*, New Left Books, London, 1970. Both these works were available in French and therefore had a wide impact in France in 1965.
9. *Urban Sociology: Critical Essays* (Ed. C. G. Pickvance), Tavistock, London, 1976, p. 5.
10. Pahl, R. E., Urban social theory and research (1969). Reprinted in Pahl, R. E., *Whose City?*, 2nd ed., Penguin, Harmondsworth, 1975, pp. 195–212.
11. Rex, J. A., and Moore, R., *Race, Community and Conflict*, Oxford University Press, London, 1967.
12. A good summary of recent British work from this perspective and some of the problems are contained in Norman, P., Managerialism—a review of recent work,

in *Proceedings of the Conference on Urban Change and Conflict* (Ed. M. Harloe), Centre for Environmental Studies, London, 1975, pp. 62–86.

13. See, for example, Davis, J. G., *The Evangelistic Bureaucrat*, Tavistock, London, 1972, and Dennis, N., *Public Participation and Planner's Blight* and *People and Planning*, Faber and Faber, London, 1972 and 1970. For a critical review of this 'radical' sociology see Harloe, M., Inner urban areas—a review article, *CES W.N. 356*, Centre for Environmental Studies, London, 1972.

14. Pahl, R. E., *Whose City?*, 2nd ed., Penguin, Harmondsworth, 1975, p. 6.

15. Pahl, R. E., A perspective on urban sociology, in Pahl, R. E. (Ed.), *Readings in Urban Sociology*, Pergamon, London, 1968, p. 13.

16. Mingione has suggested that a different pattern, dissolving the Western urban forms, may be emerging in China (Mingione, E., Sull' uso socialista del territerio, in CRMP, *Citta e Campagna in Cina*, Calusca, Milan, 1976.).

17. Pahl, R. E., Urban processes and social structure, in Pahl, R. E., *Whose City?*, 2nd ed., Penguin, Harmondsworth, 1975, p. 250.

18. Anderson, J., *The Political Economy of Urbanism. An Introduction and Bibliography*, Architectural Association, London, 1975, p. i.

19. Published quarterly since 1970 by Editions Anthropos, Paris.

20. Strictly speaking of course, 'Marxist theory' in the abstract does not exist; the reference is always to a specific social formation and dominant mode of production or a transitional period. Thus the remarks here refer to modern Western societies dominated by the capitalist mode of production.

21. 'Class has a double significance: firstly as factors or *objective conditions* of production... and secondly as the *political agents* of the whole human social process'. (Marxism as a sociology, in Colletti, L., *From Rousseau to Lenin, Studies in Ideology and Society*, New Left Books, London, 1972, p. 14.)

22. Poulantzas, N., The capitalist state: a reply to Miliband and Laclau, *New Left Review*, **95**, 74, 1976.

23. Quoted by E. Balibar in Althusser, L. and Balibar, E., *Reading Capital*, New Left Books, London, 1970, p. 308.

24. See Poulantzas, N., *Political Power and Social Classes*, New Left Books, London, 1973.

25. Mellor and others have recently suggested a new basis for urban sociology which draws on the analysis of the relation between more and less developed countries developed by Frank and others. (Mellor, R., Urban sociology in an urbanised society, *British Journal of Sociology*, **XXVI**, No. 3, 276–293, 1975). However, as she mentions, there are many problems surrounding Frank's key distinction between 'surplus expropriation/appropriation', and 'metropolis/satellite polarisation'. For relevant critiques, see Booth, D., Andre Gunder Frank: An introduction and appreciation, in I. Oxaal *et. al.*, *Beyond the Sociology of Development: Economy and Society in Africa and Latin America*, Routledge, London, 1974, and Laclau, E., Feudalism and capitalism in Latin America, *New Left Review*, **67**, 19–38, 1971. For an attempt to apply Frank's analysis to regional development see Carter, I., The Highlands of Scotland as an underdeveloped region, in Kadt, E. de, and Williams, G., *Sociology and Development*, Tavistock, London, 1974, pp. 279–311.

26. See the works by Althusser and Poulantzas cited above and also Poulantzas, N., *Classes in Contemporary Capitalism*, New Left Books, London, 1975.

27. Weber, M., *Economy and Society*, Vol. III, Bedminster Press, New York, 1968, Chap. XVI, The city (nonlegitimate domination). Merrington has recently analysed the relation between urban development and the growth of capitalism, suggesting that 'It is wrong to interpret the "freedom" of the medieval towns in a one-sided, unilateral sense outside the feudal context which both determined the "externality" of this freedom of merchant capital and defined its limits. The town's autonomy was not that of a "non-feudal island" (Postan); its freedom and development as

a corporate enclave was not "according to its *own* propensities", as in Weber's historicist formulations'. (Merrington, J., Town and country in the transition to capitalism, *New Left Review*, **93**, 71–92, 1975.)

28. *Ibid.*, p. 1309.
29. Bendix, R., *Max Weber: An Intellectual Portrait*, Methuen, London, 1966, p. 382.
30. Gerth, H., and Mills, C. W., *From Max Weber*, Routledge, London, 1964, p. 49.
31. *Ibid.*, p. 47.
32. Marx, K., *Grundrisse*, Penguin, Harmondsworth, 1973, p. 265.
33. Tristram, R., Ontology and theory. A comment on Marx's analysis of some of the problems, *Sociological Review (NS)*, **23**, No. 4, 764–765, 1975.
34. *Ibid.*, p. 767.
35. Marx, K., *Grundrisse*, Penguin, Harmondsworth, 1973, p. 86.
36. *Ibid.*, pp. 85–88.
37. A term which is in no sense intended to convey some average or mean abstracted from real-world situations around which the latter are distributed in some obscure manner.
38. Tristram, R., Ontology and theory. A comment on Marx's analysis of some of the problems, *Sociological Review (NS)*, **23**, No. 4, 721, 1975.
39. See Nagel, E., *Principles of the Theory of Probability*, University of Chicago Press, Chicago, 1970; Popper, K. R., *Logic of Scientific Discovery*, Hutchinson, London, 1959, and *Conjectures and Refutations*, 3rd ed (rev.), Routledge, London, 1969; Kuhn, T. S., *The Stucture of Scientific Revolutions*, (2nd ed., University of Chicago Press, Chicago, 1970. For a critical discussion of Popper and Kuhn see *Criticism and Growth of Knowledge* (Eds. Latakos, I. and Musgrave, S.), Cambridge University Press, London, 1970, especially the papers by Kuhn, Popper, Latakos and Feyeraband. For a Marxist view of some aspects of this work (and of the origin of Althusser's epistemology) see Counihan, T., Epistemology of science—Feyeraband and Lecourt, *Economy and Society*, **5**, No. 1, 74–110, February 1976, and Williams, K., Facing reality—A critique of Karl Popper's empiricism, *Economy and Society*, **4**, No. 3, 309–358, 1974.
40. Colletti, L., *From Rousseau to Lenin, Studies in Ideology and Society*, New Left Books, London, 1972, p. 39.
41. *Ibid*, pp. 41–44.
42. Hobsbawm refers to Marx's refusal to separate the different academic disciplines and comments: 'such mechanical divisions are misleading, and entirely contrary to Marx's method ... [it is] entirely wrong ... to think of historical materialism as an *economic* (or for that matter a *sociological*) interpretation of history'. (Hobsbawm, E. J., Introduction to Marx, K., *Precapitalist Economic Formations*, Lawrence and Wishart, London, 1964, pp. 16–17.)
43. Althusser, L., and Balibar, E., *Reading Capital*, New Left Books, London, 1970, pp. 20–21, quoting Marx, K., *Capital*, Vol. 1, Lawrence and Wishart, London, n.d., pp. 208–209.
44. Althusser, L., *For Marx*, Vintage, New York, 1970, pp. 170–171 (on the materialist dialectic).
45. Geras, N., Althusser's Marxism: An account and assessment, *New Left Review*, **71**, 66, 1972.
46. See Colletti, L., *From Rousseau to Lenin, Studies in Ideology and Society*, New Left Books, London, 1972, pp. 229–236 (Marxism: science or revolution?).
47. Pahl has reevaluated his approach to urban managerialism in Pahl, R. E., *Whose City?*, 2nd ed., Penguin, Harmondsworth, 1975, pp. 265–287 ('Urban managerialism' reconsidered).
48. Pahl, R. E., and Winkler, J. T., The coming corporatism, *New Society*, 72–76, 10th October 1974; Winkler, J. T., Corporatism, *European Journal of Sociology* (forthcoming 1976); and Pahl, R. E., Collective consumption and the state in capita-

44

list and state socialist societies, in *Cleavage and Constraint: Studies in Industrial Society* (Ed. Scase, R.) Chap. 9, Allen and Unwin, London, forthcoming.

49. Giddens, A., *The Class Structure of the Advanced Societies*, Hutchinson, London, 1973.
50. Weber, M., Class, status, party, in Gerth, H. and Mills, C. W., *From Max Weber*, Routledge, 1964, pp. 180–244.
51. Harloe, M. H. (Ed.), *Proceedings of the Conference on Urban Change and Conflict*, Centre for Environmental Studies, London, 1975, p. 18.
52. Castells, M., and Godard, F., *Monopolville*, Mouton, Paris, 1974.
53. For reference to these differences, see especially Poulantzas, N., *Political Power and Social Classes*, New Left Books, London, 1973, and *Classes in Contemporary Capitalism*, New Left Books, London, 1975.
54. In particular see Castells, M., The interaction between the urban structure and the urban political process: The case of the urban crisis in the United States, in *The Urban Question*, Part V, Arnold, London, forthcoming. This new addition to the English version of Castell's book presents a significant development of his work, but became available too late to be reviewed in this introduction.
55. Althusser, L. and Balibar, E., *Reading Capital*, New Left Books, 1970, p. 97.
56. Althusser, L., *For Marx*, Vintage, New York, 1970, p. 209 (On the materialist dialectic).
57. Althusser, L., and Balibar, E., *Reading Capital*, New Left Books, 1970, p. 224.
58. *Ibid.*, p. 180.
59. Castells, M., *La Question Urbaine*, Maspero, Paris, 1972, pp. 165–166.
60. *Ibid.*, pp. 303–304 (extract trans. C. G. Pickvance).
61. Pickvance, C. G. (Ed.), *Urban Sociology: Critical Essays*, Tavistock, London, 1976, pp. 26–27.
62. Parkin, F., *A Marxist Sociology of the Superstructure*, paper given to the British Sociological Association Conference on the Advanced Industrial Societies, University of Kent, Canterbury, 1975.
63. Garnier, F., A propos de 'la question urbaine', *Espaces et Sociétiés*, **8**, 123–129, February 1973.
64. Laclau, E., The specificity of the political: the Poulantzas–Miliband debate, *Economy and Society*, **5**, No. 1, 87–110 February 1975.
65. See Geras, N., Althusser's Marxism: An account and assessment, *New Left Review*, **71**, 57–86, 1972; Glucksmann, A., A ventriloquist structuralism, *New Left Review*, **72**, 68–92, 1972; Glucksmann, M., *Structuralist Analysis in Contemporary Social Theory*, Routledge, London, 1974; and Macey, D., and Taylor, J., *The Theoreticism of 'Theoretical Practice'*, London (mimeo).
66. See Geras, *ibid.*, p. 64.
67. See Althusser, L. and Balibar, E., *Reading Capital*, New Left Books, London, 1970, Foreword to the Italian Edition, and Althusser, L., *Lenin and Philosophy and other Essays*, New Left Books, London, 1971, pp. 13–25.
68. Poulantzas, N., The capitalist state: reply to Miliband and Laclau, *New Left Review*, **95**, 1976.
69. Castells, M., *La Question Urbaine*, Maspero, Paris, 1972, p. 441 (extract trans. C. G. Pickvance).
70. *Ibid.*, p. 442.
71. Ecker, T., *Theory and Empirical Research: A Discussion*, unpublished paper, Polytechnic of Central London, June 1975.
72. Poulantzas and Castells both refer to the growing role of the state in modern capitalist society. However, Poulantzas also suggests that 'capital is directly invading all sectors "outside" the economic relations of labour in the strict sense, both those involved in the reproduction of labour-power (town planning, housing, transport, etc.) or the sphere outside of work altogether (leisure, "free time", etc.)'. (Poulantzas,

N., *Classes in Contemporary Capitalism*, New Left Books, London, 1975, p. 312; see also p. 165.) Clearly, although state intervention overall is growing, its nature and extent in any specific area is likely to vary according to the profit possibilities of such an area. These will vary over time in some cases and when profits can be realized pressure may well arise for the 'privatisation' of state provision.

73. Preteceille, E., with Pinçon, M., and Rendu, P., *Equipements Collectifs, Structures Urbaines et Consommation Sociale*, Centre de Sociologie Urbaine, Paris, 1975. Also Pahl has raised a series of interesting questions about the concept (Pahl, R. E., Collective consumption and the state in capitalist and state socialist societies, in *Cleavage and Constraint: Studies in Industrial & Society* (Ed. Scase, R.), Chap. 9, Allen and Unwin, London, forthcoming.

74. Harvey, D., *Social Justice and the City*, Arnold, London, 1973.

75. Baran, P., and Sweezy, P., *Monopoly Capital*, Penguin, Harmondsworth, 1966.

76. O'Connor, J., *The Fiscal Crisis of the State*, St. Martin's Press, New York, 1973.

77. For an outline of the theory of monopoly capital and some critiques see Gamble, A., and Walton, P., *Capitalism and Crisis*, Macmillan, London, 1976, pp. 77–110.

78. Gough, I., State expenditure in advanced capitalism, *New Left Review*, **92**, 53–92, 1975.

79. See Gamble, A. and Walton, P., *Capitalism and Crisis*, Macmillan, London, 1976. The debate about the falling rate of profit is both complex and controversial. Hodgson, for example, regards the view that the 'law' of the falling rate of profit due to a rise in the organic composition of capital is a key element in Marxist analysis as misconceived, drawing on neo-Ricardian economics in his discussion. On the other hand, Glyn and Sutcliffe do suggest that (British) capitalism is in decline because of a falling rate of profit, but they relate this not to an inevitable rise in the organic composition of capital but rather to successful trade union and working class struggle (see Glyn, A., and Sutcliffe, R., *Workers, British Capitalism and the Profits Squeeze*, Penguin, Harmondsworth, 1972, and Hodgson, G., Theory of the falling rate of profit, *New Left Review*, **84**, 55–82 1974.

80. It should be noted that, in making this criticism, Gough too seems to assume that a distinction can be made between 'laws' and the class struggle. I am indebted to Doreen Massey for pointing this out.

81. Preteceille, E., with Pinçon, M., and Rendu, P., *Equipments Collectifs, Structures Urbaines et Consommation Sociale*, Centre de Sociologie Urbaine, Paris, 1975.

82. Castells, M., *La Question Urbaine*, Maspero, Paris, 1972, pp. 117–128.

83. Harvey writes, concerning Levfebvre's thesis, 'To say that the thesis is not true at this juncture in history is not to say that it is not in the process of becoming true or that it cannot become true in the future. The evidence suggests that the forces of urbanisation are emerging strongly and moving to dominate the centre stage of world history'. (Harvey, D., *Social Justice and the City*, p. 313. Arnold, London, 1973.)

84. See the contributions by Bruegel I., and Byrne, D. and Beirne, P. in *Political Economy and the Housing Question*, Political Economy of Housing Workshop, London, 1975, pp. 34–67.

85. Poulantzas, N., *Classes in Contempory Capitalism*, New Left Books, London, 1975, pp. 93–95; Frank, A. G., *Capitalism and Underdevelopment in Latin America*, Monthly Review Press, London and New York, 1967; and Emmanuel, A., *Unequal Exchange*, New Left Books, London, 1972. In footnote 8 to his article in this collection Mingione points out that the two alternative Marxist explanations of imperialism go back to the analyses of Lenin and Luxemburg respectively. He suggests that neither Frank's nor Emmanuel's theories can be identified with one of the alternatives only; they show features of those theories which stress the generation of surplus (Lenin) and those which stress its realization (Luxemburg).

86. Poulantzas (1975), *ibid.*, p. 109.

87. Lojkine, J., Contribution to a Marxist theory of capitalist urbanisation, in Pick-vance, C. G. (Ed.), *Urban Sociology: Critical Essays*, Tavistock, London, 1976, pp. 119–146.
88. Pickvance (Ed.), *ibid.*, p. 19 (Historical materialist approaches to urban sociology).
89. Ecker, T., *Theory and Empirical Research: A Discussion*, unpublished paper, Poly-technic of Central London, June 1975.
90. Poulantzas, N., *Classes in Contemporary Capitalism*, New Left Books, London, 1975, pp. 156–174.
91. *Ibid.*, p. 107.
92. *Ibid.*, p. 157. In commenting on the draft of this introduction Pickvance suggests that Poulantzas has here confused two issues: (*a*) the independence *as entities* of state and monopolies and (*b*) the alleged determination of the policies of the former by the latter. The theory he is attacking actually consists of (*b*).
93. *Ibid.*, p. 162–163.
94. Pickvance has recently analysed the Poulantzas–Lojkine controversy at length. He suggests that, although Lojkine on one occasion did seem to suggest that the state is 'independent' from society, this was merely a slip. Certainly in the original and slightly longer version of the article reprinted in this book, Lojkine accepts Poulantzas' criticism of his 'confusion' but states that this is a lapse which is 'in complete contradiction with other analyses where on the contrary we show how the state reflects the class struggle and the dominance of one class or another' (Lojkine J., Strategies des grandes entreprises, politiques urbaines et mouvements sociaux urbains, *Sociologie du Travail*, **1**, 28, 1975, quoted in Pickvance, C. G., *Marxist Approaches to the Study of Urban Politics: Divergences Among Some Recent French Studies*, paper for the political Studies Association Conference, Nottingham, 1976, mimeo). Pickvance concludes that both Poulantzas and Lojkine misinterpret fundamental aspects of each other's approach; in fact, 'The difference dividing Lojkine and Poulantzas is one of political strategy' rather than a theoretical one with respect to the relationship between the state and social classes.
95. Pickvance, C. G., Housing: reproduction of capital and reproduction of labour power: some recent French work, *Antipode*, forthcoming. Also reprinted in Walton, J., and Masotti, L. (Eds.), *The City in Comparative Perspective*, Sage, Berkeley, 1976.
96. Poulantzas, N., *Classes in Contemporary Capitalism*, New Left Books, London, 1975, p. 186.
97. *Ibid.*, p. 23.
98. Mingione, E., Territorial division of labour and capitalist development, *Current Sociology*, 1976, forthcoming.
99. Szelenyi, I., *Regional Management and Social Class*, Centre for Environmental Studies, London, 1975.
100. See, for example, Dennis, N., *Public Participation and Planner's Blight* and *People and Planning.*, Faber and Faber, London, 1972 and 1970.
101. An important British example of this is found in Cliff, T., *Russia. A Marxist Analysis*, International Socialism, London, n.d. Miliband has recently criticized key aspects of different but somewhat similar types of analysis (Miliband, R. Bettleheim and Soviet experience, *New Left Review*, **91**, 57–66, May 1975).
102. Anderson, P., *Lineages of the Absolutist State*, New Left Books, London, 1974, pp. 462–549. (See also Notes 103 to 105 below.)
103. *Ibid.*, pp. 353–359. Hobsbawm, E. J., Introduction to Marx, K., *Precapitalist Econo-mic Formations*, Lawrence and Wishart, London, 1962, contains a valuable account of Marx and Engel's treatment of pre-capitalist modes of production and its problems and subsequent theoretical developments. From his account, and those of others, its seems difficult to see how Szelenyi's suggestion that the Asiatic *mode* was dominant in the East can be sustained (rather than a particular type of feudal

mode), even if the state apparatus did resemble the Asiatic state in certain aspects. In another essay Hobsbawm has suggested that Eastern Europe was 're-feudalised' as semi-colonies of developing Western capitalism from the mid-fifteenth century, after the earlier Asian conquest (Hobsbawm, E. J., From feudalism to capitalism, *Marxism Today*, August 1962). Possibly Szelenyi's conception of Eastern Europe might better be characterized as 'state feudalism'. His view of the nature of the state in Eastern Europe also bears comparison with Wittfogel's thesis (see Wittfogel, K., *Oriental Despotism*, Yale University Press, New Haven, 1964, especially Chaps. 9 and 10) which is usefully discussed in Hindness, B., and Hirst, P. Q., *Precapitalist Modes of Production*, Routledge, London, 1975, pp. 208–220.

104. However, this seems to have little impact on Anderson for, according to Hirst in his recent critique, Anderson in his comments on Russia is deriving the class nature of the state from the nature of its apparatus, not the nature of the dominant class as most Marxists would. As a consequence, Anderson concludes that the non-development of bourgeois democracy leaves the East with a tradition of authoritarian state rule derived from the feudal state. Interestingly, Hirst concludes that Anderson's work is 'speculative empiricism of the comparative method' and historicist. He likens Anderson's attempt to explain why capitalist development occurred in the West to Weber's work. (Hirst, P., The uniqueness of the West, *Economy and Society*, 4, No. 4, 446–475, November 1975.)

105. See, for example, Dobb, M. H., *Studies in the Development of Capitalism*, Routledge, London, 1946, pp. 446–475; Sweezy, P. et. al. *The Transition from Feudalism to Capitalism*, (new ed.), New Left Books, London, 1976; Hindness, B., and Hirst, P. Q., *Precapitalist Modes of Production*, Routledge, London, 1975. On the transition between capitalism and socialism, Bettleheim's work (a part of which is contained in the recently translated Bettleheim, C., *Economic Calculation and Forms of Property*, Routledge, London, 1976) is important. On the role of the town in the development of capitalism see Merrington, J., Town and country in the transition to capitalism, *New Left Review*, 93, 71–92, 1975.

106. Pickvance, C. G., (Ed.), p. 31 (Historical materialist approaches to urban sociology). *Urban Sociology: Critical Essays*, Tavistock, London, 1976.

107. Colletti, I., *From Rousseau to Lenin: Studies in Ideology and Society*, New Left Books, London, 1972, p. 9.

108. In commenting on this analysis of his position Pickvance has rejected the distinction made here between complementary and supplementary usages and the conclusions drawn in this paragraph. He also writes that he sees the Marxist position as unevenly developed but 'it remains an open question just what its capacities are in some areas'. However, '. . . I would argue for a materialist epistemology and insist that Marxist analysis is not just one more story, equally valid, because equally noncomparable with other stories, but that its superiority is to a considerable (though varying) degree demonstrable.'

109. Pickvance, C. G., On the study of urban social movements, in Pickvance, C. G. (Ed.), *Urban Sociology: Critical Essays*, Tavistock, London, 1976, pp. 198–218.

110. See Rex, J. A., The sociology of a zone of transition, in Pahl, R. E. (Ed.), *Readings in Urban Sociology*, Pergamon, London, 1968.

111. Pahl, R. E., *Whose City?*, 2nd ed., Penguin, Harmondsworth, 1975, p. 5.

112. *Ibid.*, p. 3, 12.

113. *Ibid.*, p. 5.

114. See Stewart, M. (Ed.), *The City: Problems of Planning*, Penguin, Harmondsworth, 1972; and Faludi, A., *Planning Theory*, Pergamon, London, 1973.

115. Harloe, M. H., (Ed.), *Proceedings of the Conference on Urban Change and Conflict*, Centre for Environmental Studies, London, 1975, p. 233.

# 1
# Managers, Technical Experts and the State: Forms of Mediation, Manipulation and Dominance in Urban and Regional Development*

*R. E. Pahl*

The study of urban and regional development is increasingly coming to be synonymous with the study of political economy. No longer need sociologists concerned with the urban question limit themselves to fruitless attempts to get theoretical yields from the now overworked ground of the Chicago ecologists. Similarly, there is a growing confidence among urban sociologists in rejecting the definitions of urban problems provided by others; such problem-definers seek to adjust their clients to specific patterns of land use or to the location and distribution of urban services and facilities. Freed from the atheoretical and ideological constraints which inhibited much previous work, a return to the concerns and levels of analysis of Marx and Weber enables those concerned with urban questions to shed new light on the sociology of the advanced societies. A focus on the sphere of consumption, on the distribution and scale of urban infrastructural investment and on the role of the state in general, raises problems and issues which have been largely neglected by sociologists until recently. Even in Giddens' recent work on *The Class Structure of the Advanced Societies*[1] there is virtually no mention of the urban problematic.

The purpose of this paper is, firstly, to set out some of the main elements in the Weberian or bureaucratic model of urban management which developed largely in Britain, and to a lesser extent in the United States. Secondly, I turn to discuss the Marxist analysis of the urban question which has developed in France: this focuses on the role of a relatively autonomous state. Finally, I mention the difficulties in incorporating analysis of the role of the state and the technical experts in Eastern Europe into the previous analyses developed in different contexts. Comparative analysis of urban and regional development in the advanced societies is the essential foundation for the political economy of space. In what follows I have been extremely selective, intentionally sacrificing the one virtue of comprehensiveness to the other of clarity. My presentation of

*I have received pertinent comments on this paper from Martin Boddy and Chris Paris. Neither of them is responsible in any way for what I have written; their most substantial points were too fundamental to respond to in this context.

the arguments of the so-called 'managerialist thesis' does not necessarily imply that I accept them in that form.

## 1. Structured and Systematic Inequalities are Said to be Generated Independently of an Individual's or a Category's Position in the Labour Market

This argument was originally put forward by Rex and Moore in 1967. In their formulation of housing classes they define them not solely by an individual's or a category's ownership of capital, or market power of skill or labour, but by their *degrees of access* to housing, 'and it is this which immediately determines the class conflicts of the city as distinct from the workplace'.[2] There are as many classes as there are kinds of access and being a member of one of them 'is of first importance in determining a man's associations, his interests, his life style, and his position in the urban social structure'.[3]

This formulation, in its strong and unqualified form, is open to criticism,[4] and Rex has responded to some of these.[5] It is unnecessary to go into these arguments here; suffice to say that Rex and Moore did much to draw attention to systems of distribution and allocation independent of those created by labour markets. They suggested that the formal bureaucratic rules and procedures operated by local authorities had systematic and punitive effects, and they argued that this could give rise to common feelings of actual or potential deprivation which would generate conflict. Further, they related these ideas to the spatial structure of the city. They are cautious about the universality of their model and it is clear from later studies that, even if their formulation had some limited temporal and spatial validity, other cities and different legislation provide substantial modifications.

## 2. The Managers of the Urban System are Claimed to Exert an Independent Influence on the Allocation of Scarce Urban Resources and Facilities which may Reinforce, Reflect or Reduce the Inequalities Engendered by the Differentially Rewarded Occupational Structure

In my original formulation of the position[6] I emphasized that the access to any scarce urban resource or facility could be seen as comprising two elements: the *spatial* element, which could be expressed in terms of time/cost distance, and the *social* element, which included on the one hand the rules and procedures which defined access for populations, defined in both social and spatial terms (e.g. old-age pensioners living in a given local authority area), and on the other hand the interpretation and administration of these rules and procedures by local managers or gatekeepers. The knowledge, awareness and understanding of the nature of the given facility by sections of the population was also seen as a factor affecting access, perhaps in a kind of 'fossilized' form. (For example, a low level of education following from previous poor provision of schooling might lead to low take-up rates of various rights and benefits at a later stage.) Quite evidently, space is a material resource which can be manipulated according to the goals and values of those responsible for deciding locations and distributions.[7] Similarly, there are those who determine the rules and procedures of all allocation and those whose access is thereby modified. This position, like the previous formulation, has had its critics and discussants,[8] and to these I have responded by largely accepting them and, indeed, enlarging on them in my own critique of managerialism.[9] Firstly, there is a clear danger, as Gouldner has reminded us, of taking the underdog's perspective and attributing too much power and influence to the middle-dogs, which may lead to an 'uncritical accommodation to the national elite and to the society's master institutions'.[10] Secondly, there is a danger of accepting local government's own 'managerialist' conception of itself and its assumed independence from market forces.[11] This may also lead to a neglect of the managers in the private sector. Finally, an urban managerialist position implies the systematic control of the same urban resources and facilities in different localities and the ineffectiveness of elected councillors or central institutions to introduce variations. In brief, it implies a degree of autonomy by the local urban technostructure, for which there is certainly some evidence[12] but which cannot be upheld with the strength I originally propounded.

### 3. Location and Access are Put Forward as the Only Independent Bases for Urban Politics

This position has been most persuasively presented by Williams.[13] Basically he is arguing that urban politics is based on conflicts over resources which have a spatial dimension and that people deploy themselves in space in order to improve their access to such resources. Coalitions can form to improve collective accessibility by using the local political structure and channelling more resources to given locations. Alternatively, access may be improved individually or collectively by migration, so that geographical mobility is seen as a fundamental aspect of urban politics. Criticisms of this position[14] could apply equally well to all short-term, locality-based, populist action. Such 'community action groups' inevitably preempt a share of scarce resources which would otherwise go elsewhere (perhaps to those objectively more needy but less well organized). Also, most evidence suggests that once such coalitions have achieved their immediate ends their political impetus declines. Nevertheless, Williams' continued emphasis on specifically *urban* political issues and the social significance of access is important.[15] A particular problem arises if urban coalitions are encouraged to see themselves as the basis for a broader social movement. Since there is no objective basis for coalitions to turn into classes (unless, perhaps, 'the people' organize and combine against 'the corporate state'), relative deprivation and dissatisfaction are bound to follow.

### 4. 'Territorial Injustice' is Inevitable

This is a question which has concerned scholars in many different fields over the past decade, but perhaps the clearest summary and synthesis has been provided by Harvey.[16] He poses the question, 'Is there some spatial structure or set of structures which will maximise equity and efficiency in the urban system or, at least, maximise our ability to control the powerful hidden mechanisms which bring about redistribution?'[17] Like Davies[18] and others before him, Harvey attempted to understand and measure the various distributive mechanisms, but flounders on the difficulties in defining his key concepts such as 'need' or 'real income'. The combination of 'modern big cities' and market mechanisms is too daunting for Harvey and he falls back on utopian non-market models in order to achieve his normative end—'an urbanism appropriate for the human species'.[19] Harvey's 'revolutionary theory' and his discussions of rent are somewhat soggy, although undoubtedly stimulating, and criticism of his work is clearly growing.[20] However, his conclusion that attempts to redistribute real income in the urban system are doomed to failure makes it clear that sociologists working with planners in capitalist society are inevitably involved in a form of urban Taylorism.[21] The need to live with territorial inequality poses particular problems in societies committed to an ideology of inequality. In theory, socialism and 'modern big cities' are incompatible. In practice, of course, socialists must make do with aspirations of territorial justice which very often lead to further inequalities. I return to this point later.

### 5. The Role of the State is Increasing in the Advanced Societies and its Intervention in the Sphere of Consumption and in Relation to the Reproduction of Labour Power is a Form of Domination to be Analysed within an Urban Problematic

This theme has been developed by a group of French sociologists influenced by Althusser and expressed most vigorously by Castells:[22]

'Technical and social change in industrial societies is leading to a progressive increase in the importance of . . . political interventions over other elements of the (urban) system. This does not mean that society is becoming more "voluntaristic" but simply that the dominant instance is shifting towards the political as the state progressively becomes not only the centre but the driving force of a social formation whose complexity requires centralised decision-making and control of processes. Consequently a sociology of the production of space must increasingly be focused on what is termed urban planning.'[23]

While there may be debate about the reasons for the increasing role of the state and arguments about whose interests it serves, there is no doubt that it has developed its own momentum and capacity for expansion. Thus, over time, the original goals and purposes may change and it does not follow that the reasons for the initial intervention apply later on, particularly if the state moves from a position where it aids and supports to one where it dominates and controls. Political pressure from the public in social democracies may lead to a shift from private to public investment which may go far beyond the original intention of serving the interests of a given fraction of capital. Further, the necessity for coordinating public provision—where everything affects everything else—comes into conflict with the vagaries of private actors in disparate, if not competing, markets. Furthermore, the solution of many of these broad problems is hindered by small political units and the local processes of democracy. Hence, both as investor and administrator, the state is impeded by the very institutions it is intending to support. Yet the role of the state must and does continue to expand so that, according to Castells, it comes to play

'the role of a full scale planner of the daily life of the masses, and under cover of "the organisation of space" it is really predetermining the way time is spent . . . . This globalisation of urban conflicts, and their systematic take-over by the authorities at every level, *has turned the urban question directly into a political issue* (my italics—REP) and made it one of the axes of political change in our societies.'[24]

However if, as Castells goes on to suggest,

'the State expresses *in the last resort and through all the necessary intermediaries* the combined interests of the dominant classes, then town planning cannot be an instrument of social change, but only one of domination, integration and regulation of conflicts.'[25]

Hence, according to this view, forces for change in the advanced societies should not be directed at the planners but rather at the central political power, and connections must ultimately be made between these new urban questions, which he discusses, and the 'basic' economic and political issues, which he assumes we all accept as the contradictions inherent in monopoly capitalism. Thus, the production of space becomes essentially a political issue.

It would be wrong to suggest that Castells' writing, particularly in *La Question Urbaine*, is very clear and straightforward. One feels that the Althusserian position of Marxist functionalism is not made any simpler by Castells' attempt to adapt it to the analysis of urban planning:

'In advanced capitalist societies, the process structuring space is that which concerns the simple and enlarged reproduction of labour power; the whole of the so-called urban practices connote the articulation of the process to the whole of the social structure. The "urban units" are to the process of reproduction what enterprises are to the process of production, provided they are not thought of solely as places but as originating specific effects on the social structure. . . . By urban systems one means the specific articulation of the instance of a social structure within a (spatial) unit of reproduction of labour power.'[26]

## 6. The State, Political Issues and the Urban Question

The sociology of urban and regional development is seen by many exponents of the 'new urban sociology' as a means of exploring the role of the state in capitalist society. The argument is that the state does not primarily serve the interests of a *specific fraction* of the ruling class, that is to say the dominant, economic elite controlling the central productive processes, but rather has a relative autonomy, which 'sometimes makes it possible to cut into the dominant classes' economic power without ever threatening their political power. It is in this context that we should locate, for example, the whole problem of the so-called "welfare state", a term which in fact merely disguises the form of the "social policy" of a capitalist state at the stage of monopoly capitalism. . . . This "social policy" though it may happen to contain real economic sacrifices *imposed on* the dominant class *by the struggle of the dominated classes*, cannot under any circumstances call into question the capitalist type of state, so long as it operates within these *limits*' (author's italics).[27]

It seems to me that this raises very interesting sociological problems, which deserve to be explored in concrete instances. 'The state' is allocating vast resources which are distributed differentially to populations defined spatially and socially. In Britain, expenditure by central and local government accounts for well over two-fifths of the national income.[28] Furthermore, a recent study has demonstrated how the political careers of ministers in government departments depend on increasing their expenditure, no matter how much the public policy of their party is committed to restraint:

'Few objective measures exist for judging a minister, but ability to hold his own and perhaps do better than his colleagues in gaining funds is one of the most well-worn touchstones in Whitehall, in Cabinet, and in the outside public.'[29]

The specific forms and contexts in which the state extends its activities is an empirical question. This *diversity* in the pattern of state activity in capitalist society is accepted by even such an abstracted theoretician as Poulantzas, who has remarked in an uncharacteristic flippant vein, 'To each his national bourgeoisie'. Thus, each 'imperialist metropole', as he refers to Western European nation states, 'constitutes a separate field and object'.[30]

This separateness and distinctiveness of the role of the state in relation to urban and regional development is further complicated by the growth of regionalism and splits in national unity which, according to Poulantzas, is directly related to the internationalization of capital in the advanced societies. This leads to 'interior colonisation' and the dominance of the metropolitan centres over their peripheries. The development of empirical research along these lines has been advocated by Mellor[31] and by Lebas in this book. This seems to follow very closely the approach developed by Castells and Godard in their study of the Dunkirk region.[32]

Quite evidently the *form* in which the state carries out its activities will vary, and in the recent discussions between Poulantzas and Miliband over the past five years, the focus has been on the state in *capitalist* society. The relative balance between central and local government structures will clearly affect the pattern and style of dominance. What Poulantzas calls 'the social categories of the State apparatuses'[33] and I call 'the managers of the urban system', will have different styles and ideologies depending on whether they identify strongly with a central authority dominating the periphery or whether, alternatively, they have a degree of local autonomy and struggle to support local interests against those of the centre. One Marxist position appears to be that the 'State is not a mere tool or instrument of the dominant classes'[34] and this independence is reflected in the allocation of resources on the ground. Hence Lebas' concern for a framework which will provide 'some conceptual understanding of the relationship between the State, the private sector and "the ground"'.[35] It seems to me that one set of urban managers and technical experts must play crucial *mediating roles* both between the state and the private sector and between central state authority and the local population. Another set of private managers control access to capital and other resources. Admittedly the main focus up to now has probably been on local or peripheral public sector managers and their relations with councillors or the local electorate. I am arguing that there are other equally important linkages or, as current jargon has it, 'interfaces', where the managers' role is crucial. Only very recently are we getting studies which, while still being limited to the middle levels of bureaucracy in the urban planning process, nevertheless look more broadly at the links between the state bureaucracy and its environment.[36] The attempt to focus on the relationship between market distributive systems and 'rational' distributive systems, seeing the urban managers as the essential mediators between and manipulators of the two systems, is extremely interesting.

Some argue that the advanced societies have reached a stage of 'monopoly capitalism' where ultimately the state is a promoter of hegemony. This view is contested by Giddens who argues that formulations are too simple. Firstly, the level of concentration of industrial capital varies markedly between even the most technologically advanced capitalist societies, and, secondly, the emergence of long-range planning has produced new conflicts between the state and industry.[37]

## 7. Urban and Regional Development under State Socialism

Unfortunately, those such as Castells and his colleagues who have applied their formalistic, almost functional,[38] analysis to the situation in France, have not so far extended analysis to other societies. It would be particularly interesting to analyse the state socialist societies of Eastern Europe within a Marxist framework. Up to now we have no intellectually rigorous Marxist analysis of urban planning and the role of the state in centrally planned societies. A systematic sociology of the *system of rational redistribution* to compare with more *price regulating systems* is urgently needed. What we do know about Eastern Europe does suggest that there is a wide discrepancy between ideal and reality. While the state has the power to achieve socially desirable goals, in practice it lacks the necessary technical knowledge and political independence to do so. The inadequacies of state planning do not lead to a random distribution of disadvantage. On the contrary, in connection with urban planning in Yugoslavia, according to one authority, 'Those least qualified i.e. least able to express their interests and needs (lowest strata, with low degree of education, workers, peasants, etc.) are most affected by the lack of empirical sociological research.'[39] The strong implication is that with such research new and different forms of inequality would be made explicit. Furthermore, this social inequality in access to urban resources and facilities is paralleled by spatial inequality: 'Large cities which could, with their economic potential, provide for the under-developed regions in their hinterland, do not activate this potential role'. Hence 'the least developed rural areas . . . can be found in the immediate surroundings of large cities.'[40] Musil has written of the conflicts in the planning process in Czechoslovakia:

'Since there are practically no price mechanisms to regulate the use of land and since there is a great scarcity of it in towns, then a non-economic allocation of the resources must be effected. This means that *the allocation becomes predominantly a socio-political process* (my italics—REP). The conflicts are solved by negotiations of political bodies with economic and interest organisations.'[41]

Turning to Hungary, Konrad and Szelenyi claim that economic and industrial interests have been stronger in recent years than they were in the late nineteenth century under the Austro-Hungarian Monarchy. In the earlier, capitalist, period, Konrad and Szelenyi claim that 50 per cent. of accumulation at that time was devoted to the development of the infrastructure, whereas in the 1960s, under state socialism, they estimate that only about a third of investments went to the infrastructure. They go on to argue that 'the standard of the supply of housing and communal services in Hungary is roughly 30 per cent below that which the general development of the country would justify'.[42] According to this analysis, a much higher proportion of state resources goes to housing in advanced capitalist societies than in Eastern Europe and the Soviet Union. This all suggests that the 'socio-political process', in Musil's phrase, does not apparently favour investment in collective consumption under state socialism. The power of those controlling industrial investment appears to be greater than in capitalist societies. If we follow Giddens and define 'exploitation' as '*any socially conditioned form of asymmetrical production of life chances*, 'life chances' here may be taken to mean the chances an individual has of sharing in the socially created economic or cultural 'goods' which typically exist in any given society',[43] then exploitation in different forms exists in both capitalist and socialist societies. I am suggesting that it is an *empirical question* to determine the nature and degree of exploitation thus defined within and between societies. Giddens is correct to stress that 'exploitation implies a separation between the social *creation* of human faculties on the one hand, and the social denial of "access" to these faculties on the other'. Since 'every developed form of society embodies relationships of exploitation, it follows that class exploitation represents only one mode of organization of such relationships'.[44]

My argument is that since territorial injustice and some form of this more broadly conceived exploitation are both inevitable and, since the role of the state in allocating the infrastructure of collective consumption is increasing in the advanced capitalist society, then the role of state bureaucrats and technical experts must be central to an understanding of urban outcomes and regional development. Further, there are indications that *some* forms of exploitation may be more acute under state socialism than under capitalism and that it is the purpose of a critical sociology of urban and regional development to compare and contrast price-regulated distributive systems and state-dominated systems of rational redistribution. In each case the focus should be on who runs the system for whose benefit. The almost complete absence of a critical Marxist analysis of state socialist societies is a serious handicap to any sustained attempt to develop the essential comparative analysis of the urban question.

## 8. Conclusions

We have seen that there is little dispute between both Marxists and non-Marxists on a number of issues. These include the notions:

(*a*) That territorial injustice is inevitable.

(*b*) That uneven development takes place in all advanced societies.

(*c*) That some form of exploitation takes place in all societies, with the possible exception of certain hunting and gathering societies.

(*d*) That the state is growing both in importance and in relative autonomy in capitalist societies.

(*e*) That Marxist theories of the capitalist state have hitherto proved inadequate.

(*f*) That there are wide differences between capitalist societies in economic structure, political organization and the power and autonomy of the state.

(*g*) That Marxist attempts to analyse and explain these differences have not proved very successful—this failure applies equally to bourgeois theories too.

(*h*) That, in particular, the lack of Marxist analyses of the state in Eastern European societies is a serious weakness.

Thus the state is playing an increasingly important role in the advanced societies in developing urban infrastructure and the means of collective consumption. It is also becoming increasingly central in determining and distributing life-chances for a given population. The role of the technical specialists employed by the state at national and local levels in determining the allocation of and access to scarce urban resources and facilities is increasing. This technical stratum is increasingly moving from a concern with means to given ends to determining these ends or goals themselves. The distributive systems of the advanced societies are moving away from price-regulated systems to systems based on plan rationality. With devolution of central state powers due to populist, ethnic, nationalistic and other pressures, urban and regional planning by local technical specialists is likely to increase. Following Konrad and Szelenyi,

'Regional planning in this sense includes not only planners and research workers specifically concerned with it, but all those, largely central, political planning and administrative organs that are called on to determine or influence the location and distribution of the instruments of urban development, that is investments in general, and particularly the structure of industrial consumption by virtue of the positions they take up, the proposals they make, or the decisions they are entitled to take.'[45]

In fact, as a result of regional planning, Konrad and Szelenyi go on to suggest that the division in Hungary between town and country could perhaps be better replaced by the division between industry and infrastructure. The great merit of the work by Konrad and Szelenyi—and also of that by Castells and Godard[46]—is that the political economy of space is expressed in a specific historical context. If Althusser and Poulantzas have been guilty of what Miliband has termed 'structuralist abstractionism',[47] then British sociologists such as Dennis may have been guilty of pragmatic empiricism. The goal of Castells and Godard is to avoid 'the sterile opposition between pragmatic empiricism and theoretical formalism',[48] but unfortunately they have not entirely convinced one sympathetic critic.[49] There now seems equal enthusiasm among Marxists and non-Marxists alike for 'the necessity of concrete analyses'[50] and for a focus on 'the national forms' of the class struggle in different capitalist societies.[51] While there is not yet much enthusiasm among Marxists to extend their comparative analysis to Eastern Europe, the Soviet Union and other societies not overtly committed to the price mechanisms as a basis for distribution, hopefully this will come. In the meantime there is considerable scope for applying the model of the Castells' school in different contexts. In my view the strength of the new urban sociology will be measured by its success in developing comparative analysis.

## Notes

1. Giddens, A., *The Class Structure of the Advanced Societies*, Hutchinson, London, 1973.
2. Rex, J., and Moore, R., *Race, Community and Conflict*, Oxford University Press. London, 1967, p. 274.
3. *Ibid.*, p. 36.
4. Brindley, T. S., and Couper, M., *Housing Classes and the Sociology of Housing*, University of Bath, Bath, 1974 (mimeo).
   Davies, J. G., and Taylor, J., Race, community and no conflict, *New Society*, 16(406), 67–69, 1970.
   Haddon, R. F., A minority in a welfare state society: the location of West Indians in the London housing market, *New Atlantis*, 2(1), 80–133, 1970.
   Karn, V., A note on race, community and conflict, *Race*, (9), 100–104, 1967.
   Lambert, J., and Filkin, C., Race relations research: some issues of approach and application, *Race*, 12(3), 329–335, 1971.
   Pahl, R. E., 'Urban managerialism' reconsidered, in *Whose City?*, 2nd ed., Penguin, Harmondsworth, 1975, pp. 265–287.
5. Rex, J., The concept of housing class and the sociology of race relations, *Race*, 12(3), 293–301, 1971, and *Race, Colonialism and the City*, Routledge, London, 1973.
6. Pahl, R. E., Urban social theory and research, *Environment and Planning*, 1, 143–153, 1969.
7. Massam, B., *Location and Space in Social Administration*, Arnold, London, 1975.
8. Eisenschitz, A., *Planning and Inequality*, Polytechnic of the South Bank, London, 1973 (mimeo).

Hooper, A., *Class, coalition and community*, paper prepared for the Urban Studies Seminar, University of Kent, 1973.

Lambert, J. R., The management of minorities, *New Atlantis*, 1(2), 49–50.

Longstaff, M. J., *Housing Improvement and Community Action in Birmingham: A Study Based on Institutional Urban Theory*, M.Sc. thesis, University of Birmingham, 1972.

Paris, C. T., and Blackaby, R., *Research Directions in Urban Sociology*, Centre for Urban and Regional Studies, Working Paper 16, University of Birmingham, Birmingham, 1973.

9. Pahl, R. E., 'Urban Managerialism' reconsidered, in *Whose City?*, 2nd ed., Penguin, Harmondsworth, 1976, pp. 265–287.
10. Gouldner, A. W., The sociologist as partisan, sociology and the welfare state, in *For Sociology*, Allen Lane, London, 1973, Chap. 2.
11. Flynn, R., *Local Government and the Allocation of Resources*, M. A. course, Dissertation, University of Kent, 1973. Stewart, J. D., *Management of Local Government*, Charles Knight, London, 1971.
12. Davies, J. G., *The Evangelistic Bureaucrat*, Tavistock, London, 1972. Dennis, N., *People and Planning* and *Public Participation and Planner's Blight*, Faber, London, 1970 and 1972. Elkin, S. L., *Politics and Land Use Planning*, Cambridge University Press, London, 1974.
    Levy, F., Meltsner, A. J., and Wildavsky, A., *Urban Outcomes*, University of California Press, Berkeley, 1974.
13. Williams, O., *Metropolitan Political Analysis*, Collier-MacMillan, London, 1971.
14. For example, see Hooper, A., *Class, Coalition and Community*, Paper prepared for the Urban Studies Seminar, University of Kent, 1973.
15. Williams, O., Urban politics as political ecology, in *Essays on the Study of Urban Politics* (Ed. K. Young), Macmillan, London, 1975.
16. Harvey, D., *Social Justice and the City*, Arnold, London, 1973.
17. *Ibid.*, p. 86.
18. Davies, B., *Social Needs and Resources in Local Services*, Joseph, London, 1968.
19. Harvey, D., *Social Justice and the City*, Arnold, London, 1973, p. 314.
20. Massey, D. B., Social justice and the city: A review, *Environment and Planning*, A(6), 229–235, 1974.
    Hooper, A., *Class, Coalition and Community*, Paper prepared for the Urban Studies Seminar, University of Kent, 1973.
21. By 'urban Taylorism' I am implying an anology between the 'human relations' school of scientific management which sought to fit the worker to the machine in the early twentieth century America and the planner's concern to fit people into the built environment. For a summary of industrial Taylorism see Blumberg, P., *Industrial Democracy*, Constable, London, 1968.
22. Castells, M., Y a-t-il une sociologic urbaine?, *Sociologie du Travail*, 1(1), 72–90, 1968, and Theorie et ideologie en sociologie urbaine, *Sociologie et Sociétiés*, 1(1), 171–190, 1969. Both are reprinted (in English) in *Urban Sociology: Critical Essays* (Ed. C. G. Pickvance), Tavistock, London, 1976.
    Castells, M., *La Question Urbaine*, Maspero, Paris, 1972.
23. Castells (1969) in Pickvance, C. G., (Ed.), *Urban Sociology: Critical Essays*, Tavistock, London, 1976, p. 80.
24. Castells, M., *Luttes Urbaine et Pouvoir Politique*, Maspero, Paris, 1973.
25. *Ibid.*
26. Castells, M., *La Question Urbaine*, Maspero, Paris, 1972. pp. 298–299.
27. Poulantzas, N., *Political Power and Social Classes*, New Left Books, London, 1973, pp. 193–194.
28. Klein, R., *et al.*, *Social Policy and Public Expenditure*, Centre for Studies in Social Policy, London, 1974.

60

29. Heclo, H., and Wildavsky, A., *The Private Government of Public Money*, Macmillan, London, 1974, p. 136.
30. Poulantzas, N., Internationalisation of capitalist relations and the nation-state, *Economy and Society*, **III**, 145–179, 1974.
31. Mellor, R., *Urbanisation in an Urban Society. Uneven Development in the Metropolitan Society*, University of Hull, 1974. (Paper prepared for a seminar of the International Sociological Association, Research Committee on the Sociology or Urban and Regional Development, mimeo.)
32. Castells, M., and Godard, F., *Monopolville*, Mouton, Paris, 1974.
33. Poulantzas, N., *Political Power and Social Classes*, New Left Books, London, 1973, p. 171.
34. *Ibid.*, p. 170.
35. Chapter 3 in this book.
36. Harloe, M., Issacharoff, R., and Minns, R., *The Organisation of Housing, Public and Private Enterprise in London*, Heinemann, London, 1974.
37. Giddens, A., *The Class Structure of the Advanced Societies*, Hutchinson, London, 1973.
38. Frank Parkin has suggested, somewhat mischievously but with considerable justification, that the Althusserian approach is simply 'radicalising Radcliffe Brown'. I am inclined to agree with him. See Parkin, F., *A Marxist theory of the superstructure*, Paper given to the British Sociological Association Conference on the Advanced Industrial Societies, University of Kent, Canterbury, 1975.
39. Mlina, Z., Social values and decision making in town planning, *New Atlantis*, **2**(2), 103–115, 1971.
40. *Ibid.*, p. 113.
41. Musil, J. Town planning as a social process, *New Atlantis*, **2**(2), 5–29, 1971.
42. Konrad, G., and Szelenyi, I., Social conflicts of underurbanization, *Valosag*, No. 12, Budapest, 1971. Revised English version published as Chapter 8 in this book.
43. Giddens, A., *The Class Structure of the Advanced Societies*, Hutchinson, London, 1972, pp. 130–131.
44. *Ibid.*, p. 131.
45. Konrad, G., and Szelenyi, I., Chapter 8 in this book, p. 163.
46. Castells, M., and Godard, F., *Monopolville*, Mouton, Paris, 1974.
47. Miliband, R., Poulantzas and the capitalist state, *New Left Review*, **82**, 83–92, 1973. See also Miliband, R., *The State in Capitalist Society*, Weidenfeld and Nicholson, London 1969, and Reply to N. Poulantzas, in *Ideology in Social Sciences* (Ed. R. Blackburn), Fontana, London, 1972.
48. Castells, M., and Godard, F., *Monopolville*, Mouton, Paris, 1974, p. 22.
49. See Lebas, E., Chapter 3 in this book.
50. Poulantzas, N., The problem of the capitalist state, in *Ideology in Social Sciences* (Ed. R. Blackburn), Fontana, London, 1972.
51. Castells, M., and Godard, F., *Monopolville*, Mouton, Paris, 1974, p. 171.

# 2
# Towards a Political Urban Sociology

*Manuel Castells*

## 1. New Trends in Urban Sociology*

We start with a paradox: while urban problems are increasingly regarded as priorities in political programs and in the daily lives of people, urban sociology seems more and more incapable of providing scientific answers to these problems; i.e., it can describe problems, but it seems incapable of *explaining* the processes at work. We can agree on the fact that even though empirical research is an indispensable moment in any demonstration, it is hardly sufficient. Research data, to be something other than simply a photograph of reality at a precise point in time (and, hence, *depasse* since reality is always changing), must be used to verify hypotheses which themselves have to be integrated into a cumulative, evolving body of knowledge. Of course, the metaphysical lucubrations associated with the search for a 'Grand Theory' have taught researchers to distrust abstract constructions that become only formal games. Yet, this distrust should not lead researchers to abandon the search for an understanding of the relationship between empirical observation and explanatory theoretical schemes; such a relationship constitutes the only means for social scientists to understand social action beyond specific concrete situations.

Moreover, this observation is particularly important given the fact that certain fields of sociology, such as the sociology of organizations, the sociology of social mobility, the sociology of development, etc., have made considerable progress in strictly scientific terms in recent years. While there is not a unified and undisputed overarching theory, there are the beginnings of some relatively circumscribed fields of knowledge which now permit exchanges and some progress in common despite their very different starting points. Such is not the case, it seems to me, for urban sociology, in American as well as in Europe, even though it is one of the oldest branches of sociology.

Our hypothesis is that such a situation is essentially due to the fact that urban sociology is not a scientific domain, nor a field for observation, but rather an ideological artifact. That is, its existence, as it was constituted historically, is justified less by the effects of the knowledge it produces than by its ideological impact on social relations.[1] Let us explain.

A scientific discipline is built either by a certain conceptual cutting up of reality, i.e. through the definition of a *scientific object*, or by a specific field of

---

*The *first part* of this paper is a revised version of a paper delivered before a session on Comparative Studies in Community Research, at the annual meeting of the American Sociological Association, Montreal, 28th August 1974, under the chairmanship of Professor M. Aiken.

observation, i.e. through the choice of a *real object*. Most of the specific fields of sociology (industrial, political, medical, etc.) are established by applying general sociological theories to a particular sphere. In other cases, it is a *social process*, abstracted in theoretical terms, which constitutes a special area of sociology; for instance, social mobility is a field of study which corresponds to a certain problematic which cuts across all of social reality.

However, *urban phenomena* or *urbanization* is neither a specific real object nor a scientific object. Indeed, what is the urban phenomenon? What is relevant to cities that is not relevant to the countryside? Is an urban phenomenon something that is not rural? But, what is rural? Is it a phenomenon that is non-urban? Is it a certain organization of the economy, defined by the nature of industry or by the division of labour? But then, why call it 'urban'? In this sense, most of what is going on in our societies is urban since the city is the major scene of action. Yet, if we consider as 'urban problems' transportation and criminality, housing and political cliques, radical tensions and green areas, educational infrastructure and leisure activities, it seems that we are far from the specificity of an observed concrete reality. Of course, we may call 'modern' society an 'urban' society, but this caprice of terminology is not without its consequences, both theoretical and ideological.

While we mean by urban a certain style of society (whose description strangely resembles either American or Western European society), we also mean by this term a certain social organization of space characterized by the concentration and interpenetration of man and his activities. But, if this space is the arena of a given sociological inquiry (in contrast to space which is 'rural'), it is because we embody within it certain *social* properties. Otherwise, we would consider this space as a factor contributing to the social activity which we study, in much the same way as if we were to consider the mineralogical structure of the land upon which a school is built as influencing its pedagogical system which we are studying.

In reality, it is this implicit, obvious, almost natural association between a certain type of space and a certain type of society which defines the possibility and utility of an urban sociology. The best attempt to provide a conceptual basis for this discipline was that of Wirth and the Chicago school who tried to define urbanism as a specific cultural system (basically, the liberal capitalist society). It was called urban because it was produced by certain specific qualities of the spatial organization of the human species: density, size and heterogeneity or urban agglomerations. In this sense, urban sociology is not an empirical or conceptual specification, but its very definition implicitly assumes an entire 'theory' of society: the forms of space produce social relations and the physical characteristics of human territorial collectivities determine their cultural models of behaviour. This is in fact one of the most advanced versions of naturalism and of the organicism of the origins of functionalism. Such a 'theory' is extremely useful to ruling political elites inasmuch as it conceptualizes social organization as depending less on social data, in particular class relations, than on natural, spatial, technical and biological data. As a consequence, any action for reform or any action for control is examined using the objective technical terminology of the organization of space. Hence, urban planning by technocrats replaces the political debates between social groups.

On the other hand, since urbanization is a natural consequence of human evolution and since it necessarily produces certain social effects, i.e. the 'Western' cultural model, human history is in fact predetermined and all countries may be ordered in terms of their greater or lesser proximity to 'urban' or 'modern' society (in effect, this means an advanced industrial society of the American type). This type of society is considered as the historical model with which we can judge the degree of progress or backwardness of other countries. For example, Toynbee did not hesitate to assimilate the terms 'urbanisation' and 'westernisation'.[2]

We would be wrong to underestimate the importance of this debate by dismissing it as a purely epistemological problem. The theses which are the basis of 'urban sociology' are also the basis for extremely important daily ideologies, such as, for example, the explanation of criminality by the size of cities or of political radicalism by the level of urbanization. All of these analyses are based on spurious correlations because, if we control for the 'social' variables, spatial variables produce different effects, depending on the circumstances. But it is easier to put the responsibility for criminality on 'the monstrous huge city' than to introduce into the explanation variables such as the growth of unemployment among ethnic minorities evicted from the South by the mechanization of agriculture.

Most of the works in urban sociology are influenced, implicitly, by such a perspective or they are descriptive empirical investigations. In neither case is it possible to explain the observed phenomena, especially since the so-called urban perspective has progressively moved from themes of social integration and the accumulation of migrants to themes of urban politics or of social conflict over issues such as some aspect of a city's infrastructure. For it is, in fact, this social evolution which explains the decreasing capacity of the old functionalist schemes to be credible and the increasing demand for a new type of 'urban sociology'.

The transformations which are at the root of an increasing, politically important new urban perspective may be summarized as follows:[3]

(a) On the one hand, the economy of advanced capitalist societies rests more and more on the process of consumption; i.e. the key problems are located at the level of the realization of surplus value or, if one prefers, on the extension of the market.

(b) The accelerated social and spatial concentration of the means of production and of management units also determines a concentration and growing interdependency between the population and distribution process. Consequently, the organization and management of the means of consumption such as housing, schools, health, services, commerce, leisure, etc., is increasingly concentrated. The concentration is not necessarily realized in the same space, however, although it is articulated around a system which is increasingly centralized from a functional point of view. So, consumption processes are increasingly organized in terms of collective consumption and it is the location of these collective facilities which determines the structure of residential space and, hence, of urban entities.

(c) Thus, a series of new social contradictions emerge at the level of consumption processes and especially at the level of processes of collective consumption in correspondence with the displacement of economic contradictions toward the sphere of consumption. The urban social movements which result from this contradiction are a new factor which directly affects the dynamics of the transformation of advanced societies to the extent that they affect those social strata (such as the middle class) which, until the moment, have not been involved in social conflicts.

(d) Finally, to the extent that these means of collective consumption are generally managed by public authorities (the state at its different levels—national, regional and local), the entire urban perspective becomes politicized, since the organization of hospitals, schools, housing and transportation are at the same time fundamental determinants of everyday life, tightly linked and interdependent networks, and political options linked to the class interests which form the social structure. Consequently, the state becomes, through its arrangement of space, the real manager of everyday life. But, on the other hand, the politicization of the urban question also politicizes the consequent social conflicts: urban movements become one of the axes of social change in advanced societies.

This increasing politicization of urban affairs has rendered even more decrepit an urban sociology based on the perspective of social integration and the adaption of migrants of rural origins to the urban culture of modern society. This is why political science has increasingly taken the lead in urban research, in particular in the study of the power processes or in communities. Urban problems have ceased to be the natural consequence of modernization. They are instead inserted into a web of social and political strategies and are redefined and transformed according to power relations. Urban political studies of a liberal bent (from Robert Dahl to Terry Clark, Nelson Polsby and Edward Banfield) accomplished a genuine change of perspective and opened the way to the *social* analysis of urban contradictions. But these studies remained enclosed within an individualist and social psychological approach to power which prevented them from probing these questions more deeply. The central object of such analyses has been the network of strategies among *actors*, each one of whom is defined by his attempt to maximize his power and gains. Thus, trade unions, the press or businessmen are considered to be on the same level, and power is viewed as an end in itself which each tries to monopolize, with the relative equilibrium of forces always forcing compromises. Such a perspective, even though it has permitted very fine descriptions of concrete situations, has been able to generalize its discoveries only through the use of highly formalist perspectives, e.g. the search for the determinants of a centralized or decentraliz- ed power structure, of a unitary or pluralist network of power, etc. But it has not accounted for the relations between political processes, urban contradic- tions, and general social interests, i.e. the economic, political and ideological interests of the social classes which form the totality of a society. This has occurred for two reasons.

Firstly, such studies usually remain at the level of a local community, while urban problems—even those which appear at the local level—are determined by general social forces and structures.[4] Of course, this determination of urban problems by social structures is expressed in a specific way in each case. But such specific traits cannot be the beginning of research. On the contrary, in order to understand the logic of these specific traits, we must locate them within their general determinants.

Secondly, one cannot analyse a social or political process independently from its structural context and from the web of structural interests which determine it.[5] Consequently, we cannot base urban research on the analysis of actors and of their strategies without first analysing urban issues and the contradictions in the social structure which these issues express. These contra- dictions will objectively define the social interests at stake and will allow an understanding of the unfolding of the political process, which possesses autono- my *vis-a-vis* the socio-economic structure, but which becomes a pure formal game, coupled with a utilitarian metaphysic, if it is not studied by starting from class relations.

This perspective on urban research has been developed in France and in other European countries by a more and more influential wave of urban research which has been forcefully developed since 1968 (and it is not without reason that it has dated from that year). The central interest of this wave of research is that, even though it attempts to pose problems theoretically starting from an anlysis of the class structure, it advances only through *empirical research* which simultaneously attempts to understand certain urban political problems as they exist as well as to verify some more general hypotheses about the nature of emerging contradictions in advanced societies.

The result is represented by more than a hundred pieces of empirical research in urban sociology carried out in France in the last five years; if these works do not provide definitive solutions to problems, at least they open the way to new theoretical and methodological perspectives towards the problems which have been posed.[6] These research results attempt simultaneously to recognize the new importance of urban contradictions, trying to give them a precise place within the social structure and to develop, starting from there, a theoreti- cal and empirical analysis of the political processes which seem to us to be at the heart of the question. It is to be expected that such an ambitious attempt is still in its infancy, but it is trying to confront real social and theoretical problems in a spirit which is both scientific and socially engaged.

We would like to present one example of this new approach by summarizing briefly the findings and methods of one of our own studies, centred on the analysis of the relationship between the urban system and the political system in the expanding industrial region of Dunkerque, France.[7] We will start by giving some background details about the concrete situation observed, then providing a presentation of our methods and finally summarizing the major aspects of our analysis which is grounded on this empirical study.

## 2. Urban Contradictions and Political Processes: A Case Study*

### a. Urban System and local Political Arena in the Dunkerque Region

In order to facilitate an understanding of the concrete analysis to be discussed below it is first necessary to set out some of the characteristic features of the Dunkerque situation emerging as a result of our research.

The Dunkerque situation is characterized by the very rapid creation of a major industrial pole around a steelworks (Usinor-Dunkerque), together with the extension of a second steelworks (Creusot-Loire), an oil refinery (B.P.–Total), shipyards, and a number of existing industrial establishments or plants to be set up in the future, which are either directly linked to the new complex (e.g. Vallourec) or else are seeking to take advantage of the technical and industrial environment it has created (e.g. Lesieur, Ciments Laffarge). This industrial pole is articulated around a new giant outer harbour which is now being built and which is capable of taking ships and tankers in the 125,000–500,000 ton range. The state is paying for the majority of the construction costs of the new infrastructure and the Port Autonome de Dunkerque [Dunkerque Port Authority] is the sole developer of the gigantic port and industrial zone currently under construction.

Industrial growth of this magnitude not only totally transforms the urban landscape but also requires a supply of labour which has to be housed, transported, provided with facilities, etc. If one adds to this the wide range of urban facilities required by the various social categories it is easy to comprehend the crisis we observed in the functioning of the urban system.

More precisely, what we observed was a total seizure in the circuit of production, distribution and management of housing, transport and collective facilities, as well as in the functioning of the city as a centre and in the symbolic elements of the urban landscape. Such a seizure is due in part to the shortage of funds in relation to existing needs. But this is not the most important reason, for the crisis persisted even after the releasing of additional resources. The primary obstacle is the inadequacy of the traditional circuit of production and planning of the urban in relation to the new demands placed on it. The persistence of the crisis is not due to the traditionalist reflex of 'resistance of change'. It is due to the opposition between political interests seeking to obtain control over these circuits of production as essential trumps in their relations with the powerful economic interests which dominate the overall functioning of the

*This section is translated by C. G. Pickvance. Translation additions are marked by square brackets.

region. In other words, what we are witnessing essentially is an attempt by the urban community (controlled by local councillors) to keep control of housing circuits in the face of manoeuvres by the state at the central level to avoid pouring large sums of money into channels which might escape its control, in an operation of the scale of the of Dunkerque.

However, this is not a case of direct opposition between the state and the 'locals', but a confrontation of social interests, a conflict between contradictory logics in urban development. More precisely, the newly emerging economy in the Dunkerque region has brought about profound changes in the social structure; new interest groups have arisen adopting new strategies, their conflicting bases and aims leading to a new network of relations in the region. The long-standing opposition between the port bourgeoisie and the traditional working class (dockers, railwaymen, textile workers) umpired by a middle class of provincial notables is displaced and transformed by the direct opposition between the big industrial interests (Usinor, Schnaider) which take control of the Chamber of Commerce and the new working class in the big firms, highly unionized and extremely militant. These varied interests are reflected in the different priorities accorded to urban development by different groupings.

Briefly, two main tendencies can be distinguished: on the one hand, priority for the development of production facilities, and an emphasis on the central city (Dunkerque), with its tertiary facilities and nearby residential and recreational areas for managers in the former resort of Malo; and, on the other hand, priority for the old and new working class housing areas (in part organized around the priority development area of la Grande Synthe, which is actually a working class housing estate at the gates of Usinor), the shacks on the building sites, single workers' hostels and rural districts which now serve as dormitories for peasants transformed into workers.

Between these two tendencies a petite bourgeoisie of officials, teachers, shopkeepers and members of the liberal professions seeks to preserve its social role as manager of the local community. It thus allies itself in turn with the two main forces emerging in the agglomeration, now moving closer to the big economic interests in the central city, now seeking support among the popular classes in the working class suburbs and small towns of the Dunkerque region (Coudekerque, Gravelines).

These varied social interests find expression in three main political tendencies: (1) the apoliticals and U.D.R. Gaullists, who control the city of Dunkerque; (2) the socialist notables of the Nord *department*, who retain predominant positions in most of the older districts; and (3) the 'Union de la gauche', socialist–communist alliance with a trade union base, whose strength lies in working class districts. The expression and mediation of these social and political interests at the urban level takes place through the transformation of the institutional system. The new industrial complex and the urban facilities resulting from it have in fact altered the spatial scale of daily life and made necessary a readjustment by the administrative institutions responsible for it. But this readjustment has not taken place according to juridical rules ensuring an optimal distribution of spheres of competence, but according to competing formulae advanced by each of the social interests mentioned above in an attempt to maintain their own hegemony. For example, the local notables, at socialist instigation, created the first voluntary Urban Community in France, giving it the maximum number of spheres of competence permitted by the law, thus providing themselves with a privileged instrument in their attempt to counteract the 'industrial power' of the economic groups by an 'urban power' based on local institutions.

In the face of this institutional mechanism which threatened to interfere with the smooth realization of an economic project of international dimension, the state at one time considered the idea of an inter-Ministerial urban planning authority, as at Fos. But due to the complexity and relative power of the local community of Dunkerque, the choice was made instead to gain support primarily in the city of Dunkerque (which was socially and politically in favour of close collaboration with big firms) by seeking to strengthen it gradually through a series of carefully planned amalgamations between *communes*. This plan, known as the 'Greater Dunkerque' scheme, has already started with the linking of Dunkerque first to Malo-les-Bains, then to Rosendael and la Petite-Synthe, thus enabling the city to grow from 27,000 inhabitants in 1963 to over 80,000 in 1972, or a total of about 150,000 inhabitants for the agglomeration as a whole.

This thrust by the 'ruling classes' met with resistance on the part of the 'opposition' which reacted by strengthening the Urban Community. The opposition retains control of the latter by means of an alliance between socialist notables and Union de la gauche which expresses politically the alliance between the traditional petite bourgeoisie and the various strata of the working class.

This, then, is the context in which we have attempted a concrete analysis of a number of general questions posed by the new urban sociology.

### b. Research Methodology

The basic hypotheses from which we start are the two fundamental laws of historical materialism according to which, in a capitalist society, the economic instance determines the social structure while it is the political relations between classes which explain and organize each conjucture for social practice as a whole. As far as the realization of economic logic is concerned, this perspective implies concretely the study of the movement of capital responsible for the creation of the industrial complex of Dunkerque, the process of concentration of the labour force and the characteristics of its various strands, and hence the conditions of its reproduction and of daily life. As for the specifically political logic, it is necessary to show both its relative autonomy and its subordinate character. This requires an analysis of the structure of class interests intervening in the industrial and urban growth of the Dunkerque littoral in terms of the positions of individuals and social groups in the economic dynamic commanded by capital and in the productive structure defining the relations of production. On the basis of this analysis, and by relating class structure to class practice (both with reference to struggles and to reproduction), it is possible to understand the complex and dislocated game of the local political arena; and, by combining the effect of the later with the general logic of the state apparatus, it is possible to begin a study of local institutions. Finally, an analysis of the structural and conjunctural logic of the urbanization process and the local political system enables one to understand the social mechanisms underlying urban politics.

In order to demonstrate these propositions as a whole, two levels must be distinguished: (1) proof of propositions specific to each of the topics and real processes we have identified and (2) validation of the general approach.

On the first point, it goes without saying that proof is specific to each concrete analysis and even to each proposition in each analysis. All we can do here is to set out the approach which has been generally followed, more or less rigorously, according to the actual possibility of obtaining proof for each proposition. In general, we sought to use a systematic set of propositions in order to give meaning to a set of observations itself systematized and from which no information had been deliberately excluded. In other words, rather than 'operationalize' each concept by means of an indicator, which implies a term by term correspondence, a completely illusory goal in the analysis of dynamic social processes, we have attempted to find a correspondence between a 'theoretical chain' and a 'chain of observations', by means of logical connections, in such a way that the totality of facts is illuminated and interpreted in a coherent and theoretically meaningful way.

Such an approach requires extreme care in the establishment of facts and a very close correspondence between the observations made and the questions posed at the outset. It is thus that the theoretical perspective adopted directly conditioned the way in which the research was carried out; a wide variety of techniques was made use of, always with the aim of obtaining in the most appropriate way the specific information required to answer a particular question.

In general, and without going into technical details, the study developed in a number of simultaneous sequences during the two years of fieldwork. The various levels of approach used can be summarized as follows:

(1) Examination, analysis, classification and interpretation of a vast quantity of economic, geographical, sociological, political and administrative documentation relating to the problems being researched.

(2) Examination and analytical classification of daily newspapers and of certain periodicals, as well as of various leaflets, internal documents and reports of different bodies, and minutes of the local councils of the different *communes*.

(3) Information obtained by letter from government authorities, firms and associations. Thus, for example, we sent a questionnaire concerning a

number of precisely defined points of information to the main firms in the agglomeration, who kindly provided detailed replies.

(4) An exploratory study to make contact with the area observed using interviews, participant observation and the collection of documents, during the municipal elections of March 1971, in order to familiarize ourselves with the urban problems of Dunkerque in a 'hot' conjuncture.

(5) Interviews with 'key informants' or significant 'actors' in the process studies. These persons were chosen after an examination of the points of information they were capable of providing. For each interview we drew up an interview guide. The guide was as flexible but also as specific as possible, and took account of all the information already available to us on each subject, thus enabling us to check and interpret on the spot the information and points of view expressed in the course of the interview. At no time were we concerned with the psychological or individual attitude of the interviewee, or his 'values'. Each interview contributed to the universe of information available to us on each topic studied, and new information arising from one interview was often pursued in subsequent interviews with other information. Our informants and actors represented the main points in the spectrum of social, urban political and ideological situations. In total about one hundred interviews were conducted, lasting on average $1\frac{1}{2}$ hours. They were mostly tape-recorded, then transcribed, analysed and classified.

(6) Ethnographic study and participant observation, firstly, during a number of short stays lasting several days made by the team as a whole during the two years of the research, and, secondly, during an uninterrupted stay of several months by one member of the team who participated in the social and political life of several parts of the city. Throughout these stays we held group discussions (with a number of local councils, political militants, employers' committees, urban planning teams, etc.) and attended a variety of political and organizational events (sessions of the Urban Community, meetings, local neighbourhood gatherings, meetings in the youth centre and social centre, etc.). We also actively participated in the pleasures of local life, from the waterfront cafes to long walks in the region, and gained a knowledge of all the industrial and port establishments, and the various districts and neighbourhoods of the agglomeration.

(7) Production of a forty-minute film, with soundtrack, presenting the main results of our research. This film, shown to and discussed with research workers from other teams, is intended to make the study known to the various social groups in Dunkerque, in order to obtain some feedback from our research.

(8) Direct observation of families from different social backgrounds, involving the completion of (a limited number of) time–budget diaries and the drawing up of profiles of daily activity.

(9) A study of urban symbolism, with photographic transcription of the results.

The sum total of the information obtained in these ways in itself proves nothing.

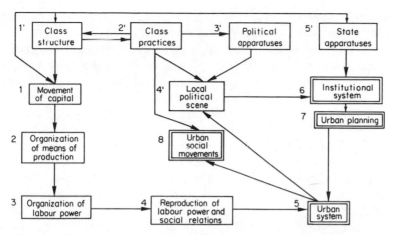

Figure 1 Theoretical order of determination of the real process observed

It is for this reason that we neither collected it for descriptive purposes nor presented it in the order in which it was collected. Rather it has served as the raw material on which to found our specific analyses and has provided an empirical basis for the articulation of a coherent picture of the social process as a whole.

In our view it is at the level of the logic of development of the process as a whole that the validation of our general approach and of the specific propositions can best be carried out. The propositions mutually reinforce one another in that they are interwoven within a single theoretical register and show the logic and hierarchical order of the determination order of the determinations and interactions postulated by the general theoretical perspective. This perspective organizes the real process observed in order of social determination as set out in Figure 1.

Now by analysing these different processes in the numerical order indicated (where 1′, 2′, ..., 5′ represent the simultaneity of the structural order in relation to 1, 2, ..., 5) we arrive at a twofold result:

(1) The totality of the real process observed is explained by interpreting it within a single theoretical perspective and by relating together all the facts observed.

(2) Each level expresses and specifies the structural logic of the preceding level, and it is solely in this way that it is possible to understand the concrete effects actually observed at this former level. For example, the urban system may be understood by starting from the logic of reproduction of the different strands of the labour force, itself the result of the organization of the means of production which in turn derives from the logic of capital in interaction with the class structure. Moreover, the feedback and interaction effects among the different elements of the social process observed are not arbitrarily determined: in every case they convey the structural charge which they contain as a result of the process of social production which underlies them.

## c. Principal Results

A set of closely interrelated questions underlay our study. To start with, we observed that an acute situation of crisis regarding 'urban problems' existed in the agglomeration which was emerging in the Dunkerque littoral. This led us to analyse the conditions of reproduction of labour power and social relations, together with the functioning of the urban unit in which this process took place. In fact our questions referred back to the conditions of production of an urban system, understood as a structure of contradictions resulting from the process of collective consumption.

A study of the social treatment of these contradictions revealed the decisive importance of interventions by the state apparatus and led us on to two further concrete questions: (1) the causes and consequences of the very rapid and thoroughgoing reorganization (unprecedented in France) of the whole local institutional system and (2) the social role of urban planning in a situation where conditions unquestionably justified the demands being made for rational control of the overwhelming social and functional effects of the urban growth currently occurring.

*i. The Social Process of Production of 'Urban Problems'* One of the first results of our analysis was to show the fruitfulness and relevance of the perspective which treats 'urban problems' as questions relating to the reproduction of labour power, thus giving them a precise social structural content. In fact our approach was not to start from 'urban problems' as pragmatically defined; rather we started from the requirements of the process of reproduction of labour power and it was at the conclusion of our analysis that we arrived at a concrete understanding of the set of so-called urban questions. It should also be noted that the urban unit in question, the Dunkerque agglomeration, is based on all the processes necessary to the reproduction of the labour force concentrated in it, whereas the complex unit of production requiring this concentration is in no way identical with the agglomeration.

It is in the concrete articulation of the various processes which constitute the urban system that we discover both the main features of the processes of reproduction of labour power and of urban problems as they are posed in practice. It is on the basis of this definition of the status and content of urban problems that we have been able to understand the social production of the various 'crises' as being due to the specific action, in these processes, of general social contradictions: contradictions between capital and labour, contradictions internal to the logic of capital and contradictions between the capitalist logic of the economic and the capitalist logic of the political developing in dislocated fashion and subject to the hazards of the political scene. It is mechanisms such as these that we have found to underlie the crises, bottlenecks, contradictions and conflicts of the urban system, which we regard as structural effects of these mechanisms.

In the first place, the contradiction between the requirements of capital and those of the reproduction of labour power reveal through two specific effects that they underlie the crisis of the urban system:

(1) The systematic dominance of the organization of means of production over all other elements of the urban system. *Note.* Such a situation will not occur in all cases: it derives from the key role played by the productive apparatus of Dunkerque for big French capital as a whole and for those fractions implanted in Dunkerque in particular.

(2) An inability to carry out regulatory intervention in the urban system as a whole and the limitation of any actual intervention to pragmatic responses to crises as they occur; this derives from the secondary importance of the reproduction of labour power in relation to the principal stake, part of a complex national and international chain of interdependences.

Secondly, contradictions internal to the logic of capital, which may take two forms:

(1) Previously established monopolies and monopolies seeking to establish themselves follow two differing development strategies thus obstructing the adoption of a series of measures aimed at stabilizing and controlling the quantity and type of labour required.

(2) The preference of capital, in the present instance, for the production of means of production results in a seizure in the production of certain means of consumption (e.g. housing).

Finally, the contradictions and dislocations between the requirements of capital and those of the reproduction of labour power, on the one hand, and the means available to effect this reproduction, on the other, prove to be an underlying factor in urban crisis. This lack of adjustment has three causes:

(1) The total amount and distribution of resources allocated for purposes related to the process of reproduction, in particular through the state apparatus, are not solely determined by the requirements of the economic (in its dual aspect, capital and labour); they are treated socially by the economic branch of the state apparatus and are thus subject to urban policy imperatives serving the overall interests of capital and of the class block in power.

(2) The 'ineffectiveness' or 'seizure' of the institutional means for dealing with crises in the process of reproduction of labour power are not the result of a historically accidental delay or of administrative bungling, but derive both from the variety and the complexity of the different functions which the state apparatus has to perform and from the dependence of the state on the political arena and on the contradictory social interests which confront each other there, within the last instance the logic of the structurally dominant class.

(3) Capital invested in the functioning of means of circulation or consump-

tion follows an internal and individual logic of production for profit, thereby introducing notorious 'inconsistencies' at the level of the articulation of complex urban use values.

This set of social processes, mutually interrelated in a hierarchy of reciprocal determinations, is the underlying source of the 'crises' and 'problems', so often denounced, in the urbanization process of the Dunkerque littoral. Now these 'problems' are nothing but the perception, at the level of experience, of the bottlenecks and contradictions of the urban system—themselves a reflection of the contradictory mode in which the reproduction of labour power takes place, in compliance with the structurally dominant logic of capital—in the various specific ways we have just indicated. These contradictions underly the struggles and social conflicts which are perceived as 'urban crises'.

The urbanization process we studied is characterized by the decisive strategic importance of the intervention of the state apparatus on urban contradictions, and its structural and conjunctural incapacity to cope with demands so manifold and contradictory.

Under these conditions the questions initially posed demand an analysis of the functioning and social effectiveness of state institutions intervening in urban organization. It is to this question we now turn.

*ii. Local Institutions as Social Process*   Local institutions in the Dunkerque littoral have undergone a profound transformation as a result of the exceptional changes in social relations which have taken place there. But it is not simply a matter of local government 'adjusting to new needs' nor of the straightforward replacement of one elite by another. On the contrary, at the level of real individuals and social groups holding key positions in the local apparatus, there is a remarkable continuity with the period prior to the occurrence of rapid industrialization. But this continuity at the level of individual supports conceals a major change in the interests expressed through the political arena and institutional machinery, as witnessed by the profusion of institutional formulae in this field (Urban Community, amalgamation of *communes*, joint study commissions, etc.).

These institutional changes may be explained in terms of the interaction of three elements which are indissolubly linked in the effects they produce on the institutional system:

(1) The diverse structural exigencies of the state apparatus at the local level, due in particular to the complex dialectic between dominant and dominated classes in relation to the four functions which the state apparatus must perform: domination and regulation of the interests of the dominant classes, repression and integration of the dominated classes.

(2) The local political arena, itself the resultant of the reciprocal action of political apparatus expressing in dislocated fashion the different social interests determined by relations between classes.

(3) Interaction within the different instances of the institutional system,

insofar as these instances express the social and political interests underlying each institution in each conjuncture.

The concrete progression of institutional changes in Dunkerque can be understood as due to the combined action of these three elements. Now it is essential to emphasize the need to take account of the complexity of the web of interactions in order to avoid either the mechanistic image of institutions acting simply as transmission belts for dominant interests or the liberal voluntaristic perspective of an endless struggle for power between different pressure groups, particularly as we have shown to what extent the strategies of different apparatuses and individuals reflect their position in the web of class contradictions.

Thus administrative institutions appear neither as sources of inertia nor as mere trampolines for individual ambition, as in the images to which we have been too accustomed by a certain 'sociology of organizations'. On the contrary, the case of Dunkerque reveals the striking capacity for change of institutions when change proves necessary. The source of this change lies not in the pursuit of an abstract rationality determined by the meandering course of 'natural technical progress', but rather in the social rationality of the interests of the classes and class fractions present in the different levels and branches of the state apparatus in each conjuncture. Thus at Dunkerque the position between big monopoly firms, powerfully supported by the central level of the state apparatus, and the industrial working class coincides with an internal division within the local political elite. Within local institutions, the 'regnant' bourgeoisie is divided into two fractions set against each other in terms of the interests of the opposing blocs of classes and class fractions with which they identify, given their role as managers of social interests with more significant structural roots than their own.

It is by decoding local institutions in this way that it also becomes possible to understand the conditions of their functioning, both as regards their internal division into spheres of competence and their organizational structure or financial policy. Through the various mechanisms we have analysed in the principal local institutions, we have uncovered a general tendency; modes of institutional functioning cannot be related to a rationality of means but only to a rationality of ends. The functioning of local institutions is largely dependent on the social interests predominating in each conjuncture and expresses the particular way in which these institutions ensure the realization of interests for which they are the means.

But it is first and foremost through the meaning and content of interventions on the urban system that we have been able to test the relevance of our perspective for the analysis of the social logic of local institutions. These interventions did not prove to be a direct translation of a technical rationality or even of a clearly unfolding class rationality. Rather they could be understood as relating to the articulation between the conflicting web of underlying social interests of the different apparatus present in each institution. Thus the 'seizure' produced by the logic of capital in the circuit of house production seems to be closely linked to the battle being waged between institutions and industrial monopolies, in which control over the sizeable resources (to finance house production) is a major stake; similarly, non-intervention in the public transport crisis is not a sign of irrationality but the result of local alliances dominated by big firms, alliances which are necessary for the maintenance of part of the labour force scattered throughout country districts, in accordance with the require- ments of the process of reproduction of social relations; and, finally, the adequate provision of facilities in the central city and the inadequate provision of the working class *communes* are not only an effect of segregation but the expression of a policy of the central municipality, supported by the central state, seeking to encourage the amalgamation of *communes*, a policy whose social and political logic, directly connected to the interests of the hegemonic fraction of the dominant class, we have already established.

The general tendency identified at the level of the institutional system as a whole and its interventions (of which urban planning represents a specific example) thus expresses the political logic of the dominant class, as it relates to each stake in question, conditioned by the concrete conjuncture of institutional functioning and continuously modified by the state of class relations in the social formation as a whole and in the local political arena.

*iii. The Social Effects of Urban Planning*    The social effects of urban planning may be located at two different levels: on the one hand, at the ideological level of rationalization and legitimation of social interests, particularly in the case of master plans; and, on the other hand, at the political level, where planning is a privileged instrument of negotiation and mediation which each group present seeks to appropriate in order to give itself the appearance of social and technical neutrality—without of course planners themselves being able to do anything about it. Our main findings on this point are as follows.

It was found that master plans, which appear to be the veritable embodiment of schemes for urban development, whatever their scale, have an underlying social and political logic, which varies for each plan in exact correspondence with the situation of political hegemony within the institutional apparatus on which the planning agency in question depends. This hypothesis turned out to be so precise that plans drawn up in indecisive political situations took the form of 'question mark plans', while other plans underwent substantial changes as changes took place in the political parties controlling the planning apparatus. But, in addition to this observation, which is in the nature of things, what was significant was the importance of the ideological role of urban planning, since for such an ideology to be particularly effective in the realization of the social interests it embodies, the legitimation–recognition effect characteristic of all ideologies must accommodate itself to the specific means of expression which is urban planning. Plans stamp all individual schemes with a double character: on the one hand, they come to be seen as 'reasonable', rational technical solutions to the problems posed and, on the other, they appear to bring about a convergence of the various social groups and urban functions. Town planning comes to embody social neutrality, by expressing the general interests of the community, in addition to its advantage of technical neutrality. It is for this reason that planning is a privileged instrument for the ideological embodiment of the interests of classes, fractions and groups; it increases opportunities for social integration to the maximum, a prime function of dominant ideology.

Moreover, as we have seen, the political role of urban planning is due essentially to its capacity to act as an instrument of mediation and negotiation between the different fractions of the dominant class and between the various requirements necessary to the realization of their overall interests, as well as *vis-a-vis* the pressures and demands of the dominated classes. We have seen that this mediating capacity derives from the possibility of achieving an overall relative harmony between the different corrective and regulatory interventions of the state apparatus, wherever the dominant logic pushes contradictions so far that the process of reproduction of labour power and social relations is interfered with. Now, for such mediation to take place efficiently, i.e. to avoid in the final analysis the transformation of the dominant structural logic, the 'dice must be loaded'; in other words, the process of negotiation itself must be organized in such a way that once the various interests have been expressed, the law can ultimately be brought to bear. This is achieved by a number of mechanisms ranging from direct political control to administrative regulation and control of criteria of budgetary allocation.

It is urban planning's capacity to act as a framework for conditional and institutionalized social negotiation which explains the eagerness of the various political tendencies to gain control of planning agencies, which thus become not only political instruments but political stakes in themselves.

Thus the incapacity—so often decried —of urban planning institutions to 'control growth' and to resolve the contradictions of collective consumption is revealed to be merely the reverse side of a process whose true significance lies in the ideological and political effects of urban planning on urban contradictions and social relations.

The research we presented here is still not able, of course, to answer the number of questions we raised at the more general level. But it represents an effort to move from the critical perspective of the first part of this paper to the proposition of some alternative to what is entered there for use in our research field. In spite of the present limits of this effort, our attempt has to be considered within the broader purpose of adjusting the orientations of a new urban sociology to the increasingly political status of urban problems in advanced capitalism, i.e. as a step towards a political urban sociology.

## Notes

1. See Castells, M., Theory and ideology in urban sociology, in *Critical Essays on Urban Sociology* (Ed. C. G. Pickvance), Methuen, London, 1976.
2. For a systematic discussion of the overall perspective, see Castells, M., *La Question Urbaine*, Maspero, Paris, 1972 (forthcoming English translation, Arnold, London).
3. See Castells, M., Advanced capitalism, collective consumption and urban contradic-

78

tions, in *Patterns of Change in Advanced Industrial Societies* (Ed. L. Lindberg), Council for European Studies (forthcoming), both for the development of the argument and for bibliographical references on the topic.

4. See Alford, R. R., *Social Needs, Political Demands and Administrative Responses*, unpublished paper, University of Wisconsin, Madison, 1974.

5. As do, in a masterpiece of urban political research, Cloward, R. A., and Piven, F. F., *The Politics of Turmoil*, Pantheon Books, New York, 1974.

6. Most of these research results are unpublished but they are beginning to appear, particularly in a new collection called *La Recherche Urbaine*, published by Mouton. Also, many articles representative of this new trend have been published in *Sociologie du Travail and Espaces et Sociétés*. Researchers having this general perspective include: in France, Jean Lojkine (*La Politique Urbaine dans la Region Parisienne*, Mouton, Paris, 1973, and *La Politique Urbaine dans la Region Lyonnaise*, Mouton, Paris, 1974), Edmond Preteceille (*La Production des Grands Ensembles*, Mouton, Paris, 1973, and *Jeux et Simulations: Une Critique des Jeux Urbains*, Mouton, Paris, 1974), Francis Godard (*La Renovation Urbaine à Paris*, Mouton, Paris, 1973), Christian Topalov (*Les Promoteurs Immobiliers*, Mouton, Paris, 1975, and *Capital et Propriete Fonciere*, C.S.U., Paris, 1974), Sylvie Biarez and others, (*Institution Communale et Pouvoir Politique*, Mouton, Paris, 1973), Claude Pottier. (*La Logique du Financement Publique de l'Urbanisation*, Mouton, Paris, 1975), Alain Cottereau. (two important articles on urban planning in Paris in the issues of *Sociologie du Travail*, **4**, 1969, and **4**, 1970), Suzanne Magri, (*La Politique de l'Etat pour le Logement des Travailleurs*, C.S.U., Paris, 1972), Armel Huet and others. (*Le Role Ideologigue et Politique des Comites de Quartier*, Ministere de l'Equipement, Paris, 1972), Jacques Ion and others. (*Les Equipements Socio-culturels et la Ville*, Ministere de l'Equipement, Paris, 1972), Michel Amiot and others (*Politique et Equipments Culturels*, Ministere de l'Equipement, Paris, 1973) and M. Castells, E. Cherki, F. Godard and D. Mehl, *Sociologie des Mouvements Sociaux Urbains*, Vol. 1, Mouton, Paris, 1975), etc.

In other European countries, there are researchers that by and large share the same perspective, but not always in the same way; e.g. in Italy, Enzo Mingione (*Citta e Conflitto Sociale*, Feltrinelli, Milano, 1972, in collaboration with others), Franco Ferrarotti (*Roma da Capitale a Periferia*, Roma, 1971 and *Vita dei Baracatti*, Roma, 1974), A. Daolio ((Ed.) *Le Lotte per la Casa in Italia*, *Feltrinelli*, Milano, 1974) and Giuliano della Pergola (*Lotte Urbane e Diritto alla Citta*, Feltrinelli, Milano, 1974); in England, Tom Davies, Michael Harloe, Ray Pahl, Christopher Pickvance, Rosemary Mellor, etc.; in Spain, Jordi Borja, Jose Olives, etc.; in the Socialist countries, Jiri Musil, Ivan Szelenyi, etc.

We do not want to oppose France to the United States by establishing a geographical separation between these intellectual trends. Some excellent French researchers such as Gremion, Worms and Birnbaum are more linked to the liberal tradition while certain American works such as those of Robert Alford, Dorothy Nelkin or Frances Piven have many similarities with the French ones we have mentioned. However, it is certainly true that specific social situations and different intellectual traditions facilitate the development of the perspective just outlined in these different countries to a greater or lesser extent.

7. For a complete presentation of our findings and theoretical explanations, see the book reporting this research: Castells, M., and Godard, F., *Monopolville*, Mouton, Paris, 1974.

# 3
# Regional Policy Research: Some Theoretical and Methodological Problems

*Elizabeth Lebas*

## 1. Introduction

This paper is essentially a consideration of some issues and problems involved in attempting to go beyond a certain sociological perspective, a perspective which, we will say, is grounded in positivism[1] and focuses on individual social actors as the bearers of social action. It is characterized, perhaps as a consequence, by a remarkable lack of theoretical conceptualization.

The background to this essay is research on 'the impact of British industrial location policy upon relatively non-industrialised areas of Britain'.[2] The mandate is a double one and, to some extent, a contradictory one. For while it is to be an evaluative study of the possible socio-economic effects of an aspect of regional policy and planning, and entails extensive fieldwork, it is also research into the theoretical and methodological possibilities of undertaking such evaluative work. This paper is therefore about a particular set of problems encountered when attempting to redefine the object of study, namely the search for, and the use of, theory and its confrontation with empirical observations. In this sense these problems must be envisaged in an evolutionary manner, for they constitute only a moment in the realization of a study.

After a time in our thinking, regional policy was perceived as a political process, ongoing and historically delimited. This process was constitutionally and ideologically defined by the state, but its substance appeared to be complex negotiations between demands of production, the market, types and extent of labour forces, as well as of the actions of the bureaucratic and political representatives of that state. The policy process was also conceived as being vindicated by the economic and political repercussions of a capitalist national and international socio-economic system, a system whose contours and implications have yet to be fully identified or properly understood. Although the policy process was seen as a state activity designed to 'rectify' the inherent and obvious contradictions in the economic and political system, these contradictions and their constituent elements had yet to be theoretically located.

Having reached this stage of conceptualization, we began to see more of the implications of this political process. Did it provide a sufficient point of departure from which to organize field research? Would it assist us in further attempts at conceptualization? Finally, could it eventually serve an evaluative function? What further theoretical, methodological, not to mention epistemological, questions did it raise? From another viewpoint, what did this initial conceptualization signify in terms of the state of contemporary British research in the sociology of regional planning and policy?

While it may appear surprising that to us the explicit use of a Marxist notion of the state did constitute an advance, in view of the virtual lack of any concept of the state in British studies of the sociology of policy in general and planning policy in particular, this surprise becomes more understandable. But the realization of 'more Marxist' orientation in our thinking did raise some new questions. Could the naked prepositions of the Marxist theory of the state be extended into a political *sociology* of the state? Would its current theoretical interpretations[3] posit an epistemology too complex and intellectually foreign for us to transcend and use instrumentally?

Although we did not wish to become caught up in the debates revolving around the worth of Marxist structuralism as an epistemology,[4] we did make an initial choice. We were sympathetic to the argument that the construction of logical theoretical systems of understanding could be in fact no more than complex elaborations of idealized models already prevalent in systems theory.[5] Since we had yet to properly understand why there could be a relation between Marxist structuralism and certain kinds of technicism, we in fact chose a pragmatic stance, deciding that future readings based on this approach, as well as attempts to use it, could well decide the question in due course.

On second thoughts, it now seems likely that our reticence about Marxist structuralism was not so much derived from what we considered to be an insufficient understanding of the epistemology in itself, but rather from the fact that point of entry into Marxist theory had not begun, so to speak, from the 'point of production'. This is not to deny that the Marxist theory of the state, in its so-called pre-theoretical descriptive form,[6] still posed a number of difficulties for us, especially in conjunction with empirical work. We would like to examine some of these difficulties now by way of illustration.

## 2. The Realities of the Marxist State

As Louis Althusser has pointed out, the classical Marxist theory of the state is, as it stands, simply a descriptive theory, verifiable to the extent that its prepositions can be confirmed by empirical reality. This theory, however, also infers a topology of power relations in the society. These relations of power, derived from economic bases of production, are historically delimited and rest on a distinction between private and collective ownership and possession of the means of production. The state is in itself neither public nor private, but rather constitutes that very distinction.

An important problem of the classical theory of the state is that it does not analytically distinguish between 'state autonomy', state form and state activity. If one attempts to examine state autonomy in itself, one may find through circuitous ways that one is only returning to something rather akin to the Hegelian concept of essence. If one then contemplates state form, also in itself, and thus probably through an evolutionary historically comparative method, one can thus find oneself with a useful but not theoretically informative model of comparative formal institutions.

On the other hand, and perhaps closer to the letters of the theory, if one undertakes an account of the parameters of state activities in a given field of study, one may find that all one is doing is multiplying cases of empirical evidence for state activities. The classical theory of the state without its extension into the theories of production, consumption, circulation and class formation will not clearly inform one about the nexus of the state, which is state power. It is only then that one can reconsider the concept of state autonomy.

In an empirical research situation the researchers will tend to first encounter the state activity in terms of state apparatuses (distinct from state power) and moreover in terms of formal institutional apparatuses. If the researcher focuses only on these, a number of omissions and misconceptions may arise. While these apparatuses may purport to exist for practical organizational purposes, they also exist to veil the real nature of state power, which is class power. Secondly, the state pervades the entire social order. The reproduction of conditions and relations of production, as well as the cohesion and maintenance of the social formation, also depends on the internalized acceptance of authority relations. How these authority relations are established and maintained in the daily existence of individuals is also a legitimate object of enquiry, but one which is difficult to apprehend.

Furthermore, the researcher examining policy consequences will have a tendency to conceive of the state in the very way which the state wishes itself to be perceived. While he may ignore the intrusion of the state into the psyche of individuals, he may in time perceive formal bureaucratic efficient and ineluctable state intervention everywhere. The oversensitiveness of the 'state-oriented' researcher to the eminence and force of state intervention may lead him into an inability to explain class resistance to the state. It is then that he must go beyond the 'problematic of the state' in order to come to terms with the real object of his pursuit, class conflict.

But assuming at this point that the researcher is still involved in theory making, he may now come to a new set of problems. Having on the one hand a nascent theory of the state and on the other a series of empirical observations which he feels could further inform the theory, he must then ask himself what status must these observations have in his theory making. Empiricist epistemology lacks a rationale for the interconnection of events and ideas, while an epistemology resting on the logical interconnection of abstract concepts must, in order not to violate the materialist nature of Marxist analysis, integrate, in one way or another, empirical reality. Otherwise, the penalty for this non-integration is idealized deterministic reductionism.

This last, theoretical, issue can be resolved both empirically and philosophically, but, in the last instance, it rests on the concept of application. The statuses of empirical and theoretical reality depend in Marxism on the uses which these realities are going to be put to. These uses are by definition political and, in the end, praxis, both academic and political, may resolve what may retrospectively appear to be a false problem.

## 3. British Sociology of Regional Planning and Policy

British sociology of regional planning and policy as it now stands is not characterized by its rather light theoretical contents. Although it shares many of the assumptions of traditional British (and American) urban sociology, it would be unfair to accuse it of 'ideological production', as Manuel Castells has done for urban sociology.[7] One symptomatic reason is that there is so little of it.

Quite soon it became apparent to us that a sociology of regional policy and planning entailed, almost by definition, a 'global approach', able to grasp in historical context some notion of the socio-economic and political whole. Also, it had to take into account the existence of power relations and socio-economic conflict, since planning and policy were in themselves ideological and political activities. Otherwise one could not even begin by posing such basic questions as the following. What really is regional policy and planning, behind all the pronouncements and activities? Why are issues formulated or *not* formulated the way they are? What part does this form of state intervention play at a particular stage of capitalist society? After which, one could begin to ask about relationships between regional policy and planning and the management of the labour force in areas conveniently labelled 'disadvantaged', 'peripheral' or 'underdeveloped'.

Although there may be a certain 'globality' in British sociology of regional planning and policy, it is not an explicit one. It can be interpreted as a 'holding constant' of certain historical events in a particular area. The usual means of entry into 'the problem' (and this sociology bears resemblances to 'the sociology of social problems') has been through the study of medium-level bureaucratic and political figures, using more or less closely the ubiquitous 'urban managerialism thesis'. Complementing this approach have been limited attempts to account for the effects of policy execution on the receiving clientele.

Attention focusing on bureaucratic actions and ideologies has been useful in revealing contradictions between professional thinking and institutional behaviour. Furthermore, it has contributed to the demystifying of state intervention by focusing on its negotiating role and irregular aspects of the intervention. But this approach is not located within a theory of state power and tends to envisage the state only in terms of its constitutional and regulatory aspects. Consequently, it is not particularly informative about the coercive nature of planning ideologies and their roles in the context of state intervention into capitalism. In fact, the focus on ideologies has tended to obscure matters by attributing policy and planning failures to the failures of individuals in a professional category.

Not all British sociology of regional planning and policy has been so restricted in its conceptualization of the problem. Some work has been characterized by an awareness of the need for a wider, conflictual and historical framework. A paper by Ian Carter, 'The Highlands of Scotland as an underdeveloped region', has examined how the ideology and policy assumptions of the Highlands and Islands Development Board (HIDB) contrast with the socio-economic historical reality of the Highlands.[8] Carter's adoption of the Gunder Frank model of underdevelopment has enabled him to go some way in locating the role of the HIDB within the wider context of national policies of economic growth. His complementary account of the history of economic relations between Highlands and Lowlands seriously put into question HIDB assumptions about traditional backwardness of the Highlands. Moreover, Carter established, but does not develop, the relationship between increasing intervention of market forces and the further deterioration of the economic and social situation of the region.[9]

Although it is evident in Ian Carter's paper that explanatory advantages have been derived from the use of the metropolis/satellite model, a number of conceptual problems arise. Carter still envisages the HIDB as an institution in itself and does not locate it inside a conceptualization of the state. Admittedly an explanation of the rise and role of a regional state apparatus is very difficult. But perhaps even a partial analysis could have been further elaborated, based on his observations that a number of contradictions did exist between HIDB institutional regional ideology and national economic policies. The observation of contradictions is only the beginning of analysis.

Another reflection which could be made about Ian Carter's analysis and which could be extended to most attempts at using formally coherent theoretical models is that their application is often subject to weaknesses inherent in the models themselves. For example, a criticism which could be directed against Frank could also be directed against Carter. It concerns the roles and composition of 'regional' notables. These are not properly categorized and nor are their precise roles in exploitation and accumulation demonstrated in practice.

A group of British sociologists who have tried to confront regional policy as political activity rather than take it for granted as a constitutional fixed entity have been the Rowntree Research Unit at Durham University.[10] Their occasional papers have shown, as has Ian Carter, the contributions which socio-economic history can make in contrasting contemporary state interpretations of situations with a history of regional economic exploitation. Nevertheless, their work demonstrates some of the problems entailed in the use of a historical perspective for sociological analysis. The first problem is that of regression. How far does one 'go back' in history? Without an interpretation of history in terms of production and relations of production, no theoretical 'cut-off' point can be conveniently established. Even then, the adoption of 'historical materialism' does not guarantee success when faced with the existence of 'coexistant' and interrelated modes of production. The use of historical analysis, besides demanding a rigour and meticulousness not achieveable by researchers working on a sparse grant and in a limited time period, also introduces the problem of scope. As soon as it is realized that the history of the region is connected to that of the nation and of imperialism, the perspective within which interpretations can be made becomes very wide indeed.

On the other hand, the use of historical analysis can act as a check against 'creeping parochialism', a characteristic often noted of research groups doing work 'on their region'. This incipient parochialism, compounded with the lack of concerted theoretical perspective, leads researchers to establish the questionable existence of 'regional bourgeoisies'.

The Rowntree Research Unit's absence of theoretical coherence is illustrated by the end-product of their work. It adds up to a series of papers varying from discussions of working class consciousness to accounts of the history of regional organizations, without identifying an interconnecting rationale. In view of our search for theory, this group demonstrates a problem which can arise when one only acknowledges the theoretical perspective without attempting to apply it and develop a critique of it. Good and sometimes fashionable intentions are not sufficient. Theoretical references are not enough to guarantee their extensions into a mode of explanation.

Having criticized our British colleagues, it may now be useful to mention how two of our research exercises have demonstrated our theoretical limitations while at the same time they have led us to consider new possibilities.

## 4. Observations Arising from Two Field Visits

Retrospectively, the decision to engage in preliminary visits to separate fields sites prior to choosing a definite one to focus on may be interpreted in two ways. This decision may have been symptomatic of an underlying empiricism, epitomized by the belief that one could not 'generalize' before 'knowing facts better'. On the other hand, we also felt, in a rather inarticulate way, that only empirical research practice in a field situation could really highlight for us, in a way no academically situated debates could achieve, our true methodological and theoretical problems. Both field sites were located in areas which were perceived in different ways by official state policy as being 'non-industrialized'. These were also experiencing the relatively recent appearance of large manufacturing plants. Otherwise, the sites were quite different; they were culturally different, they had experienced seemingly separate local histories of exploitation and capital formation and they had different locations *vis-a-vis* large industrial towns and London.

The first observation, which arose as a result of writing to all the regional headquarters of the Department of Trade and Industry, was that very few large industrial investments could be said to have been attracted to 'peripheral' regions as a result of formal regional policy. Indeed, despite the political propaganda centred around 'regional policy', state expenditure on the capitalist means of production appeared to be comparatively small. The attraction of large plants to the periphery appeared to be the result of the locational advantages of natural resources, lack of pollution control and, in some cases, cheap and unspecialized labour. State support appeared to be sectional rather than regional. What did this mean in terms of the increased tendency for state economic intervention? Was regional policy really a form of political and ideological, rather than economic, intervention? If so, why? Did it relate to the positions of economic groups in the regions?

The second observation was that very few areas of Britain had not undergone in their history some form of capitalist industrialization and involvement in an international market economy. This seemed to contradict the assumptions of policy-makers and executives with regard to these areas. It became evident that the so-called lack of local entrepreneurial spirit was certainly not due to a lack of industrial experience. We had then to examine why these areas were consistently categorized as 'rural' and suitable for large capital investments.

The local politics of policy implementation provided us with a further means of focusing our problem. The local political notability was in fact differentiated in terms of economic interests and of relations with the metropolitan centre of decision making. Local residence was no indicator of local power, as the existence of a metropolitan-oriented gentry showed us. Although the local bourgeosie appeared to put forward a common ideological front in identifying the ills of their areas and invoking state intervention, it was divided over the best means of 'introducing industry' and managing it once it came. It was faced with a decreasing and more expensive supply of labour as well as a larger and more socialized working class, not to mention the political burden of administering increasing expenditures on infrastructure which had to be paid by local taxes (rates).

The third set of observations may have been the most useful one. State intervention was no longer seen as an idealized phenomenon, but as a concrete kind of activity affecting the relations between classes in a locality and responding to both local and extra-local economic and political pressures. Perhaps it was then that we also realized that state power was constituted in the relation between class and state. We also observed the situation of the working class. Detailed knowledge of state policy and the activities of the firms and local notables during the implantation stage confirmed that the labour force, both local and imported, was being managed and socialized in a way which was congruent with the conditions of production. The conceptual acceptance of the existence of a working class has of course posed new problems for us, problems whose discussion and presentation may well lead to a new series of project working papers.

The above account of our observations was included in this essay in an attempt to show one way in which redefinitions of sociological problems are arrived at. Our preliminary field visits did help us to move away from a constitutional conception of regional policy to one which perceived it as a form of ideological and political state intervention. The economic aspects of this type of intervention were accounted for more in terms of their extended social implications rather than their role in the financing of an economic operation.

Obviously conceptual redefinitions do not occur in sequential form. While we were examining the work of some of our British colleagues and gaining experience from the field, we were also becoming aware of the new body of literature which appeared also to be looking at capitalist development and state policies, but in a rather more cogent and theoretical manner. We came across authors such as Jean Lojkine, Danielle Bleitrach and Edmond Preteceille, and found their work influential and revealing. It is evident at this stage that we are not yet fully prepared for a constructive and comprehensive critique of these authors' works, especially in view of the fact that they themselves differ considerably on emphases and methods. Nevertheless, for argumentative purposes and as further illustration of the directions our thinking is taking us, it may be useful to consider one text in particular. This text is *Monopolville*, written by Manuel Castells and Francis Godard.[11]

## 5. Monopolville

It was noted above that in Marxist structuralism the location and status of empirical reality posed a particularly important question. How do the authors of *Monopolville* conceive the empirical existence of Dunkerque? Dunkerque appears to have an expressive function. Dunkerque is not 'a town in itself' but the expression of a configuration of processes related to induced urbanization under French growth pole policy. Dunkerque is thus raised to the status of a conceptual category symbolizing a kind of urbanization characteristic of a particular set of interactions between capital and state and the imperial stage of monopoly capitalism. Dunkerque as an urban form has a particular mandate; it demonstrates the fundamental contradictions arising from the socialization and reproduction of labour in a social formation dominated by monopoly capital.

This epistemological treatment does appear to resolve an important methodological problem. Whereas we had been asking ourselves how an analysis of a particular place can be made valid for another, Castells and Godard presumably resolve the issue by implying that one location, if taken conceptually, can be made to represent other locations, as these fulfil a number of 'given' conditions. However, given their bias, the authors are singularly unreflective about limit conditions of their theoretical construction. Although we may know that Dunkerque is a construct derived from a complex empirical reality, we are never very certain why it must be so, why the town cannot be put forward as the 'thing in itself' and why doing this would weaken the explanatory force of the authors.

It is true that the authors are clearer about their theoretical methodology. It is about the discovery of a 'logical chain of correspondence' between theory and a 'chain of observation' and not, as it is usually assumed, the 'operationalization' of concepts. Thus the theoretical methodology is one of juxtaposition between a theoretical system and a complex account of processes grounded and chosen from a complex reality. The question which immediately arises is whether this theoretical juxtaposition is more of an imposition. The authors appear to be somehow uncertain about the ability of the empirical world to reveal just what they want to say about the nature of state and capital.

Interestingly, it is precisely when they allow the situations in Dunkerque 'to speak for themselves' that the force of their argument and what it reveals becomes the most apparent and the most exciting.

In *La Question Urbaine*, Castells was very clear about the purpose of his efforts, which was an emancipation from conventional sociology and ideological fabrications in order to develop theoretical tools for the analysis of a redefined problematic of urbanization. In *Monopolville*, the authors do effectively use their theoretical tools in the sense that they do achieve their aim of unveiling the nature of state economic intervention and social manipulation for a dominant mode of production. On the other hand, they fail in part to fulfil the original intention in *La Question Urbaine* in that they do not, in our estimation, allow research praxis to sharpen and develop their theoretical instruments. The inexorable unfolding of their chain of explanation can only allow a controlled intrusion of what is in fact the chaotic and reified reality of capitalism. Their formation, compounded by a conscious and explicit ahistoricism, has, moreover, some unfortuitous and perhaps unintended consequences for the explanatory effectiveness of the text.

Leaving aside more detailed criticisms of actual content and definitions, it is evident to us that the 'input'-oriented and hence cursory treatment of the history of capital investment and exploitation in the North-East region of France since the 1950s led the authors to an overestimation of the force of monopoly capital over other modes. Other less developed modes of capitalist exploitation obviously affect monopoly investment in one location, for no other reason than the fact that classes are historically defined and that their adaptation or resistance to the massive introduction of advanced capital constitutes in itself a new series of struggles both within and between classes. The meticulous categorization of fractions of capital and fractions of classes without a historical account of their interrelated struggles and conjectural uniqueness will tend to make the operationalization of theoretically located contradictions such as to not only lead back into the very economism which the authors implicitly wished to avoid, but also to lead to the evasion of what is presumably the real interest of the authors, class conflict.

This very partial and broad critique of *Monopolville* in no way denies the worth of its authors' approach. *Monopolville* indicates to us the legitimacy of Marxist theorization and the possibilities of its application to real, concrete situations. It also shows, as other texts on induced and highly managed urbanization do, that the use of a well-defined and precise theoretical model creates much greater demands on the empirical craftsmanship of the researcher. Since the appearance of works such as this one, theoretically concerned researchers can no longer be accused of ivory-tower speculation at the expense of a disregard for the urgent reality of a concrete world.

## Notes

1. For our conceptualisation of positivism, see Kolakowski, L., *Positivist Philosophy from Hegel to the Vienna Circle*, Penguin, Harmondsworth, 1972.

2. Davies, T., Ecker, T., Lebas, E., and Psenicka, R., *The Impact of Regional Industrial Policy upon Receiving Areas in Europe: A Sociological Study*, work carried out at the Polytechnic of Central London with a grant from funds supplied to the Centre for Environmental Studies by the Ford Foundation.

3. For example, the work of Althusser, L., Ideologie et appareils ideologiques d'etat: Notes pour une recherche, *La Pensee*, **151**, 3–38, mai–juin 1970, and that of Poulantzas, N., *Pouvoir Politiques et Classes Sociales*, Vols. I and II, Maspero, Paris, 1968.

4. The two sides of this debate are outlined in Miliband, R., Poulantzas and the capitalist state, *New Left Review*, **82**, 83–92, November—December 1973, and Poulantzas, N., The problem of the capitalist state, in *Ideology in Social Sciences* (Ed. R. Blackburn), Fontana, London, 1972.

5. Kolakowski, L., Althusser's Marx, in *Socialist Register*, Merlin, London, 1971, footnote 2, pp. 127–128.

6. Althusser, L., Ideologie et appareils ideologiques d'etat: Notes pour une recherche, *La Pensee*, **151**, 3–38, mai—juin 1970.

7. Castells, M., *La Question Urbaine*, Maspero, Paris, 1972.

8. Carter, I., The Highlands of Scotland as an underdeveloped region, in *Development and Sociology* (Eds. E. de Kadt and G. Williams), Tavistock, London, 1974.

9. *Ibid.*, p. 302.

10. Rowntree Research Unit, *Community Studies: Studies of the Promotion of Regional Policy and the Organisation of a Bibliography of Regional Material*, 1971–1974. See *Urban and Regional Research in the United Kingdom, An Annotated List*, CES Information Paper 23, CES, London, August, 1973.

11. Castells, M., and Godard, F., *Monopolville*, Mouton, Paris, 1974.

# 4
# Theoretical Elements for a Marxist Analysis of Urban Development

*Enzo Mingione*

## 1. Introduction

In this brief account I shall try to bring together as systematically as possible some of the main theoretical and methodological elements which are required for a Marxist analysis of the social problems of urban and regional development. In addition I shall set out a preliminary and necessarily tentative examination of the Italian situation in this respect. This work is limited by the fact that, for reasons of brevity, simplicity and organization, I am taking for granted without serious critical scrutiny three lines of research and discussion which form the basis of my analysis in this paper.

In the first place I will not enter here into the debate over the Marxist approach to socio-territorial analysis, although I do have a fairly clearly formulated position.[1]

In the second place I assume the acceptance of the critique of traditional urban sociology and 'ecological' analysis, though this critique is not wholly satisfactory. Furthermore, although the view that neither urban nor rural socio-territorial relationships constitute an autonomous research objective in a 'social science'[2] is shared by several scholars, and the critique of the Chicago school's ecological analysis has been a point of departure of the new methods of research and analysis, the end results of these efforts are often quite different and not at all compatible with each other or acceptable. Thus some of these studies have given particular emphasis to viewing urban problems as phenomena of collective consumption,[3] others have placed a strong emphasis on analysing urban development as the construction of the social infrastructure, i.e. the formation of fixed immovable capital,[4] and others have emphasized the processes of distribution and redistribution of the resources which exist within the urban territorial structure.[5] There are in fact widely differing theoretical and methodological approaches, varying from different interpretations of Marxist method to non-Marxist 'eclecticism'. In this latter case some authors consider themselves to be Marxist insofar as macro analysis is concerned, but they drop this approach when entering into the concrete analysis of fractions of society.[6] This is analogous to the situation in economics where the labour theory of value has often been completely repudiated, even by Marxist scholars doing micro economic research into company behaviour, for example, in preference to the approaches concerned with production factors and costs which typify the neo-classical and marginalist schools.

Finally, the text will not contain a detailed review of the research and debate concerning Italian development and, in particular, urban and regional development[7] from which derives my references here to the Italian situation. This must mean that the present paper can be little more than a preliminary and tentative examination of some theoretical elements, a series of suggestions for further research work.

Despite the dangers of these limitations and of this approach I believe that it is methodologically sound and will serve to stimulate a systematic debate on the theoretical axioms which Marxist scholars can apply to the study of socio-territorial problems. The first step is to set out what appears to be the main significance of the recent critique of traditional urban sociology. This is the starting point for my subsequent review of the principal theoretical and methodological developments in the new series of studies of socio-territorial problems which have followed this critique.

It seems that these developments can be summarized in the following four points:

(a) Most importantly, sociological relationships in a territory are not of a special kind but are an inseparable aspect of the general set of relationships. This means that social research on the city must necessarily take into account the whole gamut of social relationships.

(b) Since all social relationships have a territorial aspect and since territory is in short supply, every social change has effects on the structure of the territory. Furthermore, these effects are clearly not independent of their causes.

(c) Since territory is the material basis for all social relationships (territory/ nature with its historical and geographical characteristics), social relationships in general will be conditioned by the territorial characteristics.

(d) There are a series of individual interrelationships, different ways of perceiving and manifesting the need for territory and different forms of general social relationships, which all constitute an important element of social relationships in territorial terms and therefore require study. But of course if urban analysis merely consists of cataloguing the various phenomena found in a territory, it will amount to little more than a mainly descriptive social ecology.

Clearly, then, the social relationships which exist in a territory can only be analysed on the basis of theory of more general social relationships. And it is for this reason above all that in Europe, at least, the Marxist view has regained considerable ground. This does not mean, as has already been pointed out, that Marxism is the only basis for a criticism of traditional urban sociology or that a Marxist point of view is sufficient to finally determine the nature of such criticism. It should be remembered that the crisis of urban sociology was already well advanced before the recent diffusion of Marxist analysis. Furthermore, a number of Marxists had in the meantime, even if indirectly, favoured the classic approach to urban social analysis.

What follows is solely concerned with the Marxist approach because it is undoubtedly the most systematic, and also because it incorporates a number of the positive elements of other critiques of classical urban sociology. In the interests of simplicity, though, these will not be dealt with in detail.

## 2. Social Classes as a Subject and Method of Analysis of Urban Problems

The Marxist view of history is that it is the history of struggles and relationships between the social classes. It follows that territorial problems must also be considered in the light of these relationships in particular countries and at given historical moments. This simple statement contains innumerable complications, problems caused by, for example, identification of specific class relationships or the need to grasp the dynamics of the relationships between classes in order to understand the problems of territorial development. I shall therefore make a number of simplifications in order to arrive at generalizations which can broadly speaking be derived from the most recent Marxist studies of these problems. I shall provide a definition of the relationship between territory and the dominant productive and class system, i.e. capitalism. Then, in the course of giving a detailed account of this definition, I shall try to specify, with the help of examples, the temporal and spatial dimensions and the main trends of the socio-territorial relationship.

There are three aspects to a definition of territory:

(*a*) Territory is a map of the social relationships of production because it is fundamental to all these relationships.

(*b*) Territory is itself a means of production.

(*c*) Territory is a consumer good in short supply.

It now remains to be seen what follows from these in terms of class relationships, first in general terms and then in the real world situation.

(*a*) This is the most general aspect of the definition and refers to the complex synthesis of the social relationships of production in their spatial form and is not, as it might seem, merely a descriptive geographical aspect of socio-territorial relationsips. The relationships between social classes, which are ultimately relationships of exploitation, are not equally distributed over the territory. In other words, the distribution of wealth (or development) lacks balance and certain regions (or, more clearly, the classes in those regions) exploit certain other regions (i.e. classes present there).

Therefore it is possible to give a socio-territorial interpretation of the social division of labour and of exploitation which is essentially an interpretation of inter-class relationships. The approach amounts to examining the socio-territorial consequences of capitalist accumulation and this in turn consists of the analysis of exploitative social relations which are historically determined. Thus territorial imbalances appear to be connected with three specific form-phases (this expression is used here to show that capitalist accumulation is always, or almost always, a complex articulation of its three forms, but that each phase is predominant in three successive historical periods) of capitalist accumulation: primitive accumulation, capitalist accumulation in the strict sense and imperialist accumulation.

The territorial dialectic which corresponds with each of these three aspects of capitalist accumulation respectively are as follows:

(i) The contradictions between city and country, which are determined by the process of expropriation of resources and productive capacity in the latter areas for the development of modern industry in the cities.

(ii) The contradictions between centre and periphery (both terms being used in the broadest sense), which are determined by the process of centralization, a product of the exploitation of workers which also involves the progressive ruin of small capitalists.

(iii) The contradiction between development and underdevelopment, which is determined by the overexploitation of underdeveloped areas by imperialism.

(*b*) Territory is a means of production both directly in agriculture, because it is the initial basis for the process by which the increase of value of agricultural products is achieved, and indirectly in the towns, because it is the prerequisite for building, whether for consumption (for which see below) or for production units. Since it is a means of production, its ownership or control is an essential social relationship; hence the importance of land ownership and territorial planning as expressions of the social relationships between classes. Therefore, among the social relationships of production, the relationships of disposition (ownership or control) of land are fundamental. Ownership of land constitutes an exceptional social relationship because it is a relationship older than the capitalist system of production, because land is limited and cannot be increased by the development of productive forces (as in the case of other means of production) and because territory is, at one and the same time, an instrument of production and a consumer good.

So land ownership and territorial planning can be seen as coercive social relationships which control a factor which is both a means of production and a consumer good in short supply. Therefore they are of fundamental interest to students of the social problems of territory.

The relationship between land ownership and capitalist accumulation, which must be the subject of specific case studies if it is to be fully understood, lies at the heart of the analysis of the management of a territory as an instrument of production. In theory, land income is in conflict with capitalist accumulation, as it abstracts surplus value from this accumulation, but as the conflict between the working class and capital develops even land income becomes an instrument of capital, serving to control the territory to the detriment of the working class. Land income and speculation are no longer alternatives to capitalist development but complementary to the conservation of the system, and this naturally has a considerable influence on class relationships in the territory, as we shall subsequently explain in greater detail.

(c) The analysis of territory as a consumer good in short supply which is unequally distributed among the various social classes was the main focus for traditional urban sociology, and it continues to be a central feature of many studies of social relationships in a territory. This is the so-called 'housing problem'. Since housing is one of the main consumer goods, it gives rise to three class-based processes. Firstly, *the stratification of the quality of housing* reflects the general stratification of the population; some people are forced to live in very poor accommodation, others are not. The process of stratification can be determined by the cost of the housing alone and also by the political intervention of the state (e.g. provision of council houses). Apart from this, it is also the case that many members of the poorer strata, on moving to the towns, fail to find a house altogether and others are placed in an insecure situation. Secondly, *the cost of housing*, which is often artificially raised and in many Western countries is one of the commodities showing the greatest increase in price, results in the less well-off classes paying the owners a considerable part of the pay rises which they have struggled for in the factories. Finally, *the control of the consumption of territory by the state and/or by property speculation* is itself an important instrument of class repression and control. All these social relationships which exist in territory are of course part of the more general class struggle and so-called urban struggles are merely one form of expression of this wider struggle. Consideration of this latter factor involves examination of the generation and nature of consciousness, and of the organization of social conflict and of the specific conditions which give rise to urban unrest.

### 3. Territory in the Social Division of Labour

A comprehensive discussion of this point would be extremely complex and beyond the scope of this paper. It would be necessary to isolate the particular types of exploitation which correspond with each of the three phases of capitalist accumulation, and then show in concrete historical terms the interconnections between the main phase and the secondary phases of accumulation, thus indicating the socio-territorial relevance of the exploitation. Even though the analysis of primitive accumulation and true capitalist accumulation are clearly set out in the classics of Marxism, the problems concerning imperialist accumulation are extremely complex and still debatable.[8] Even if the mechanism of exploitation in this latter case was clearly understood it would still be necessary to demonstrate the socio-territorial consequences of the various processes of accumulation. This cannot be done without systematic and well-documented evidence and this is only, as yet, readily available for the initial phase of capitalism, by virtue of the monumental documentation used by Marx in the first book of *Capital*.

Therefore this paper will only attempt to bring together in a fully coherent way the material on primitive accumulation. In addition, less systematic observations will be made concerning the other two processes of accumulation. Finally, some limited aspects of the current Italian situation, namely the socio-territorial effects of recent capitalist development, will be examined. But the complex questions concerning how primitive accumulation benefited the North more than the South and how present-day development tends to accentuate the imbalances and the regional contradictions rather than resolving them will not be discussed here.[9]

Primitive accumulation,[10] or more correctly the initial phase of capitalist accumulation, involves a massive removal of resources from the countryside in order to centralize them in cities. In industrial societies, throughout the nineteenth century at least, the map of the social relationships of production clearly showed the increasing imbalance between town and countryside due to the fact that rapidly developing industrial production utilized the resources of the countryside in ever-growing quantities, removing labour and the agricultural products needed to feed a continuously increasing urban population, as well as the agricultural raw materials needed for the growth of industry.

With the world-wide expansion of capitalism, with the progressive exhaustion of the reserve supply of industrial labour which was provided by drawing on the underemployed rural population, with highly developed means of transport facilitating the diffusion of new customs and ways of life, with mass consumption extending its grasp to the rural population and with the rapid growth of the large cities and the possibility of decentralizing industrial production towards the periphery, the socio-territorial situation has acquired some new aspects which, although not less contradictory than before, are more complex. In fact the main contradiction is no longer the classical opposition of town and country but rather the imbalance between centre and periphery and between developed and underdeveloped areas.

Both the urban analyses of the Chicago school and the various theories of underdevelopment take note of the phenomenological aspects of territorial imbalance. However, all too often they ignore the crucial point, which is that this imbalance is a necessary result of the social relationships of production, not merely a defect which can be eliminated by political means. Territorial imbalance, as has been stated already, is a symptom of the underlying situation of class exploitation and conflict.

In Italy it is not difficult to see that there is a relationship between capitalist accumulation and the widening of regional imbalances, i.e. the progressive underdevelopment of the South. On the other hand, it is very difficult to give a complete explanation of this relationship, thus fully revealing the social relations of exploitation which are contained and developed in the territorial imbalances. My hypothesis, which cannot be fully presented here, is that the massive concentration of resources which typifies post-war Italian development is a product of the simultaneous occurrence of delayed primitive accumulation, of rapid capitalist expansion (involving the massive extraction of surplus value and the ruin of small capitalists) and of a related process of imperialist accumulation (based on the partial decentralization of industry towards those areas with a lower organic composition of capital, on agricultural specialization in the South and on financial and other forms of speculation). However, it seems

Table 1. Resident population of various areas of Italy

|  | 1951 | 1971 | % 1971/1951 |
|---|---|---|---|
| North and Centre | 29,735,973 | 35,223,708 | 118.45 |
| Industrialized South | | | |
| (10 provinces)* | 7,525,315 | 8,955,201 | 119.02 |
| Non-industrialized South | | | |
| (22 or 23 provinces) | 10,254,249 | 9,846,302 | 96.02 |
| Total Italy | 47,515,537 | 54,025,211 | 113.70 |
| Industrial triangle** | 6,040,725 | 8,821,875 | 146.04 |

*These are the provinces of Caserta, Naples, Salerno, Pescara, Bari, Taranto, Catania, Syracuse, Sassari and Cagliari. They are not the only Southern provinces to maintain their populations (Palermo has, for example), but they have been the scene of large operations of industrial decentralization and may be considered, to use Rossi—Doria's term, the 'pulp' of Southern Italy.

**These are the five provinces in which industrial development has been most marked: Milan, Turin, Genoa, Bergamo and Varese.

certain that the *internal* regional imbalances which exist are not principly a result of imperialist exploitation as is the case of a large part of the Third World. Rather they result from a process of centralization and specialization which is common to all capitalist development.[11]

The effect on territorial imbalances of this rapid capitalist development in post-war Italy is evident. In the last thirty years, which have been characterized by unprecedented economic growth, the abstraction of the resources of backward areas by more advanced areas has been clearly seen.

Between 1951 and 1971 the population dropped (in absolute and percentage terms) in all those parts of Southern Italy not being industrialized.[12] In fact this decline occurred in the greater part of the South (twenty-three provinces out of thirty-three); this was entirely due to migration moreover because the birth rate in these areas is above the Italian average (see Table 1). This development is particularly serious because the emigration was selective. A disproportionate number of young and old people and women were left behind and they were unlikely to be able to constitute the basis for a labour force which could serve local industry. The economic policies of the government increased this territorial imbalance since they led to a more rapid depopulation of the interior, particularly agricultural areas, in favour of large non-industrialized cities such as Naples and Palermo. More general relationships of class and production lie behind this policy, namely the need to create and control the flow of labour needed for the development of Italian and European industry which is concentrated in a small number of areas in the North.

Also in the last twenty years there has been a marked centralization of all the other economic resources and political decision-making power in two areas: the Milan—Turin axis which controls industry and private finance and Rome, the centre of political and public decision making. There are other studies which document this process of abstraction of resources and centralization,[13] but the main trends may be seen in the following phenomena:

(*a*) The process of concentration of the ownership of industry, accentuated after the economic crises of 1963 and 1969/1970, destroyed many small- and medium-sized firms and led them to be absorbed by (i) financial groups controlled by the large Milanese Banks, (ii) the monopolistic industrial groups of the Milan–Turin axis, (iii) state companies (IRI–ENI) and (iv) foreign capital, which penetrated Italy either through the Milanese private banks or through the decision-making centres in Rome.

(*b*) A concurrent process of financial concentration, most clearly manifest when credit is short, has increasingly brought the control of finance into the hands of large private banks in Milan and the public finance organizations in Rome.

(*c*) The process, which began in the 1950s, of restructuring the political parties of the majority, and above all the Christian Democrats, has favoured the centralization of power at the expense of local political interests. The result has been a strengthening of central political strategies against the local and peripheral interests which, though they constituted political relationships fraught with favouritism and mafia-like practices, nevertheless insured a greater degree of decentralization of resources than is the case today. (They were in fact rather dubious forms of decentralization of decision making.)

(*d*) In addition, the economic policy of intervention in underdeveloped areas either destroyed all the local economic activities and resources or subjected them to the needs of large public or private concerns. These only decentralized their productive activity; they left their decision centres in Milan, Turin and Rome.

In conclusion the problem of the division of labour in a territory is essentially one of class relationships and conflict, as the Italian example makes evident.

The existence of an increasingly violent conflict between opposite interests at the level of the social division of labour and of territorial production is demonstrated by trade union struggles for the abolition of wage zones, for the development of Southern Italy and for stable employment in underdeveloped areas, by the debate on the poles of development and on investment in underdeveloped areas and also by the risings in Reggio Calabria and in many other Southern towns. Such conflicts have tended to be underestimated by social scientists studying territorial problems, but they are vitally important.

### 4. Territory and Production: The Problem of Land Ownership and Planning

The social scientist is less interested in investigating the utilization of territory as a means of production in itself than in studying the social relationships which govern its disposal both as a means of production and as a consumer good, i.e. ownership and planning. The following points are relevant in this context:

(*a*) Land ownership is a pre-capitalist social relationship and was the basis of feudal production. The land owner was the only non-worker who had a right to receive an income because of his ownership. Ownership of land is also a monopolistic right because land is in limited supply, each piece of land has different characteristics and the owner is the only person who can dispose of any particular piece of this property.

(b) Its characteristics as a pre-capitalist social relationship and monopolistic form of property differentiate land ownership from ownership of capital and, at least in certain conditions, create antagonistic relations between them. This is because the owners of the industrial means of production have to pay rent to the land owners abstracted out of the surplus value which could otherwise be accumulated as capital.

(c) Ground rent consists of two components: an absolute component received by virtue of ownership and a differential component which depends on the particular characteristics of the land—whether it is fertile and close to agricultural markets, or urbanized and therefore useful for residential or industrial building, for example.

(d) The contradiction between accumulation of capital and ground rent was very marked in the early stages of capitalism, when capital needed to maximize all the new resources available in order to achieve rapid growth. In specific cases agrarian rent and ownership can itself be a means to achieve capitalist accumulation. This was so in England, where the landlords played a very important role in the Industrial Revolution through the rationalization of agriculture and the more efficient exploitation of the mines.

In a subsequent phase two factors intervened, with the result that ground rent no longer constitutes an absolute contradiction to capitalism, even though it continues to represent an abstraction of surplus value. The first factor was the development of the contradiction between capital and the workers, making it extremely dangerous to abolish a form of property such as ground rent because it might stimulate demands on the part of the workers for the abolition of capitalist ownership itself. The second factor was that the bourgeoisie had bought land and so land ownership was playing a part in capitalist accumulation in the way referred to above, as occurred in England.[14] This last point merits discussion at greater length and can be demonstrated by consideration of urbanization processes and building speculation in Italy.

Ground rent and industrial profit have been closely linked in economic development in Italy since the Second World War. In the case of urban ground rent there have been a number of other reasons for the interpenetration of these two interests apart from the two factors already referred to above. The ownership of urban land is the fundamental prerequisite for an important branch of industry, the building trade. Building speculation combines high profit with high differential ground rent. The building trade, furthermore, is a key sector of Italian economic development because it has played and still plays an important part in the control of the migratory flow and of marginal employment. This is possible because of the relatively small amount of capital required to enter the industry, the fact that it is not much affected by technological innovation and does not require highly qualified labour, and the low level of concentration of the productive units and the temporary nature of their organization (when a building is completed the productive unit may even be dissolved until a later date). Such an industry is an ideal 'stepping stone' to a later phase when some of the immigrants are able to find more stable employment in manufacturing industry. Furthermore, by means of controlling the supply of housing it is possible to control a key element in the basic consumption needs of the whole population, influence living standards and maintain at a low level and means of subsistence of large numbers of workers.

Land speculation has an important role in the integration and reproduction of the Southern ruling class.[15] Due to the fact that it was impossible to begin industrial accumulation in the South and to develop a local bourgeoisie, a ruling class has been reproduced, consisting at first of the large agrarian property holders and then of building speculators and those earning high bureaucratic salaries. This ruling class is certainly unproductive and therefore parasitic, but it functions to maintain the political and economic *status quo*.

For all these reasons capitalist development has never been able to abolish ground rent. In fact, in Italy the speculative gain from this source in both urban and rural situations has increased continuously. This is to the serious detriment of social progress, because it has abstracted resources from the accumulation of industrial capital, on the one hand, and from the growth of demand for essential goods by the workers, on the other, by keeping the prices of housing and food at a high level. Also, indiscriminate land speculation has accentuated the territorial imbalances, leading to the chaotic and disorderly growth of towns and the abandonment of agricultural activities in the countryside. This raises the question of the advantages and defects of the second capitalist method for the disposal of territory, land-use planning.

Planning can reduce the cost of land for specific purposes, e.g. housing or agriculture, by regulating its use and it can also eliminate inconveniences such as inadequate services or urban congestion. In these ways planning is a method of controlling the consumption and living conditions of a large part of the population. But under capitalism, in practice land-use planning does not solve the social contradictions in a territory or become a substitute for ground rent as a means for the disposal of territory. One can see how, in Italy, ground rent and planning can operate together to accentuate the subordination of the exploited classes and the territorial imbalance and contradictions.

Ground rent, building speculation and land-use planning in Italy in the period since the war have had the following functions and the following effects:

(*a*) The use of public and private capital for financial speculation connected with building and real estate has appropriated vast sums which could not advantageously be invested in production. This has accentuated or even led to deflation and, in the long term, stagnation. And this in turn has hindered

Italian economic development and the consequential level of employment, thus reducing the bargaining power of the workers. Furthermore, this speculative activity, by boosting urbanization and hastening the abandonment of the depressed areas, has created very serious social problems.

(b) Land speculation and land-use planning have together exerted monopolistic control over the markets for housing and agricultural produce. As a result they have inflated the cost of living and accentuated housing stratification and social segregation.

(c) By means of this control over agricultural production and building activity, ground rent and land-use and economic planning have largely created and controlled the migratory flow of labour. There has been a complex history of social and economic intervention. Firstly, between 1945 and 1955 approximately, a succession of planning measures favouring agricultural areas helped to create substantial underemployment in such areas. Subsequently, the land reform of 1951 effectively initiated a controlled expulsion of the workers from agriculture. In the meantime, the artificially based expansion of building activity in the large towns, above all in the South, provided employment which served to introduce the exagricultural workers to industrial work and city life. Finally, the cyclical expansion of the building industry provided a source of insecure and seasonal employment which helped to avert the occurrence of explosive social tensions which massive unemployment would have generated. But of course these processes did create social tension and conflict.

In the South, land speculation is the key instrument of social control and of social and political integration. Because of the absence of industrial production, urbanization without industrialization based on speculation is the fundamental instrument for the conservation of existing social relationships and for ensuring the accumulation of capital and the stability of the system. This then serves to ensure the reproduction of the dominant and non-productive bourgeois class. There are many examples of major urban and rural land speculation which are the responsibility of the local ruling class. Attempts to combine the interests of reproduction of capital, reproduction of the labour force and the conservation of the general political concensus by land-use planning have been far less significant than these speculative activities.[16]

Furthermore, it is worth adding that in general urban renewal faces severe problems if land ownership is the only means of controlling land use. For this reason increasingly radical attempts are being made to use planning as a means by which the various social interests in the territory can be combined in order to provide a more 'rational' and completely controllable means by which modern large-scale capitalism can regulate social relationships. But planning is not 'rational' in any neutral sense, because it is a relationship of domination of the many by the few. It cannot therefore resolve the grave contradictions which arise from the incompatability and the conflict between interests which are competing for the use of the scarce supply of land.

### 5. Consumption of Territory: The Housing Problem

The consumption of land and the housing problem were linked by the need to reproduce the labour force in the least costly way. It is fairly obvious that plentiful housing at a reasonable price, fast transport and comfortable, cheap and efficient social services would help to create a very productive labour force at low cost. Why are these conditions not found in our society and why in particular is the housing problem still unsolved? The answer is a complex one and in this paper we shall only consider the implications of the problem rather than its theoretical aspects. We shall set out some factors which illustrate the nature of the housing problem and enable it to be seen in the correct perspective.

(a) A distribution of territorial resources based on the distribution of needs is not possible while these resources are in short supply and are the object of conflicting interests.

(b) The use of territory as a means of consumption conflicts with the use of territory as a means of production, in the same way that the reproduction of capital (or of the relationships of capitalist production) are inconsistent with a 'rational' reproduction of the labour force. Recent analyses of the urban question which demonstrate the constant conflict between the requirements of productivity and efficiency of the system and those of control, conservation and reproduction of the system are referring above all to this last point. An economy which is based on international competition will gain advantages if it is able to increase the productivity of its labour force and also to reduce the cost of production. The consequences, in territorial terms, would be that opportunities should be maximized to increase the mobility of labour in order to suit the characteristics of the labour market. Among the other requirements would be adequate housing for the workers moving to the towns and efficient transport and social services. The aim would be to produce a healthy work force, able to travel to work easily and quickly, with good schools available close to home for the children, and adequate recreational facilities for use after work. Such a work force would then be able to maximize this productive effort.

But currently the maximization of social control at the cost of productivity often occurs, although the incidence of this varies in intensity. This stagnation occurs because an increase of productivity threatens class relationships and the present social and economic status quo, and because an equitable territorial distribution of social resources which favours the type of labour force referred to above is incompatible with the rigid system of social stratification which results from the coercive social division of labour that is a characteristic of the present social relationships of production.

As capitalism develops the need to control, dominate and conserve, it comes increasingly into conflict with the need for productivity and efficiency. As a consequence the distribution by the ruling class of resources in a territory is increasingly oriented towards achieving repressive control rather than greater 'rationality'. So the conflict between the divergent interests of the exploiting and the exploited classes becomes increasingly bitter and open, and as a result both sides become increasingly aware of its existence.

The various factors which contribute to the Italian housing problem are;

(a) The shortage of housing. The traditional shortage of housing for new arrivals in the cities and the persistence of forms of homelessness continues to be contradictory, for it has both functional and dysfunctional consequences for political and economic systems. It functions to maintain high housing costs for the less well off (whereas there are many luxury dwellings which remain empty) and hence it maximizes ground rent. The shortage of housing is also used politically to split the workers and other subordinate classes in general into those who have proper housing and those who have not, and hence to weaken them.

But there are seriously dysfunctional consequences of the shortage of housing as well. The difficulty of finding urban housing and its excessively high price discourages migration and thus limits the movement of the labour force to localities where there is a high demand for it. This results in a surplus of labour in some areas while in others the demand for labour, and thus the cost of labour and the bargaining power of the workers, increases rapidly. Such developments have been common in Italy in the past. Another point is that the great increase in ground rent and speculation and the shortage of working class housing helps to discourage industrial investment and to weaken the economy, while at the same time increasing the political weight of the speculators. In the long run the result is a deflationary spiral from which it is impossible to escape. This undermines the capacity of the national industries to compete on international markets, while increasing unemployment and social tension at home. This spiral can be seen in the economic history of Italy in the last ten years, as can the progressive increase of speculation which has been either connected with urban building, with purely financial activities, or with the transfer of agricultural property.

(b) The high price of housing. This has partially been discussed already as a consequence of the shortage of housing. However, it is also clear that the cost of housing accounts for a considerable proportion of the expenditure of the less well off (between 15 and 45 per cent. in workers' families). Therefore control of housing prices is essential for control of the level and composition of the workers' expenditure and hence for maintaining or altering the distribution of income between the classes. To do this effectively it is necessary to have the means, whether it be land ownership or urban planning, by which to exercise monopolistic control over the supply of housing. This explains why, in the case of Italy, the use of the public sector to provide improved social services and a supply of housing which matches demand has been abandoned. Such public provision would inevitably reduce the price of housing and the opportunities for building speculation.

Another dysfunctional result of the high cost of housing is that it reduces the amount available to be spent on other goods. This reduces the level of domestic demand for industrial products and hinders the development of manufacturing industry which depends on this market above all. In Italy the absence of any attempt to limit the cost of housing has weakened and destabilized the economy.

(*c*) The segregation of working class areas and their inadequate infrastructures. This characteristic is typical of the present conservative tendencies of capitalist development. The need for social control via increased stratification reinforced by differential access to territorial resources results in particular types of urban structure in which the working class areas are isolated and are badly served by transport, social and recreational services. The only certain links with the exterior are by using the means of transport to the work place. These, however, are not necessarily fast or comfortable owing to the tendency of capital to prefer the logic of conservation to that of productivity. In Italy this process of maximization of control has coincided with the strengthening of the urban workers' bargaining power and it has given rise to severe social conflicts which will be discussed later.

(*d*) The tendency to destroy and waste territorial resources. The tendency to useless development which is inherent in mature capitalism, a result of the need for industry to continually develop production, results in a wasteful use of territorial resources. To give some examples: the life expectancy of housing in the nineteenth century was fifty to one hundred years, now it is twenty to thirty years. Relatively new housing is demolished to make way for sky-scraper offices for commerce, industry and the bureaucracy. This destruction of material resources is accompanied by the destruction of social relationships and the creation of social conflict. This process of city centre redevelopment has destroyed the businesses of a large stratum of petit bourgeois shopkeepers and craftsman who had survived the process of industrial concentration and centralization of capital in the favourable environment created by the old quarters in the city centre. This has been particularly apparent in Italy which had a large petit bourgeois stratum. Parallel processes, less conspicuous but perhaps even more serious from the point of view of social relationships, have taken place in the countryside. Here the processes of urbanization not only result in the destruction of resources but also in the complete abandonment of productive activity. Land formerly cultivated by the peasants lies fallow, a populated region becomes deserted and agricultural villages become ghost towns. In Italy, as we have already seen, this process is concentrated in certain parts of the South and has given rise to particular forms of social imbalance.

## 6. Concluding Remarks on Urban Social Conflict

This brief analysis of the social problems of urban and regional development as a consequence of the contradictions and social relationships of production has revealed a number of basic causes of social conflict. Rather than discussing the possible typologies of such conflict or describing specific cases[17] it seems worthwhile setting out some of the more contentious areas which need to be discussed further. The first concerns the nature of the parties in conflict and the second the question of social consciousness and the organization of urban conflict.

Regarding the first point, our analysis suggests that the interests of the various strata of the dominant class do not always coincide. However, although land owners, industrial entrepreneurs, property speculators and the civil service may have contrasting territorial interests and development strategies, in practice these differences are subordinate to the higher common interest of capitalist development and maintenance of political and social equilibrium. We have emphasized the fact that, in the face of the intense conflict between capital and the working class, the contradictions between capitalist development and land ownership are contained within the structure of capitalism. Thus ground rent ends up by being used as a means of controlling and repressing the workers. But this is not strictly true, for divergences of interest within the dominant class are not always totally absorbed by it (although this virtually happens in certain European countries such as France and Italy). There are in fact countries where the working class is strongly integrated within the system, such as, in different ways, Scandinavia, Great Britain, the United States and West Germany. Here there may be a much more marked incompatability between backward and reformist sectors of the dominant class, partly because strategies for the use of territory must take into account the need to integrate at least a part of the working class and thus to make concessions to it.

In the case of the working class it is even more difficult to distinguish conflicting parties and their interests. It seems that in the Italian case, and also probably in France, one can identify a working class (in a definition which does not imply class consciousness) including white collar and marginal workers which plays a leading role in territorial conflict and a petit bourgeoisie (meaning craftsmen, shopkeepers, small farmers, small industrialists and professionals) which plays a secondary role. Thus in cases where political and economic intervention in agriculture favours emigration and depopulation of the countryside, thus expropriating the small peasants, or when the process of urban renewal ruins a part of the urban petit bourgeoisie, the struggle which ensues between these strata and the dominant class conceals the real essence of the conflict which is that between capitalism's need to develop or preserve its exploitation of the working class (by creating unemployment and thus competition between the workers, by creating migrant labour or by economic concentration) and the workers desire to strengthen their position (by obtaining better living and working conditions, and a distribution of resources which is advantageous to them).

But in other countries such an analysis can be very difficult. The ability of the ruling class to distribute advantages to large sectors of the working class (an ability which is a product of imperialist relations within the country, or with its political traditions) can split class interests up into many more particular interests which are held by local communities, specific groups, professions, etc. And even where the contending fractions and their interests are identifiable there are other complications, e.g. the differences that exist between white collar workers and blue collar workers in relatively secure employment, and other less secure workers.

Only if the most important sector of the working class, i.e. the workers employed in large modern industry, can achieve a level of consciousness and of political and trade union organization which enables them to serve as a constant point of reference for other working class strata can there be a unity of the interests between these strata, and hence of the working class as a whole, with regard to the territorial problem. For this reason an able and mature working class leadership is the key to the transcendence of the limited, sectoral character of territorial conflict. Without this the struggle for housing, for better social services or for a different urban structure will be a limited and partial one in which the real antagonists are not identified and the root causes of the conflict unaffected. No effective strategy of conflict, nor any real alternative to the logic of the ruling class, can develop in these circumstances.

This brings us to the question of social consciousness and the organization of urban conflict which, as is remarked elsewhere in this book,[18] has often been underestimated in contemporary studies. These have usually confined themselves to clarifying the objective conditions which underly conflict and the basic class interests which exist, without investigation the way in which these interests are actually perceived by those to whom they belong or the way the conflict is organized. In fact the way in which potential conflict becomes realized is very complex and difficult to make generalizations about. However, some broad conclusions can be drawn.

First of all, it is necessary to distinguish between situations where the working class is highly integrated and situations where the working class and its traditional organizations (trade unions and the Communist Party, for example) are in more general conflict. In the first case, social conflict in general and urban struggles in particular will be fragmentary and will be unlikely to develop a unity, a class identification and a national organization. Essentially a series of local conflicts of interest will occur, involving socially heterogenous groups. *Ad hoc* organizations will be set up which will be political expressions of the social consciousness of specific problems and, when these problems are resolved, such organizations will disintegrate. Sometimes of course these organizations persist longer, but in general even these reflect the same specific and limited consciousness and lack of connection with the fundamental conflict. But as the objective conditions change and profit margins diminish the increasingly worthless and stagnant character of capitalist development makes it ever more difficult to give better living conditions to large strata of the population and the processes of integration collapse, revealing the conflict which lies behind this fragile facade.

However, where this conflict exists openly things are very different. Even if particular conflicts are expressed at sectoral level and those who are in conflict have a low level of consciousness (and both of these are often true of urban conflicts), they take place in the context of the working class movement in its complex political and trade union organization and become part of this organization's strategy. The organizations in conflict may lack any clear integration with the working class movement (which consists of more than its traditional organizations anyway). For example, in Italy there have been struggles inspired by the neo-fascists, especially in the South, but even these conflicts have an ultimate relationship with the working class movement because of their working class composition, their strategy of class struggle and their consequent class alignment. Therefore where there is open conflict between the rulers and the ruled, even sectoral and partial conflicts (and those which have an intra-class basis too) which are often not among the traditional subjects and organizations for political participation are a part of the more general logic of the struggle between a working class movement and the dominant class.

The Italian experience has illustrated this point. This experience explains why, to a large extent, the problem of formation of consciousness in organizations is taken for granted by Italian studies of urban conflict. In Italy conflicts have often started quite spontaneously and have then led to new forms of organization being set up.[19] It did not matter that often these organizations were unstable, only surviving by reason of the conflict. Nor was the social composition of the conflict group important—whether it was the petit urban bourgeoisie, or ordinary workers, or white collar employees, or marginal workers, or recent immigrants—because, in the last analysis, all these struggles ended up by involving the whole working class movement. The unions reorganized themselves on a territorial basis when involved in housing and other urban struggles, thus enabling them to incorporate such conflicts into their political and trade union activities. In fact their strategies were reconstructed by basing them on these urban struggles which had come to be a dominant characteristic of the Italian situation. The left wing parties and the extra-parliamentary groups also conducted the struggle (badly or well depending on their strategies) in the same manner. This gave organized outlets for the growth of social consciousness which had been originally formed at the partial and sectoral levels which have been referred to in this paper.

## Notes

1. The debate in question is vast and very complex, dating from the establishment of the Marxist theory of land income; it is further investigated by Kautsky, K. and Lenin, V. I. (*Teoria della questione Agraria*, Ristampa, Ed. Riuniti, Roma, 1973) as far as agricultural income is concerned. For an analysis of urban land speculation, see the different interpretation of F. Engels (*The housing question*, in *Marx–Engels, Selected Works*, Vol. 2, Progress Publishers, Moscow, 1973, pp. 295–375).

   The debate on the socialist use of territory has been particularly interesting as Stalin's theory of urban development policy has been opposed to Engels' determined antiurban stand. In *Antidüring*, Engels maintains that 'Civilisation has bequeathed us a heritage which will take much time and trouble to get rid of. But it must and will be got rid of, however protracted a process it may be' (Engels, F., *Antidüring*, Lawrence and Wishart, London, 1955, p. 412). Stalin and the soviet planners have maintained instead that 'The large cities will not only fall into ruin, but they will give birth to other large new cities, which will be centres of a major cultural development, centres not only for major industry, but also for the processing of agricultural products and for a powerful development of all the branches of the food industry....' (Stalin, J., *Economic Problems of Socialism in the USSR*, Foreign Publishing House, Moscow, 1972; *Problemi Economici del Socialismo dell'USSR*, Ed. Rinascita, Roma, 1953, p. 38).

Finally, much more recently, there is the debate between two French Marxist scholars: Henri Lefvbre (*Le Droit a la Ville*, Anthropos, Paris 1968; *Du Rural à l'Urbain*, Anthropos, Paris, 1970; *Revolution Urbaine*, Gallimard, Paris 1970; *La Production de l'Espace*, Gallimard, Paris, 1972) and Manuel Castells (most importantly in *La Question Urbaine*, Maspero, Paris, 1972), where the latter condemns Lefevbre for a generally too pro-urban conception and thus an interpretation which is not shared with Marxism.

2. 'Urban sociology is noted more for the cogency of its internal criticism than for its capacity to generate concepts of wider significance. An area of study has developed whose main discipline and body of knowledge exists to show that those who traditionally argued for a distinctive urban sociology were mistaken....' (Pahl, R. E., Urban processes and social structure, in *Whose City*, (2nd ed., Penguin, Harmondsworth, 1975, p. 234). 'Our hypothesis is that such a situation is essentially due to the fact that urban sociology is not a scientific domain, nor a field for observation, but rather an ideological artifact. ...' (Castells, M., Towards a political urban sociology, Chapter 2 in this book).

3. I am reporting here an example of this first approach, as I will do later for the others. The examples are chosen arbitrarily and represent neither the ideal sample nor the only topic which these authors write about. 'Les "problemes urbains", c'est-à-dire les processus sociaux de consomation collective, deviennent centraux dans la société industrielle avancée' (Castells, M., Vers une theorie sociologique de la planification urbaine, *Sociologie du Travail*, 4, 413, 1969.)

The identification of urban problems with the social process of collective consumption also remains in Castells' volume (*La Question Urbaine*, Maspero, Paris, 1972), but it appears to me to have become strongly attenuated in his most recent work (Castells, M., and Godard, F., *Monopolville*, Mouton, Paris, 1974).

In passing I would like to add that not only do I not share this identification of consumption with urban problems (and this will be clarified in the context of this article), but it seems to me that Castells also overemphasizes the role of the bourgeoisie and the managerial class in such a way that the dialectic aspects of class in urban problems is often lost.

4. The example I have chosen for this approach is David Harvey, who says, 'The processes or urbanisation involve the creation of a built environment which subsequently functions as a vast man-made resource system—a reservoir of fixed and immobile capital assets to be used in all phases of commodity production and final consumption' (Harvey, D., *The Political Economy of Urbanisation in Advanced Capitalist Societies—The Case of the United States*, duplicated, VIII World Congress of Sociology, Toronto, 1974). I believe that one can maintain that the same emphasis on urban problems as fixed capital can also be found in Harvey's principal work (*Social Justice and the City*, Arnold, London, 1973).

5. It is more difficult to give an example of the third approach, even if in conclusion it appears to be the most widespread today. It seems to me that one can discover the essence of a distributive emphasis in the following fragment: 'Cities, then, are bits of society on the ground. They occupy a distinctive spatial configuration and resources are allocated in a distinctive pattern as a result of particular historical, economic, political or, indeed, social circumstances' (Pahl, R. E., *Whose City?*, 2nd ed., Penguin, Harmondsworth, 1975, p. 236). This seems to me to be the point of view of those authors who centre their analyses on housing stratification and thus on the distribution of residential resources in connection with diverse social variables (profession or class).

6. There are many specific examples which one could give of this tendency toward a certain type of eclecticism (it seems to me that among the others one could give two very different English examples in Ruth Glass, who combines a Marxist sensitivity for socio-urban problems with a research methodology tied to traditional socio-ecological research, and in Ray Pahl, who does not exclude the possibility of being able to arrive at some Marxist conclusions by using traditional methods of observing society and theoretical assumptions alien to Marxism); I would only like to point out that the first approach mentioned is most prevalent in Anglo-Saxon countries, where neither the old nor the new Marxist schools have succeeded in using an alternative and coherent critical apparatus to eradicate the methodologies of social positivistic or neo-empiricist research.

I would like to add that this methodological point carries no value-judgement on my part. One must admit that recent empirical Marxist research on urban problems (I am referring as much to my personal experience and that of other Italians as to the works of many young French and Spanish researchers) has not succeeded in systematically elaborating the logical connections between theoretical apparatus and empirical observation. Therefore we need a very much wider and deeper discussion before we can dismiss the eclectic methodology which, if nothing else, at least expresses a rigorous attempt to depart from concrete reality in order to arrive progressively at more and more encompassing generalizations.

7. Although this is not the place to provide yet another partial bibliography on the problems of housing and territory in Italy, perhaps it is worth remembering the names of some researchers and scholars who have recently published on the subject—in Milan: Boffi, Daolio, Della Pergola, Di Ciaccia, Bottero and Todisco; in Rome: Ferrarotti, Lelli and Marcelloni; in Naples: Drago; in Venice: Folin, Indovina and Ceccarelli. But, given the importance that the urban problem has assumed from 1968 to the present day, a complete list of the workers in this field would contain many more names.

8. There are at least two different schools of interpretation of the essence of imperialist exploitation and imperialist accumulation which can be found in the Marxist tradition. The first comes from Lenin and puts the accent on the productive reorganization of imperialism by means of the export of capital toward those areas with a low organic composition of capital where additional profits can be extracted. One could see in the recent work of A. Emmanuel (*Inequal Exchange*, New Left Books, London, 1972) a very debatable reelaboration of the thesis that the roots of imperialist exploitation lie in the diverse quantities of work (and thus of surplus value) contained in products.

The second school of thought centres around Rosa Luxemburg and insists that imperialism is the moment of realization of capitalist overproduction (in this sense Emmanuel could also be connected with the Luxemburgian theory). The authors who have best expressed this approach recently are Baran P. and Sweezy P. (*Monopoly Capital,* Penguin Books, Harmondsworth, 1970). Finally, A. Gunder Frank has proposed a complex theory in which, in the same mode of production, the necessity to underdevelop and to dominate vast regions of the world is rooted in capitalist development, a thesis which, like that of Emmanuel, can, in certain aspects, be connected with Lenin's view and, in others, with Luxemburg.

9. *Apropos* of the links between North and South in the process of Italian capitalist accumulation, I should like to set out a few points which I intend to investigate more deeply in future work.

For the most part I am inclined to accept the Gramscian thesis (Gramsci, A., *Il Risorgimento*, Einaudi, Torino, 1949) that the bourgeois revolution in the last century was not completed and did not involve the South. In my opinion, this means that the process of primitive and capitalist accumulation, which permitted the collapse, however controversial, of industry in the North 'used' the Northern countryside rather than the Southern countryside as a principal front for such an accumulation. Here we find ourselves in difficulty because Gramsci justified his thesis on historical and political grounds while our reading is largely historical and economic. In order to prove the validity of the Gramscian thesis in an economically based article such as this one and to refute the contrary theory of Rosario Romeo (*Risorgimento e Capitalismo*, Laterza, Bari, 1959), it is necessary to demonstrate that in the Southern countryside at the end of the last century those phenomena typical to agricultural areas subjected to primitive accumulation did not occur. In particular, one must demonstrate: (*a*) that there was no diffused breakdown in pre-capitalistic relationships, not so much of the large productive landed estates (latifundi) but the non-productive latifundi, agricultural units and craftsmen who produced only for self-consumption; (*b*) that farm produce did not increase to any considerable extent and that the limited increment served more to benefit anew the dominant Southern class than to finance Northern industrial development directly; (*c*) that the reserve labour force which was expelled from the Southern land did not feed the demand for labour from Northern industrial expansion; and (*d*) that there was not a substantial increase in the aggregate demand for products from Northern industrial manufacturing by the large Southern masses that could encourage the process of industrialization.

In this way it could be proved that primitive accumulation in the last century was concentrated in the Northern countryside and that there remained frozen in the South a series of typically pre-capitalistic production relations, among them the large landed estates owned by absentees and agriculture and artisanry which, if they had a role in Italian economic development, had a more negative than a positive one, i.e. they contributed to making Italian capitalism particularly weak by absorbing capital.

Our hypotheses are not particularly unrealistic if one considers that the annual increment in the national agricultural product in the last twenty years of the last century was not much above 4–5 per cent. (Gerschenkron, A., *Economic Backwardness in Historical Perspectives*, Belknap Press of Harvard University Press, Cambridge, Massachusetts, 1962) and was due principally to a result of innovations in Northern agriculture, that the corn law protected a farming structure which was particularly impervious to innovations which, however, spread abroad and hence lowered the price of grain, that the Southern farming structure changed little and with extreme slowness and that the surplus of Southern workers emigrated mostly to America or abroad, and not to the North. All that we have said up until now does not exclude the fact that the Northern industrial bourgeoisie partially benefited from its alliance with Southern land owners, and from the Southern feudal immobility. First of all, it benefited from a long-lasting, almost monopolistic position because it did not face the danger of competition in industrial production from a (non-existent) Southern bourgeoisie (in this sense the destruction of the Southern heavy industry that did exist at the beginning of industrialization constituted an enormous advantage). This meant also that, even if the farm 'surplus' which directly or indirectly (as a result of payment or of consumption of manufactured products) went from the Southern countryside to the Northern city was limited, it did not have to be shared with Southern competitors. In the second place, one must take into account the political stability of the system which permitted the systematic repression of the Northern working class and its overexploitation for a long period of time. In the third place, the South always remained a virgin territory available for future capitalist accumulation; we saw how true this was after the Second World War.

It is difficult to see in the Italian South after unification the 'countryside' of a primitive accumulation; it is just as difficult to see there the 'colony' of an anticipated imperialist accumulation (Capecelatro e Carlo, *Contro la Questione Meridionale, Studio Sulle Origini dello Sviluppo Capitalistico in Italia*, La nuova sinistra, Roma, 1972). In fact, one sees neither the additional surplus value which weak Italian industrial development might draw from the progressive underdevelopment of the South nor the systematic rape of Southern raw materials in order to feed Northern industry.

10. I have tended to give primitive accumulation a broader definition than that given to it by Marx himself (at least according to a literal interpretation) in Chapter XXIV of the first book of *Capital*. Not only does 'primitive' seem to me to refer to the long phase of accumulation which dissolves the pre-capitalist mode of production and prepares it for the take-off of the capitalist economy as the dominant mode of production but also the following progressive penetration of capital into residual non-capitalist areas in order to take resources from them (raw materials, labour force, markets).

11. For this purpose I do not share the analysis of those authors who mechanically extend theories of imperialism to apply them to underdeveloped regions. The divergence becomes yet wider when one considers the political conclusions which these authors draw, ending by giving theoretical support to separatism, local nationalism and the rebellion of all the classes in underdeveloped areas against a hypothetical colonial domination. For such theses on Southern Italy, see particularly Zitara, N., *Il Proletariato Esterno*, Jaca Book, Milano, 1972.

12. More recent industrialization in the South has been realized in particular areas commonly called development poles. In general, these areas are near-large or medium-sized cities (with some relevant exceptions in the 'poles' of Naples and Taranto), not at the periphery but rather in the hinterland of the city (within 50 kilometres), in irrigated farming areas or rich areas, on the coast or along the great communications arteries.

13. See mainly the monumental work of the French geographer Etienne Dalmasso on financial concentration in the Milanese area (*Milano: Capitale Economica e Finanziaria d'Italia*, Angeli, Milano, 1971).

14. See, for example, Kautsky, K. and Lenin, V. I., *Teoria della Questione Agraria*, Ristampa, Ed. Riuniti, Roma, 1973.

15. See also the following interesting hypothesis on the integration of the Catholic Roman aristocracy through building speculation, suggested by Alessandro Pizzorno (Three types of urban social structure and the development of industrial society, in *Modernization, Urbanization and the Urban Crisis* (Ed. G. Germani), Little Brown and Co., New York, 1973, pp. 130–131).

16. See, for example, the paper of Ginatempo, N., and Cammarota, A., in this book, Chapter 5.

17. For a typology of some conflicts in the city of Milan, see Mingione, E., *Urban Development and Social Conflict: The Case of Milan*, duplicated, ISA Berlin seminar, July 1972; and Daolio, A., Le lotte per la casa a Milano, in *Le Lotte per la Casa in Italia* (Ed. A. Daolio), Feltrinelli, Milano, 1974.

18. See Pickvance, C. G., From social base to social force, Chapter 9 in this book.

19. District committees of tenants are the most notable example. These were later consolidated by the establishment of a main organization, the Tenants' Union, which is now very well established in the larger towns.

# 5
# Land and Social Conflict in the Cities of Southern Italy: An Analysis of the Housing Question in Messina

*Nella Ginatempo and Antonella Cammarota*

## 1. Introduction

This paper analyses the social contradictions associated with land use in underdeveloped areas, concentrating on the problems arising from urban growth in Southern Italy, particularly those concerned with housing and services. It has become clear that these are social problems and that they arise from class relationships and from the contradictions in the reproduction of capital and in the development process. Taking this as our starting point we assume that

(a) The spatial and geographical aspects of the development of land cannot be isolated for study as they are closely linked to the development of the social contradictions inherent in capitalism.

(b) Land, both as a means of production and as a scarce consumer good, is a means of development which the bourgeoisie attempts to control. This control is based on a structure of exploitation in which the contradictions between classes in the use of land is manifest.

Therefore the development of land is not simply a spatial consequence of the activity of a social organization; it is also a process which is used by the bourgeoisie for its benefit to the detriment of the proletariat and hence it generates conflicts. Our aim here is to analyse land use in this manner (and thus the housing problem) in the Southern Italian cities,[1] taking land use to be a key element in the specific locally determined class relationships within a context which is formed by the contradictions inherent in the capitalist division of labour and the process of Italian economic development.

The urbanization which has occurred in Southern Italy is the expression of a non-productive form of economic activity and a set of local class relationships which result from a situation of economic underdevelopment. In fact urban growth operates in the developed areas to support the processes which dominate the capitalist system (extraction from surplus value), while in the underdeveloped areas it helps to maintain this underdevelopment and facilitates processes such as building speculation which serve the interests of the dominant class.

## 2. The Southern City and its Contradictions

The Southern city differs greatly from the developed metropolis. Unlike the latter it is not well integrated with its surroundings, being cut off from the neighbouring agricultural land by lack of proper communication and trading links. There is clear-cut social stratification by area in these Southern cities, but on the other hand there are no clearly differentiated areas which are based on different economic activities. This is because such cities are based on a single type of economic activity which involves the plunder of resources and the waste of the labour force. Because of this lack of a more complex structure, the Southern city amounts to little more than a mass of houses (many of them untenanted) and the offices of the many organizations which are engaged in the above-mentioned unproductive economic activity.

There are few public services available for the mass of the population of these Southern cities, despite the rapid growth of public administration (whose main function, based on a patronage system, is to provide a limited and insufficient source of jobs for some of the many who are unemployed). However, there are far better housing and services in the bourgeois zones of the city (mainly privately provided) than in the proletarian and lumpen-proletarian zones. The overall urban structure is, at the same time,

(a) A spatial expression of a particular historically determined process of economic growth which exists in the absence of the process of industrialization.

(b) An instrument which expresses the power of the locally dominant class and which gives rise to increasingly serious social contradictions.

Regarding the first point, Southern cities have played a key role in the pattern of Italian development since the end of the war. As is well known, industrial development has been concentrated in the Northern triangle and the South has supplied a reserve labour force which has been available for development in the North and even beyond Italy. The South has also had a role to play as a secondary market for the consumption of the products of industry.

The policies of using the South as a labour reservoir and as a market have together been responsible for the size of these Southern towns which provide the means by which the surplus labour force (which has been forced off the land) can be managed and his secondary market created. A consequence of this role was that the Southern cities came to consist of a large urban marginal proletariat which lived and worked[2] in insecure conditions and a non-productive bourgeoisie which was not involved in industry but in financial and property speculation and the exercise of corrupt power. These activities serve to maintain stability, keeping the tensions generated by underdevelopment among the urban marginal proletariat in check, principally by preventing the development of a stable and coherent working class.

One of the prime causes of the chaos and lack of facilities that has been referred to is the local bourgeoisie's exclusive and unrestrained interest in building speculation; this follows from the fact that the main interest of this bourgeoisie is not the process of extraction of surplus value but rather a distributive and financial process.

The consequence of this general situation is that there is neither a significantly large stable working class nor an industrial reserve army in these cities. In fact with the exception of a few small factories there is no locally based industrial development here. Furthermore, the crisis in capitalist development which first arose in Italy in 1963 has meant that national industrial development has been insufficient to absorb all the reserve labour force, which has therefore grown steadily larger and become a group which is now only on the margin of the regular labour force.[3]

This marginal mass, which Marx called 'stagnant relative surplus population',[4] is especially concentrated in the ghettos and shanty towns of the Southern cities and, apart from the factor referred to above, it has also been affected by the progressive reduction of local availability of steady work because of the decline in commercial, small-scale industrial and public service employment in recent times. The main source of employment is now various kinds of irregular work, particularly building and public works which pay poor wages as a consequence of the labour surplus.

Under present conditions the contradictions in the South between the local bourgeoisie and the interests of the large monopolies as well as those between the Southern bourgeoisie and the marginal proletariat are worsening steadily. These contradictions result from the evolution of the more general contradictions of capitalism and of the pattern of Italian development, and they are worsening for two reasons. The first is that during the 1950 to 1963 economic boom the monopolistic bourgeoisie was willing to finance the activities of the Southern bourgeoisie through public expenditure, because it gained from the South the economic advantage of a reserve army of labour and the political advantage of control of the tensions generated by underdevelopment. Now, however, since the Southern labour force, because of the economic crisis, is no longer usable as a reserve army and is becoming more difficult to control, the resulting alliance between monopolistic and the Southern bourgeoisies is weakened and is wholly politically based. As profits have diminished public expenditure must be cut and therefore so must the financing of this Southern bourgeoisie.

Of course, the difficulty of controlling the marginal workers in the South is also a product of the declining employment possibilities and hence the declining possibilities for patronage as well.

## 3. Class Relationships and the Housing Question in Southern Cities

In order to show how the control of land use in the Southern city has been a powerful instrument in the hands of the locally dominant class it is necessary to clarify the link between class relationships, social conflict and land use. In a capitalist society land use, as is the case with other resources, tends to be irrational and contradictory. This is because capitalism substitutes exchange values for use values. But, apart from this, there are also some more particular historical and social factors which apply in the case of housing.[5] In general capitalism is interested in reproducing capital and the labour force in the most efficient way. However, this interest, which is linked to the need for growth of production and economic development, can be contradictory and hence generate conflict within the dominant class. In towns where this criterion of development is dominant there will be a tendency towards greater efficiency in the use of land and in the reduction of the costs of reproducing the labour force through a rationalization of the housing situation. But in Italy, where there is a weak base for economic development, the existence of a bourgeoisie which depends more on speculation and financial operation is an important factor. As already mentioned, this unproductive economic activity, which results in a growth of ground rent, operates as a means of helping to repress the working class; it does this by controlling consumption, reducing salaries and in general managing the living conditions of the masses. However, it must be noted that these operations have certain contradictory and harmful consequences for capitalism itself.

In the South these contradictions have a particular characteristic arising from the fact that land speculation rather than industrial development is the basis for the key features of the relationship between the classes, and because the interest in the efficient reproduction of the labour force is for this reason very weak in comparison with the situation in the more developed areas of the country. As has been stated, the Southern cities contain a large and underemployed labour force and the control of land is used, as is public expenditure and the patronage system, to keep the tensions arising from this situation in check. Policies which result in deceptive promises of housing for shanty-town dwellers and the creation by this means of a mass of marginal workers isolated in peripheral ghettos have helped to reduce the capacity and the will to struggle and have attempted to create a subservient population.

This use of land for purposes of political control has some dramatic affects. For example, there are higher than national average percentages in the South both of owner-occupied housing and of empty and unfit lodgings. The building speculation which occurs is primarily a way of investing excessive savings and is not dependent on the immediate realization of these assets (by sale or lease) or use by the new owner. Therefore many flats remain untenanted, while on the other hand there is an acute shortage of low-cost public housing for which there is a great and unfulfilled demand by workers such as construction, occasional and marginal workers. Furthermore, these people are not even able to pay the price for what little public housing is available and thus become shanty-town dwellers. In general, therefore, the urban land is not useful for consumption by the population or by industrial processes. The expansion of the central business districts in Southern cities is not based on an industrial development and its associated commercial, service and management functions (as in Milan, for example) but on purely speculative activity which is in fact inimical to efficient industrial development. This is one reason why the central government has in the South located its 'poles of industrial development' in areas away from the Southern cities, in semi-urban zones or in minor urban centres (another is the need to ensure that major new factories do not disturb the low wage, insecure labour markets in these cities and create a new source of political power in the form of an organized working class).

In conclusion, land in the Southern city provides a means, via speculation, of expanding the income of the local bourgeoisie and, apart from a portion which is spent, it becomes a means of constantly reproducing a non-productive form of finance capital. In the Southern cities the intra-class contradictions which exist in the big bourgeoisie elsewhere between those who wish to maximize ground rent and those who wish to maximize profits is not very evident. The desire to maximize ground rent is dominant and the fundamental contradiction so far as land use is concerned is between this unproductive speculative capital and a marginal labour force. This is clearly a class-based conflict because those who suffer from poor housing are also in many cases construction workers. Their lives are therefore dominated at home in the shanty towns and also at work on the building sites by the same bosses. However, neither their class consciousness nor their level of organization is sufficiently developed to enable them to take effective action, principally because of their weak and fragmented position in the labour market. Nevertheless, the contradictions are worsening and mass movements and protest (centring on problems of land and work) are beginning to occur in many Southern cities. Furthermore, in a few cases (e.g. in Naples) these marginal workers have shown a great capacity for struggle and a high degree of political maturity.

### 4. Messina and the Housing Question

This analysis is little more than an explanatory outline which, in order to be verified, requires the comparative analysis of Southern cities. We have limited ourselves to analysing the situation in Messina, remembering that the contradictions which arise from the processes of land use are particularly accentuated there by the effects of the earthquake of 1908.

In Messina approximately 35,000 people live in the shanty towns—14 per cent. of the resident population. More than 50,000 people live without services, in overcrowded accommodation in a poor state of repair. Almost 40 per cent. of the population live in housing conditions greatly inferior to the norm. There is a complete lack of green space and very few fundamental services such as nursery schools, dispensaries and public transport. In Messina there are 1·8 square metres of neighbourhood services per inhabitant (compared with the legal standard of 18 square metres) and the few services which do exist are almost all concentrated in the bourgeois zones. The structure of the city is determined by the distribution of social classes. The expensive houses have been built on the Tyrrenian coast on a panoramic road to the north, eliminating groups of poor housing. The more major services (e.g. universities and sports facilities) are located there. Worker's houses are pushed into areas to the south or to the bottom of the little valleys which run through the town. The streets, because they are not built solely for transportation but rather for the enrichment of speculators, are chaotic. Repeated speculative bids for asphalting have succeeded in raising many roads above the level of the pavements, stopping up storm drains, so that heavy rain paralyses the city. Messina is a city of 250,000 inhabitants in which water is lacking and where, rather than trying to improve the situation, the city government wastes money on useless roadworks.

This is a consequence of the fact that land use is based on the interests of the local bourgeois class. The shanty towns in particular derive their existence from this fact. Key factors in their creation are

(a) The limited necessity locally to reproduce the resident labour force as an element of a process of local production which would then require the development of the city as well. Instead, the ghetto performs a management function by helping to achieve the social disintegration of this group. A consequence is that little public housing is provided, and that only on a speculative basis. A similar condition applies to planning and to the city administration generally.

(b) Overproduction of better quality, middle class houses when more low-cost houses are needed.

(c) The lack of a sufficient, stable income for the large marginal strata, as a result of the structure of the local labour market. Some consequences of this are the relative absence of an established working class and an enormous discrepancy between the need and the effective demand for housing.

The shanty towns grew up soon after the earthquake of 1908. More than 22,000 shanties were constructed but, at the same time that these shanties were built, it was decided that permanent private housing should be built for speculative reasons. A proposal for public ownership of all formerly private land (made by the Chamber of Commerce) was not accepted because of strong private opposition. Owners of houses damaged by the earthquake formed a consortium which gave loans for reconstruction[7] repayable over thirty years. However, people who had rented accommodation before the earthquake had no rights. The large proprietors benefited more than the small ones, who frequently had to sell their loans (which were negotiable), being unable to pay the debt charges. As a result the old property fortunes were reestablished.

At the beginning of the Fascist period, the Curia of Messina obtained a legal monopoly on the negotiability of rights to loan[8] and the city became a haven for speculators. There was some public building during this period and 'poor public housing' was constructed designed 'to satisfy the exigencies of the most needy'. These houses are on the periphery of the city and are quite unfit.

The city was almost completely destroyed in the last war. The subsidies of the post-war period led to the production of about 5,600 units of public housing, but in 1955 a law (No. 556) allowed such houses to be sold off cheaply to their occupants and in 1959 another law made this situation worse. In a few years the whole stock was sold off for 1·6 billion lire, i.e. one-nineteenth of its real value. The petit bourgeoisie rather than the shanty-town dwellers were the main beneficiaries of this (and perhaps also the large bourgeoisie).[9]

This is only the most glaring example of a process which still takes place. It can be seen in the juggling with the municipal plans for Law 167 (the main Italian public housing law passed in 1962) and the clear attempt to make sure that most of the areas for public housing provided under this law go to private cooperatives. Even now there is no aspect of public housing in Messina that does not involve speculative activity (and this is a national problem as well). This activity includes:

(a) Speculative operations linked to the local authority purchase of land at inflated prices.

(b) Speculative contracts granted to private companies.

(c) Bank financing of the public housing agency deficit and consequent interest payments.

(d) The deposition in banks for a long time of appropriated but unspent funds for public housing which they are therefore able to use.

(e) The assignment of tenancies through patronage.

(f) A racket in the buying and selling of rights to occupy public housing to poverty stricken shanty-town dwellers.

(g) Infrastructural investment in certain areas with the consequential increase of values in adjacent areas.

(h) The use of corruptly obtained contracts for the clearance of shanty towns and for the building of temporary housing elsewhere, in order to accommodate the displaced populations while rebuilding. As this rebuilding subsequently fails to occur the 'temporary' housing becomes permanent and new shanty towns are created.

(i) The inefficiency and lack of public housing in Messina generally. This is in itself speculation because it raises the price of private housing and allows areas to be despoiled without interference. It also results in the maintenance of the shanty towns, operating as instruments of segregation and for the political and economic subjugation of the marginal proletariat.

In Messina these speculative activities are not the product of the highly organized operation of monopolistic property companies linked to a modern building industry concerned, *inter alia*, to exploit a demand for public housing. There is no mass working class financially capable of supporting such a demand, construction companies are backward, labour intensive and small scale, and speculation occurs to fulfil the needs of the middle and upper classes. The savings of these groups are not being channelled towards productive sectors and this is, of course, due to the economic underdevelopment of the area. Thus the housing speculation is the only possible investment and form of savings. There are many people in Messina who buy two, three or four flats, thus preventing these flats from being absorbed into the market for rented accommodation. In these cases, where housing construction is taking the place of industrial development, it tends to become a more and more purely speculative operation, with increasingly little relevance to the need for low-priced rented accommodation. Such tendencies have been aggravated by the policy of increasing home ownership (which has greatly benefited finance capital) rather than providing low-rent housing. One result is that only 3·8 per cent. of the housing stock in Messina in 1961 was unoccupied, whereas this had risen to 10·7 per cent. by 1971.

But the shanty towns are not simply a product of speculation in the housing market and in public building. As in the case with the marginal and lumpen proletariat themselves, shanties can no longer be explained in terms of the crisis of the surrounding countryside, but must be explained in terms of the crisis of the city, of growing urban underdevelopment which has also been aggravated by the location of a 'pole of industrial development' nearby. The existence of the marginal working class is a product of the effects of the earthquake, the previous failure of many small productive activities, the progressive decay of small local industry and the establishment of a dependent economy with a sharply rising level of unemployment during the past few years.

Before 1961 the provincial population declined but that of the city increased, but between 1961 and 1971 the city's population also decreased.[10] From our analysis of data contained in municipal records it appears that about 80,000 people left the city between 1961 and 1971. But even in the earlier period the city was only growing from natural reasons; it did not attract population from the province to any great degree (e.g. between 1962 and 1969 only 8 per cent. of those leaving the rest of the province went to Messina). Thus the overwhelming majority of those who migrate from the province by pass the city, not even stopping in an area which, even though it is urban, is an underdeveloped area and itself therefore a cause of emigration. True there is some insecure employment, dependent on patronage, to be found there, but for workers this is a poor alternative to the misery of the countryside.

The situation is evident in other ways as well. In 1961 the economically active population was 30·5 per cent. of the resident population. In 1971 it was 30 per cent and the total number employed in industry (approximately 30,000) was lower than the number of those employed in public administration and services (approximately 45,000). It is interesting to make a close analysis of this latter sector. Many of these people are public employees, great numbers of which obtain jobs by patronage rather than by ability or because a job needs to be done. Others are street traders or people in insecure or temporary employment.

We have calculated, by means of a comparison between the industrial, commercial and population censuses,[11] the approximate percentage of insecure, underemployed and unemployed workers in all these sectors, in the industrial sector and in the two main subdivisions of this latter sector (manufacturing and extractive, and construction). There are more than 29,000 employed in insecure trades, not economically active or looking for work overall. According to the census of industry, this is almost equal to the number of those in stable employment in the private sector of industry and commerce (just over 30,000). The construction sector has the largest percentage of these insecure employees. This has been, for the reasons already mentioned, the substitute for industrial development in the town and has resulted in the fact that the marginal proletariat is exploited in housing and jobs by this activity, which leads to the shanty towns and the low incomes that accompany them.

In this situation it is not difficult for the dominant classes and especially the Christian Democrat Party to use promises of houses, subsidies and employment to buy the votes of these marginal workers and to prevent their political development. The Christian Democrat bosses have succeeded in monopolizing the management of public offices, welfare organizations and financial and credit offices, and now in this way control approximately 80 per cent. of the Messina labour market.[12]

Recent surveys confirmed some of the points which have been made above. A survey of one hundred families in the shanty towns of Messina in September 1973 showed that most people had been there a long time and only 5 per cent. had come to Messina in the last ten years.[13] Surveys in two other towns demonstrate the social composition of the shanty towns (Table 1), and the relationship between shanty-town dwellers and building speculation is clear from the first survey, referred to above as well. Of the twelve heads of household who were not originally from Messina ten said that their first job on arrival had been in construction and 29 per cent. of the sample overall now worked in this sector. The marginality of much of the rest of the sample was also evident. Thus 22 per cent. defined themselves as jacks-of-all-trades (this category is growing as a result of the recent building crisis), 8 per cent. were permanently unemployed (mainly because of disabilities connected with their previous employment in construction) and the remaining 41 per cent. were in various

Table 1. Social composition of two shanty towns, 1972

| Trade | Giostra (224 interviews) | Fondo Pugliatti (37 interviews) |
|---|---|---|
| Small artisan | 7·1 | 5·4 |
| Small businessman and street trader | 7·1 | 5·4 |
| Construction worker | 28·3 | 37·9 |
| Sautafossi* | 4·0 | 10·8 |
| Labourer | 7·6 | 2·7 |
| Workers employed in the service sector | 17·8 | 13·5 |
| Pensioners | 22·3 | 13·5 |
| Unemployed through illness | 2·2 | — |
| Others | 3·6 | 10·8 |

*A term used in Messina for a jack-of-all-trades.
*Note.* This survey was done in 1972 by Antonella Cammarota in collaboration with students from the Faculty of Political Science, University of Messina; 261 interviews were carried out in the two areas.

semi-artisan trades or in jobs as drivers, shoe-shine boys, street traders, dustmen, carpenters, shoe makers, etc. Shanty towns contain a pool of labour which can be employed cheaply and without proper overtime arrangements or social security payments, and is easy to dispose of when no longer required or unsatisfactory. The result is incomes which do not allow access to public housing, so condemning the workers to remain in the shanty towns.

In an inquiry into the shanty towns of Messina which took place in 1968, when over 1,300 were questioned, 51·15 per cent. of those interviewed said they could not pay more than 5,000 lire a month in rent, 48·51 per cent. not more than 10,000 lire and only 3·7 per cent. could pay more than 10,000 lire per month. Thus shanty-town dwellers were almost entirely excluded from the private market and even in part from the public sector, since then, as now, the rents in public housing range from approximately 12,000 to 20,000 lire a month.[14]

In fact, there are three labour markets in the Messina *region*. There is a working class labour market tied to the 'pole of industrial development' which, because of its distance from Messina itself, does not provide employment for people living in this town. There is the rural labour market, of course, and finally there is the labour market in Messina. This, as we have seen, consists of low-wage employment in other than manufacturing industry and it creates a fragmented working class with little possibility at present of mounting collective political action or generating class consciousness. But this is not an inert mass of individuals, ideologically subordinated to the dominant class and therefore having the political characteristics of the lumpen proletariat. The sporadic, rebellious explosions which occur are not necessarily controllable by the local bourgeoisie. The shanty-town dwellers of Messina are capable of discussing their own living conditions and of expressing some political judgements. Thus a higher percentage of the shanty-town dwellers were in favour of the divorce law than on average in Messina, and this was a considerably high proportion by comparison with the rural villages in the provinces.[15] It is easier to find the subordinated and dependent masses in the rural hamlets than it is to identify them among the urban proletariat.

The many struggles which have occurred (e.g. occupations of housing and the Town Hall) have failed because of internal division, poor leadership and the lack of political organization. It is necessary to analyse the potentialities and limits of these possibilities for conflict, for on them depend the perspectives for the class struggle in Messina.

## Notes

1. By 'Southern city' we mean the most traditional type of non-industrialized urban centre in the South, both medium-sized and large.
2. The best picture of the social and economic aspects of the employment situation in the South may be gained by reference to recent issues of *Inchiesta e Quaderni Piacenti*. See also Mezzogiorno e classe operaria, *Quaderni del Centro Operaio*, Coines, 1972.
3. Among others, see Mantovani, E., *Mercato del Lavoro, Accumulazione e Sovrappopolazione Relativa*, Inchiesta n. 9, gennaio–marzo 1973; Paci, M., *Mercato del Lavoro*

*e Classi Sociali in Italia*, Il Mulino, Bologna, 1974; Salvati, M., *Offerta di Lavoro ed Esercito Industriale di Riserva*, Inchiesta n. 7, estate 1972; Leon, P., and Marocchi, M., *Sviluppo Economico Italiano e Forza Lavoro*, Marsilio, Padova, 1973; Parlato, V., *Su ogni tre abitanti uno solo in Italia lavora ufficialmente. Un primato capitalistico*, *Il Manifesto*, 5 aprile 1972; Centro Ricerche sui Modi di Produzione, *Dispensa sul Mercato del Lavoro*, n. 7 (serie verde), collettivo editoriale Calusca, Milano, 1974.

4. Marx, Karl, *Capital*, Vol. 1, Lawrence and Wishart, London, 1974, Chap. XXV, s. 4, p. 602 (Libro I, capit. 23, para. 3, p. 78, E. Riuniti, VII edizione, Roma, 1970).

5. See Mingione, E., Theoretical considerations for a Marxist analysis of urban development, Chapter 4 in this book.

6. For an interesting analysis of Rome, the capital city of underdevelopment, and its shanty-town ghettos, see Ferrarotti, Franco, *Roma da Capitale e Periferia*, Laterza, Roma, 1970.

7. See Cammarota, A., *Urbanizzazione e Sottosviluppo Urbano*, tesi di laurea, facoltà di Scienze Politiche di Messina, anno 1971–1972.

8. See Ginatempo, N., *Il Problema della Casa e le Sue Implicazioni Sociali. Studio su Messina*, tesi di laurea, facoltà di Scienze Politiche di Milano, anno 1972–1973.

9. See Ginatempo, *ibid.*, and also Conosciani, D'Albergo, Mattioni and Tortoreto, *L'Organizzazione Pubblica dell'Edilizia*, Angeli, Milano, 1969, pp. 75–76, where other information on this scandal is reported.

10. This is based on data which, like all the official data which follow, are from ISTAT (Italian state statistical) sources. We have used The Census of Population and of Housing, the Census of Industry and Commerce, the Directory of Construction, Activity and Public Works, the Directory of Demographic Statistics, 'Popolazione e Movimento Anagrafico dei Communi'.

11. The first process to calculate figures for insecure employment using the difference between the population and industrial censuses was Paolo Sylos Labini, "L'emloi precaire en Sicile", *Revue Internationale du Travail*, 1964; the same method has been used subsequently by M. Paci, M. Meldolesi and P. Braghin, E. Mingione and P. Trivellato. In fact, the difference between the results of the two censuses can be ascribed to the fact that in the industrial census those responsible for the productive units did not list a large number of irregular workers who, in the population census, said that they worked in the relevant sector. For more precise calculations, the number of those who were absent because they were working outside the city (temporary emigrations) should be subtracted from the results of the population census. Such a calculation could be made for all the sectors and, in order to quantify the marginal proletariat, we would need to add to the result of the difference between the two sets of census data the number of workers in small firms (employing up to ten workers), excluding self-employed workers, small family businesses and clerks. However, in the case of Messina, we do not place great trust in official statistics, insofar as the service sector is concerned, because of the high labour mobility in this sector and consequent unreliability of any calculation of the numbers in various trades. Besides, since we are not making a detailed analysis of social classes in this paper, we have limited ourselves to giving an indication of the grave levels of unemployment and underemployment in Messina without attempting more detailed estimates (see, for example, Braghin, P., Mingione, E., Trivellato, P., Per una analisi della structura di classe dell' Italia contemporanea, *La Critica Sociologica*, **30**, estate 1974).

12. See the following list from the Christian Democratic Centri di Potere.
    Banks: Cassa di Risparmio, Banca del Sud, Banco di Sicilia.
    Public Organizations: Camera di Commercio, Ente Fiera, IACP, Nucleo Industrializzazione Tirreno, Ente Porto, Consorzio Autostrade Messina-Catania e Messina-Palermo, Consorzio dei Patronati Scolastici, CONI, ENPAS, INAM, Consorzio di Bonifica Alcantara, Centro Avicolo Messina, Consorzio Antitubercolare, Com-

missione provinciale di Controllo, Cantina Sperimentale di Milazzo, Centre Speri-
mentale Pesca e Frutti del Mare di ME, Azienda Speciale zona industriale di
Messina, Consorzio anticoccidico di Barcellona, Presidenza Ospedali Riuniti.
Medical Aid Centres: Casse mutue artigiani, commercianti e coldiretti.
Boards of Directors: Presidenza Istituti Tecnici e d'Arte, Istituto Regionale d'Arte
de Santo Stefano di Camastra.
Welfare Organizations: ECA, ONMI, Opera Universitaria.
This list is largely incomplete. It refers only to some of the centres of power directly
controlled by the Christian Democratic party. Not only is officially controlled infor-
mation omitted, but so are some key areas, like the offices linked to the ministries, the
schools and the Town Hall.

13. This survey was done by Nella Ginatempo with one hundred interviews in the areas of
Gazzi, Ritiro, Camaro, Bisconte and Maregrosso.

14. From the survey done by Antonella Cammarota there are several data regarding the
shanty-dwellers' income that can be used to clearly illustrate their ability to pay current
rent prices. This table represents a very approximate calculation of those in regular
employment:

| Approximate monthly wage during 1972 | Giostra % | Fondo Pugliatti % |
|---|---|---|
| Up to 50,000 lire | 27·8 | 32·4 |
| From 50,000 to 70,000 lire | 8·0 | 18·9 |
| From 71,000 to 100,000 lire | 38·6 | 10·8 |
| From 101,000 to 150,000 lire* | 23·8 | 24·3 |
| No reply | 1·8 | — |

*Note that this income was often that of the heads of nuclear families with many children and
that the rent of a two-room flat in the periphery is around 35,000 to 40,000 lire per month and,
by the end of 1974, exceeded 50,000 lire.

15. The research to which we refer is actually in progress and is being done by the Faculty
of Political Science, University of Messina. The director of the research is Professor
E. Taliani and the researchers are Antonella Cammarota, Anna Caravello, Nunzio
Carianni, Orazio Lanza and Cettina Pitrone.

# 6
# Government Policies, Financial Institutions and Neighbourhood Change in United States Cities

*David Harvey*

In this paper I shall attempt to document how certain policies fashioned at the national level with respect to housing are translated into tangible events at the local level by means of certain institutional and market arrangements. I shall also seek to demonstrate how local community activism around housing issues in the United States relates to shifting national housing policies which are primarily designed to deal with the macro economic growth problems in the United States economy.

## 1. National Housing Policies in the United States

National housing policies in the United States have typically been concerned with

(*a*) The general relationships between housing finance, construction, economic growth and capital accumulation, new household formation and population growth.

(*b*) The short-term utility of the construction industry and the housing sector as 'Keynesian regulators' through which cyclical swings in the economy at large can be ironed out.

(*c*) The relationships between housing provision, the distribution of real income (welfare) in society and levels of social discontent.

To be properly understood, these policies have to be set in the context of the extraordinary dynamism of capitalism in the United States. In 1945, for example, the United States found itself with an enormously enhanced productive capacity and a defence budget which absorbed about 40 per cent. of the Gross National Product. With the 'overproduction' and unemployment problems of the 1930s still fresh in everyone's mind, the spectre of renewed depression and consequent social unrest loomed large. The problem to be resolved at this point was to find ways to keep the productive capacity of the United States economy employed and to prevent widespread unemployment of labour. A variety of means were devised, including the export of surplus product in the form of aid to Europe and Japan and the absorption of surplus capacity by the armaments industry. Within the United States, however, a variety of strategies emerged for stimulating consumption, not least of which were a set of fiscal and monetary policies designed to accelerate and enhance the suburbanization process. In the post-war period, the 'underconsumption' problems of the 1930s were largely to be resolved by forcing a rising effective demand *via* the suburbanization process—a process that embraced the construction of highways and utilities, housing and public facilities, shopping centres and commercial functions as well as a rising demand for automobiles, energy, and the like.

The response to the crisis conditions of the 1930s had been an extended debate not over whether but over how the state should intervene to stabilize the capitalist order. The National Resources Committee,[1] for example, explored the possibility for strong centralized state planning, but the option which eventually won out was a reorganization of the financial superstructure together with the development of fiscal and monetary policies on the part of the federal government which could serve as indirect controls over the market mechanism. These fiscal and monetary policies in fact emerged as part of the New Deal legislation of the 1930s. In the housing sphere they served to stabilize and subsidize mortgage markets primarily for middle-income Americans. And it was these fiscal and monetary policies, devised in the 1930s, which were to bear the fruit in the accelerating suburbanization process of the post-war period.[2]

The range of the fiscal and monetary devices is considerable. It encompasses what amounted to a $7 billion subsidy by 1969 to home ownership through tax deductions and a variety of tax arrangements distinctly advantageous to developers and the construction industry.[3] The Federal Housing Administration (set up during the 1930s) insured home mortgages and took the risk out of middle income home ownership, thereby stimulating investment in home construction. The setting up of the federal savings and loans institutions, together with the relatively advantaged treatment which they received through federal regulation and insurance, served to channel finance towards single-family owner occupancy. As a consequence, the proportion of dwelling units owner-occupied, which stood at 47·8 per cent. in 1890 and fluctuated gently downwards to 43·6 per cent. in 1940, rose dramatically to 62·9 per cent by 1970. The construction rate of one to four family dwelling units more than doubled after 1945 compared to the pre-war period, and the United States in general experienced its greatest ever residential construction boom.

All of this made low-density single-unit home ownership highly advantageous to the mass of the population in the United States. The consequences were (a) low density suburban sprawl, (b) strong multiplier effects from housing construction through complementary investments and through the rising costs of operating and servicing a high energy consuming, low-density urban space economy and (c) an assumption that urban expansion was inevitable which led to self-fulfilling speculative activity on the part of both private and public decision-makers (the consequence being a pattern of development which became growth dependent in the sense that it was anticipated that future growth would pay for much of the delayed costs of current development). Relatively low land costs and the mobility conferred by the automobile enhanced these trends. Only in the last few years—particularly since the mid-1960s—have rising land prices, no-growth movements in the suburbs, congestion and pollution costs, and questions surrounding the high energy inputs necessary to support sprawling development, indicated that there are limits to the suburbanization of America.

The accelerated suburbanization process of the post-war period has served goals other than the artificial stimulation of an effective consumer demand for product. By a variety of indirect mechanisms, such as the monetary policy of the Federal Reserve Board and the borrowings of government housing agencies, the construction industry has functioned fairly effectively, at least until the recent debacle, as a powerful regulator within the economy at large through which cyclical movements could be contained within bounds. The evident social discontent of the 1930s has, to a great degree, been successfully defused by a governmental policy which has created a large wedge of debt-encumbered home owners who are unlikely to rock the boat because they are both debt-encumbered and reasonably well-satisfied owner occupiers. Home ownership, seen as early as President Hoover's *Conference on Home of Ownership* in 1931 as a device for achieving social stability, went hand in hand in the post-war period with the drive to stimulate consumption through suburbanization.

But all of these developments have been bought at a price. The post-war boom in the United States economy has been in large degree debt-financed. As *Business Week* (12th October 1974) recently put it:

'The U.S. economy stands atop a mountain of debt $2·5-trillion high—a mountain built of all the cars and houses, all the factories and machines that have made this the biggest, richest economy in the history of the world.... The U.S. is the Debt Economy without peer.... The numbers are so vast that they simply numb the mind: $1 trillion in corporate debt, $600 billion in mortgage debt, $500 billion in U.S. government debt, $200 billion in state and local government debt, $200 billion in consumer debt. To fuel nearly three decades of post-war economic boom at home and export it abroad, this nation has borrowed an average net $200 million a day, each and every day, since the close of World War II'.

The residential component of this indebtedness has grown from 9·5 per cent. of total private and public debt in 1947 to 23·7 per cent. in 1972 and residential mortgage debt has become a vital component underpinning the viability and security of the financial system. *Per capita* indebtedness has also risen rapidly in proportion to a rising disposable personal income (it roughly doubled during the post-war period). The social consequences of such debt encumbrance are not entirely positive when viewed from the standpoint of the stability of the capitalist order. The defensive attitudes of owner occupiers towards social change—ultimately registered as no-growth movements in the suburbs—have a lot to do with the fact that personal savings are locked into real estate values. And it has to be remembered that the stability of the financial system, the ability of surplus capital to find profitable outlets in real estate development, the maintenance of effective demand and the ability of individuals to bear the burden of long-term indebtedness are separate facets of the same thing. Any massive fall in personal disposable income, for example, would generate widespread mortgage foreclosures which would, in turn, collapse the financial system and generate chaos in capital markets.

At the national level, then, policies appear to have been designed to maintain an existing structure of society intact in its basic configurations, while facilitating economic growth and capital accumulation, eliminating cyclical influence and defusing social discontent. In the post-war period these general aims have been accomplished by a massive debt-financed boom. Within this context, housing policy, by contributing to an accelerated suburbanization process, provided a vital and effective tool for stabilizing and perpetuating the social structure of an advanced, market-based, capitalist system. These policies by and large worked up until the mid-1960s, but the credit crunches of 1966 and 1969–70, followed by the vast speculative boom of 1971–72 and the onset of recession and depression conditions in 1974 appear to indicate that we are at the end of an era and entering upon a new period of crisis in which a further structural adaptation of the capitalist order is required if it is to be perpetuated.[4] Significantly, the debate of the 1930s is being echoed as on the one hand the possibilities of strongly centralized planning (in the form, for example, of a national urban growth policy) are explored as an alternative to a reorganization of financial institutions and a refashioning of governmental strategies for indirect interventions.

## 2. Institutional Mediations and National Housing Policies

The policies and programme fashioned at the national level are transmitted to the local level and ultimately to individuals making choices with respect to housing services in different locations by a complex set of mechanisms. Some of these are contained within hierarchically organized governmental structures, but the bulk of them are to be found in the complex mix of private and public institutions which mediate the flow of investment funds to housing. That this is the case is easily understandable since, for the majority of people in the United States, it is ability to obtain a mortgage which is crucial for finding a place to live.

The financial structure of the United States is fragmented into numerous types of financial intermediary, all of which are subject to government (either state of federal) regulation and supervision. The overwhelming impression created by this financial structure is of a chaos of private activity under an incoherent and arbitrary constructed umbrella of government supervision. The financial superstructure as a whole does not appear so arbitrary a construct when it is viewed in historical perspective, since the regulatory framework and the financial institutions themselves have evolved as a response to financial crisis—particularly those during the Civil War years, the period from 1907 to 1914 and the depression years from 1927 to 1935.[5] The financial superstructure has undergone major transformations during each economic crisis. The current structure in the United States still closely resembles that created during the 1930s, although the stresses in the financial system at the present time indicate that we are in for another bout of radical restructuring, perhaps along the lines indicated in the Hunt Commission Report of 1971 on Financial Regulation or as presaged in the Bank Holdings Act legislation of 1971 (which permits a far greater degree of financial consolidation and integration than was possible prior to 1971).

The current structure of financial institutions in relationship to housing has still to be interpreted in relation to the reorganization brought about in the 1930s with a few additions since 1968. Savings and loan institutions (dealing almost entirely in residential mortgages and small savings), mutual savings banks, credit unions, commercial banks, life insurance companies, pension funds, real estate investment trusts and mortgage banks are all private institutions involved in some way with the provision of housing finance. Each kind of institution functions under different legal constraints and regulatory controls and each, by virtue of its functions, has a very specific objective in mind when it allocated capital resources to the housing market. Pensions and insurance funds, for example, are looking for good secure investments and look to real estate to provide them. Savings and loan associations, and to a lesser extent mutual savings banks, are institutions specializing in small savings for purposes of financing home ownership. Federal, state and local governments have created in addition an assortment of finance and credit agencies through which the flow of investment funds into housing is also mediated. Chief among these is the Federal Housing Administration (the FHA) set up in the 1930s to help rationalize the mortgage market by taking the risk out of long-term mortgages secured against the mortgagee's income rather than against his or her wealth. The government insurance of residential mortgage debt has been vital in permitting the debt-financed residential construction boom. The FHA could not have accomplished its function effectively, however, without the creation of a secondary mortgage market through which government insured mortgages could be packaged and sold to institutions operating in the capital market in general (such as the insurance companies and the pension funds). The Federal National Mortgage Association was set up to facilitate the formation of such a secondary mortgage market and government power exists to pump money into the housing market by buying up mortgages in the secondary market when the supply of funds to housing slackens. The federal government also insures deposits both in the savings and loan associations and in other thrift institutions. In addition, state and sometimes local jurisdictions have set up their own mechanisms for intervening in the flow of mortgage funds in various ways.[6]

Mortgage moneys flow into housing down a variety of channels with all manner of taps and regulators attached. Consequently, the capital market assumes a fragmented appearance and in certain important respects is indeed fragmented. Deposits in savings and loan associations (S & Ls as we shall call them) tend to flow exclusively into residential activity, but the volume of funds within these institutions depends on the volume of deposits which, in turn, is interest-rate sensitive. By government regulation, interest payable on deposits in the S & Ls is higher than that obtainable in other savings institutions, but when the government itself borrows heavily in the market at an even higher interest rate, funds may be drawn away from the S & Ls—a process which has its ironic aspect as the government borrowings are in part designed to pump more money into housing finance (this robbing of the S & Ls to finance the government became very important during the 'credit crunch' of 1974 and had a lot to do with the almost complete collapse of home building during that year). Other institutions, by way of contrast, have almost total flexibility in their capital allocation mechanisms compared with the S & Ls, which are specifically designed 'to promote the thrift of people locally to finance their own homes and the homes of their neighbours'.[7] Mortgage bankers and commercial banks, for example, utilize their resources according to the competition for funds in general. In the capital market as a whole, housing finance is best regarded as a residual that is left over after basic governmental and corporate needs are met. But the numerous taps and regulators which attach to the various channels through which capital can be allocated mean that the capital allocation process is not a perfectly competitive one—a characteristic which the Hunt Commission found to be highly detrimental to efficient capital allocation.[8]

The diversity of channels through which mortgage funds can flow makes it very difficult to trace in detail how national policies, such as tight money policies on the part of the Federal Reserve Board, are transmitted into housing markets, although there can be no question as to the aggregate effects on housing finance in general when the housing slumps of 1966, 1969 and 1970, and 1974–75 coincide so perfectly with periods of tight monetary policy.

### 3. Effects on the Ground—Baltimore in 1970

We may not be able to trace all the flows, but we can see where, when and how they emerge within the housing market of some local jurisdiction such as Baltimore City. Consider first of all the behaviour of the different kinds of institution with respect of house sales in different price categories. The 'commercial' institutions clearly prefer to operate in the higher price ranges (because servicing costs on mortgage loans are constant, which means that the larger the mortgage the greater the profit margin for the institution servicing it). State-chartered S & Ls tend not to be particularly profit-oriented and to be highly integrated into the community in which they are located. These institutions take up the finance of housing in the lower price ranges. The health of the housing market in this lower price category is closely tied to the health of the small state S & Ls and the perpetuation of their community-based, non-profit orientation. Federal S & Ls and mortgage banks typically originate mortgages in the intermediate price ranges. There is, clearly, a highly structured relationship between different types of institution and different segments of the housing stock as far as mortgage finance over different price ranges is concerned.

Table 1. Distribution of mortgage activity in different price categories by type of institution, Baltimore City, 1972

|  | Under $7,000 | $7,000– $9,999 | $10,000– $11,999 | $12,000– $14,999 | Over $15,000 |
|---|---|---|---|---|---|
| Private | 39 | 16 | 13 | 7 | 7 |
| State S & Ls | 42 | 33 | 21 | 21 | 20 |
| Federal S & Ls | 10 | 22 | 30 | 31 | 35 |
| Mortgage banks | 7 | 24 | 29 | 23 | 12 |
| Savings banks | — | 3 | 5 | 15 | 19 |
| Commercial banks | 1 | 1 | 2 | 3 | 7 |
| Percentage of city's trans- actions in category | 21 | 19 | 15 | 20 | 24 |

*Source. Homeownership and the Baltimore Mortgage Market,* Draft Report of the Home Owner-ship Development Program, Department of Housing and Community Development, Baltimore City, 1973.

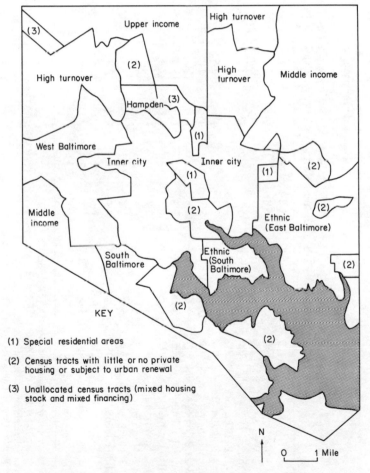

Figure 1 Baltimore city housing submarkets, 1970

Table 2. Housing submarkets—Baltimore City, 1970

| | Total houses sold | Sales per 100 proper-ties | % Transactions by source of funds | | | | | | | | % Sales insured | | Average sale price ($)** |
|---|---|---|---|---|---|---|---|---|---|---|---|---|---|
| | | | Cash | Private | Federal S & Ls | State S & Ls | Mort-gage bank | Commer-cial bank | Savings bank | Other* | FHA | VA | |
| Inner city | 1,199 | 1·86 | 65·7 | 15·0 | 3·0 | 12·0 | 2·2 | 0·5 | 0·2 | 1·7 | 2·9 | 1·1 | 3,498 |
| 1. East | 646 | 2·33 | 64·7 | 15·0 | 2·2 | 14·3 | 2·2 | 0·5 | 0·1 | 1·2 | 3·4 | 1·4 | 3,437 |
| 2. West | 553 | 1·51 | 67·0 | 15·1 | 4·0 | 9·2 | 2·3 | 0·4 | 0·4 | 2·2 | 2·3 | 0·6 | 3,568 |
| Ethnic | 760 | 3·34 | 39·9 | 5·5 | 6·1 | 43·2 | 2·0 | 0·8 | 0·9 | 2·2 | 2·6 | 0·7 | 6,372 |
| 1. E. Baltimore | 579 | 3·40 | 39·7 | 4·8 | 5·5 | 43·7 | 2·4 | 1·0 | | 2·2 | 3·2 | 0·7 | 6,769 |
| 2. S. Baltimore | 181 | 3·20 | 40·3 | 7·7 | 7·7 | 41·4 | 0·6 | 1·2 | | 2·2 | 0·6 | 0·6 | 5,102 |
| Hampden | 99 | 2·40 | 40·4 | 8·1 | 18·2 | 26·3 | 4·0 | | 3·0 | | 14·1 | 2·0 | 7,059 |
| West Baltimore | 497 | 2·32 | 30·6 | 12·5 | 12·1 | 11·7 | 22·3 | 1·6 | 3·1 | 6·0 | 25·8 | 4·2 | 8,664 |
| South Baltimore | 322 | 3·16 | 28·3 | 7·4 | 22·7 | 13·4 | 13·4 | 1·9 | 4·0 | 9·0 | 22·7 | 10·6 | 8,751 |
| High turnover | 2,072 | 5·28 | 19·1 | 6·1 | 13·6 | 14·9 | 32·8 | 1·2 | 5·7 | 6·2 | 38·2 | 9·5 | 9,902 |
| 1. North-west | 1,071 | 5·42 | 20·0 | 7·2 | 9·7 | 13·8 | 40·9 | 1·1 | 2·9 | 4·5 | 46·8 | 7·4 | 9,312 |
| 2. North-east | 693 | 5·07 | 20·6 | 6·4 | 14·4 | 16·5 | 29·0 | 1·4 | 5·6 | 5·9 | 34·5 | 10·2 | 9,779 |
| 3. North | 308 | 5·35 | 12·7 | 1·4 | 25·3 | 18·1 | 13·3 | 0·7 | 15·9 | 12·7 | 31·5 | 15·5 | 12,330 |
| Middle income | 1,077 | 3·15 | 20·8 | 4·4 | 29·8 | 17·0 | 8·6 | 1·9 | 8·7 | 9·0 | 17·7 | 11·1 | 12,760 |
| 1. South-west | 212 | 3·46 | 17·0 | 6·6 | 29·2 | 8·5 | 15·1 | 1·0 | 10·8 | 11·7 | 30·2 | 17·0 | 12,848 |
| 2. North-east | 865 | 3·09 | 21·7 | 3·8 | 30·0 | 19·2 | 7·0 | 2·0 | 8·2 | 8·2 | 14·7 | 9·7 | 12,751 |
| Upper income | 361 | 3·84 | 19·4 | 6·9 | 23·5 | 10·5 | 8·6 | 7·2 | 21·1 | 2·8 | 11·9 | 3·6 | 27,413 |

*Assumed mortgages and subject to mortgage.

**Ground rent is sometimes included in the sales price and this distorts the averages in certain respects. The relative differentials between the submarkets are of the right order, however.

Source. City Planning Department Tabulations from Lusk Reports.

This structured relationship has a geographical manifestation. Different intermediaries serve different geographical areas and act to form distinctive housing submarkets as far as housing finance is concerned. Figure 1 and Tables 2 and 3 provide a snapshot of activity for Baltimore City in 1970.[9] The inner city manifests scarcely any institutional involvement of any sort and housing transactions there were typically financed by cash or private mortgages. Small-scale, community-based S & Ls dominated housing finance in the traditional ethnic areas of South and East Baltimore, while the middle-income white areas of North-east and South-east Baltimore were basically served by the federal S & Ls. The affluent areas drew upon the financial resources of savings banks and commercial banks as well as the federal S & Ls, while areas of high turnover (and racial change) were characterized by mortgage bank finance in combination with FHA insurance. The black community of West Baltimore, historically much discriminated against in its quest for mortgage finance, relied heavily upon mortgage banker originations and FHA insurance, even though its income characteristics were broadly similar to those white areas served by the federal S & Ls.

The structure of financing across the various housing submarkets and the residential differentiation which this implies (see Table 3) has a history and is constantly in the course of evolution. Changes occurring within the submarkets promote boundary shifts. On occasion whole new submarkets may be dramatically created. Such changes are a response to a variety of forces

Table 3. Housing submarkets — Baltimore City, 1970 (census data)

| | Median income* | % Black occupied D.U.'s | % Units owner occupied | Mean $ value of owner occupied | % Renter occupied | Mean monthly rent |
|---|---|---|---|---|---|---|
| Inner city | 6,259 | 72·2 | 28·5 | 6,259 | 71·5 | 77·5 |
| 1. East | 6,201 | 65·1 | 29·3 | 6,380 | 70·7 | 75·2 |
| 2. West | 6,297 | 76·9 | 27·9 | 6,963 | 72·1 | 78·9 |
| Ethnic | 8,822 | 1·0 | 66·0 | 8,005 | 34·0 | 76·8 |
| 1. E. Baltimore | 8,836 | 1·2 | 66·3 | 8,368 | 33·7 | 78·7 |
| 2. S. Baltimore | 8,785 | 0·2 | 64·7 | 6,504 | 35·3 | 69·6 |
| Hampden | 8,730 | 0·3 | 58·8 | 7,960 | 41·2 | 76·8 |
| W. Baltimore | 9,566 | 84·1 | 50·0 | 13,842 | 50·0 | 103·7 |
| S. Baltimore | 8,941 | 0·1 | 56·9 | 9,741 | 43·1 | 82·0 |
| High turnover | 10,413 | 34·3 | 53·5 | 11,886 | 46·5 | 113·8 |
| 1. North-west | 9,483 | 55·4 | 49·3 | 11,867 | 50·7 | 110·6 |
| 2. North-east | 10,753 | 30·4 | 58·5 | 11,533 | 41·5 | 111·5 |
| 3. North | 11,510 | 1·3 | 49·0 | 12,726 | 51·0 | 125·1 |
| Middle income | 10,639 | 2·8 | 62·6 | 13,221 | 37·5 | 104·1 |
| 1. South-west | 10,655 | 4·4 | 48·8 | 13,470 | 51·2 | 108·1 |
| 2 North-east | 10,634 | 2·3 | 66·2 | 13,174 | 33·8 | 103·0 |
| Upper income | 17,577 | 1·7 | 50·8 | 27,097 | 49·2 | 141·4 |

*Weighted average of median incomes for census tracts in submarket.
*Source.* 1970 Census.

which stem from changing relative wage rates and job security among groups in the population, changing job opportunities within a changing structure of the division of labour, migratory movements and the like, as well as from alterations within the financing of housing itself. But all of these forces are marshalled and given coherence in the urban context through the mediating power of the financial superstructure. The contemporary history of residential differentiation in Baltimore can be used to illustrate this process.

### a. A Changed Neighbourhood; West Baltimore and the Land-installment Contract

The snapshot of activity in 1970 shows West Baltimore as a quiet almost stagnant housing submarket populated largely by blacks, many of whom had achieved the status of moderate-income home owners. This submarket had not always been this way. Throughout much of the 1960s it had been the scene of turmoil, rapid social and racial change, community conflict and outrage. At issue during this time was how could blacks, many of whom were experiencing modest gains in income and rising expectations, gain access to reasonable quality housing on a home ownership basis. In the 1960s financial institutions were reluctant to provide mortagage finance to this social group. Government institutions rarely intervened and when they did so, as was the case with the FHA prior to 1964, they frequently acted to formalize discrimination by a process known as 'red-lining' (not insuring mortgages within a certain area occupied by a particular social group).

Into this vacuum of rising effective demand and the failure of financial intermediaries to provide mortgage finance crept the landlord-speculator making use of a device called the land-installment contract.[10] Under the land-installment contract arrangement, speculators would typically pick up a house from a fleeing white family for around $7,000 and then sell it, providing mortgage finance, to a black family for $12,000 or so. The net mark-up, called the 'black tax', became the centre of controversy as did the very high rate of turnover in the housing stock in areas like West Baltimore.

A strong community group arose to combat what was generally regarded as excessive profiteering on the part of speculators. In the course of their investigation, the community group discovered that several S & Ls were financing the speculators' activities and that some of the major commercial banks in the city were providing credit to what appeared to be sound business ventures in the field of housing speculation. The community group sought to confront the speculators directly (by picketing and court cases) and put strong pressure on the financial institutions to provide 'normal' mortgage credit to prospective black home owners.

By 1969 the use of the land-installment contract and the speculative activity associated with it were much diminished and the level of community activism faded rapidly thereafter. The urban riots (in which discontent over housing exploitation played an important role), public pressure on the S & Ls not to finance this kind of activity (backed by tightened control of the federal S & Ls via the Federal Loan Bank Board) and the public pillorying of landlord-speculators were the most important factors in this change. But by 1969 the new submarket of West Baltimore had been created and the land-installment contract had served its purpose. The immediate purpose was, of course, to generate profits (and in some cases, excess profits) for landlord-speculators and to yield relatively high rates of return to the financial institutions. But we can identify a deeper and more general purpose.

The financial institutions, by denying funds to certain groups in particular areas and channelling investment to preferred speculative borrowers, created a decision context in which speculative activity was almost bound to succeed. In so doing, a new submarket was created by displacing a middle-income white population by a process I have elsewhere dubbed an urban 'blow-out'.[11] This population was forced, as a consequence, to look elsewhere for new housing opportunities, most of which were being created on the suburban fringe. A new effective demand was being registered at the suburban periphery as a result of inner-city speculative activity. And at the suburban fringe, land-speculation, developers, construction interests and the like were all actively engaged in promoting a suburbanization process which was itself beholden to governmental and financial policies designed to promote capital accumulation and the expansion of effective demand.[12]

The creation of the submarket of West Baltimore has to be interpreted as an example of the operation of those processes, coordinated through the financial and governmental superstructure, which give sufficient dynamism to the urbanization process to match the dynamics of capital accumulation in general. And the rise and fall of community activism which paralleled the rise and fall of the use of the land-installment contract has to be interpreted as a localized response to a local manifestation of what is a general urban process.

### b. A Changing Neighbourhood; North-east Baltimore and the FHA

The 1968 Housing Act was to a large degree an attempt to find an institutional response to the urban discontents of the 1960s. Among the provisions of that act were a whole series of measures designed to bring the social and economic 'benefits' of home ownership to people of limited means. If the social discontent of the 1930s had been successfully countered by turning the middle classes into suburban owner occupiers, then why could the same remedy not work for people of limited means in the inner cities? One of the programmes promoted in the 1968 act was the 221 (d) (2) programme, which permitted the purchase of a house within a certain low-income and price range without any downpayment.

The D2 programme (as we will call it) effectively replaced the land-installment contract as the means to obtain low-income home ownership in Baltimore after 1968. It therefore held out the prospect of continuing the processes of neighbourhood change but doing so *via* a very different set of financial inter-mediaries. It brought together mortgage bankers (who originate mortgages and then usually sell them in the secondary market) and the FHA as guarantor or the mortgages.

The effects in Baltimore were quite dramatic. Firstly, there was a marked decline in the use of the land-installment contract and this helped to defuse much of the passion that the latter had aroused. Secondly, the D2 programme produced a strong clustering of mortgage banker and FHA activity in both North-east and North-west Baltimore (see Figure 2). And in these areas the combination of mortgage banker originations and FHA guarantees began to produce very high rates of turnover in the housing stock and the beginning of radical and class change.

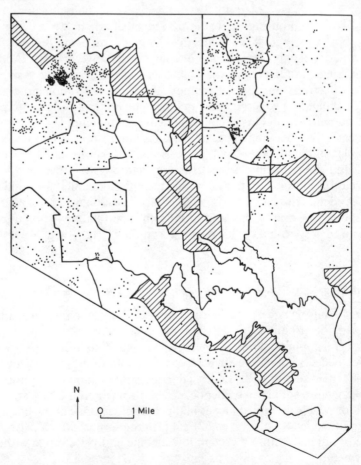

Figure 2 Distribution of FHA-insured mortgages across housing submarkets, Baltimore city, 1970

The pattern of FHA activity in 1970 (Figure 2) indicates that at that time the FHA was functioning as a line of last resort in the provision of housing finance. The FHA was drawn into insuring mortgages in between the 'respectable' middle-income areas where financial institutions were content to operate without FHA guarantees and the untouchable zone of the inner city—the area of hard-core poverty and residential decay. In such an intermediate position, the combination of the FHA and mortgage banker finance started to become the financial lever for extensive neighbourhood change. Speculators could make use of the D2 programme; they could pick up a house for, say, $8,000, make some improvements and add all the usual expenses and the profit margin before selling it under the D2 programme for, say, $13,000. But perhaps most active of all in the high turnover submarkets were the realtors who, by a variety of techniques, were undoubtedly stimulating turnover. Community reaction was fast and direct. A community organization adopted confrontation tactics first against realtors and second against the FHA which, it was claimed, was forcing neighbourhood change and artificially depressing housing prices. Community activism reached a peak in 1971–72. But thereafter FHA and mortgage banker involvement in these areas steadily declined and the levels of community activism declined simultaneously.[13]

Yet the withdrawal of the FHA–mortgage banker combination had little to do with the level of community activism. By 1972 the D2 and 235 programme scandals had erupted in Detroit and the FHA was required to adopt stringent new consumer-protection measures and to adjust its appraisal practices. At the same time, mortgage companies were finding FHA mortgages less profitable because of relative movements in interest rates. The credit crunch in housing finance which set in by the spring of 1973 quietened the turnover in the North-eastern submarket and with it died the final remnants of confrontation tactics and even community activism. It may seem odd to suggest that community activism is interest-rate sensitive, but this proved to be at least in part the case in the high turnover submarket of North-east Baltimore.

The general point, of course, is that events in the economy as a whole were registering in a certain way in a local market situation. The land-installment contract had successfully fashioned a new submarket in West Baltimore and in the process produced community opposition which disappeared when the land-installment contract disappeared from general use. The rise of the FHA–mortgage banker combination riding hard on the D2 programme continued the processes of neighbourhood change in a different manner and in a different area, but with the same underlying logic. Here, too, an opposition group formed only to disappear as the mortgage bankers began to withdraw from servicing FHA mortgages and as the funds for housing finance began to dry up in general during 1973–74. But by then substantial changes had been wrought, particularly in North-east Baltimore. The penchant for promoting neighbourhood change through the financial superstructure can be detected in this case also.

*c. Neighbourhoods Ripe for Change; the Ethnic Submarkets and the
Reorganization of the Financial Superstructure*

The submarkets designated 'ethnic' in Figure 1 are dominated by relatively small-scale state-chartered S & Ls as far as mortgage finance is concerned (see Tables 2 and 3). The intermediaries typically take in savings from the community and then, making use of detailed knowledge about housing and people, apply these savings to foster home ownership within the community. Although they are frequently exclusionary towards other groups (particularly blacks) these ethnic-based S & Ls have managed to provide mortgage finance on relatively low-priced housing for not very affluent blue-collar workers. In this case, savings, far from entering into the mainstream of capital markets, remain locked into the community from which they originate.

Over the years these community-based S & Ls have weakened somewhat. Some fell into the hands of speculators, others became larger and began to lose their neighbourhood identity and, as they became larger and more successful, so they became oriented to doing 'good business' which meant financing suburban development rather than servicing the needs of the blue-collar worker. These profit-oriented and expansion-minded S & Ls appeared to be exporting savings from the city as investment capital to the suburban periphery. The Baltimore City authorities cast a jaundiced eye on these practices and began to put pressure, with the help of some activism, on the S & Ls to commit a greater proportion of their funds to the city.[14] In return for city delegation votes for raising the usury ceiling in the State of Maryland, the financial community agreed to commit a certain minimum of mortgage finance to the needs of Baltimore City. The city has, thus, put pressure on the financial community to do more business in areas from which the savings originate.

This logic flies in the face of the recommendations made by the Hunt Commission on *Financial Structure and Regulation.* The Hunt proposals were drawn up because of the obvious problems in national capital and credit markets at a time of rapid inflation and, as we have seen, represent just one option for the reform of the financial superstructure in the United States at a time when structural adaptation of some sort seems imperative. The Report was fundamentally concerned to eliminate barriers and inequities in the competitive flow of credit in general.

The Report recommended, for example, that S & Ls should compete on an equal footing with other financial institutions for deposits (the interest rate advantage of S & Ls would be abolished), but that the S & Ls should be permitted to offer a wide range of credit facilities and consumer services; they would become, in effect, mini-banks. Such a reorganization of the S & Ls would probably increase their profitability and their profit orientation without necessarily generating any additional funds for the housing market. Indeed, at a time of general capital shortage it would probably mean a reduced flow of capital into residential real estate.

If the S & Ls are forced to become more business-like and competitive, then the small, community-based S & Ls will not survive long. The effects in Baltimore could be quite devastating. Financing for low-value mortgages would become hard to obtain. Savings which usually get channelled into housing finance would not be even slightly protected against the depredations of corporations hungry for external sources of funds. The flow of funds to meet the needs of the not-so-affluent, white, ethnic, blue-collar worker would be much curtailed, particularly in times of credit shortage. A major mechanism for ensuring neighbourhood social stability would be destroyed and the disruption of communities by external speculative forces made that much easier.

## 4. Some Conclusions

The land-installment contract was used in a decision context created by financial intermediaries to devastate existing communities and to create new ones in their place. The FHA's 221 (d) (2) programme took over where the land-installment contract left off. Now before the Congress, as the FHA and all of its programmes lie in disrepute, are a set of proposals for the reform of the financial superstructure in the United States which would be likely to perpetuate the process of neighbourhood change and displacement merely by merging the channels through which mortgage funds flow to facilitate a more competitive flow of finance to wherever the rate of return is highest. In capital markets in general this has meant in the past that government and corporate needs dominate over housing finance. Within housing finance this has meant that the needs of the more affluent (high value mortgages in the most secure areas) are given priority over lower value mortgages in less secure areas. These priorities will be emphasized under the Hunt Commission proposals and the least attractive investment will become even less protected than it currently is.

For a generation or more now, the American city has been promoted as a consumption artifact in the cause of promoting that consumerism which was fashioned as a response to the underconsumption problems of the 1930s. The contemporary history of residential differentiation in any city in the United States (and Baltimore has been used as an example here) shows that communities are disrupted, populations moved (often against their will) and the whole structure of the city altered as the urbanization process, coordinated in its major outlines through the mediations of governmental and financial structures, is utilized as a vehicle to sustain an effective demand for product. An accelerating rate of 'planned obsolescence' in our cities appears as a necessary evil to feed the dynamics of capital accumulation and growth within the United States economy.

The difficulty is, of course, that people who live in the communities being 'obsolesced' resist and resent the process for the most part. Community activism arises as a response to the pressures for change. The necessity to contain levels of social discontent within acceptable bounds is therefore in potential conflict with the necessity to sustain an effective demand for product by means of planned obsolescence.[15]

The history of residential differentiation in Baltimore also indicates that the contradiction between accelerating rates of planned obsolescence and the need to contain social discontent is 'managed' to a large degree by changing both the form and the location of the process of neighbourhood disruption. Moving the problem around geographically prevents a solid opposition forming. The constant revisions of government programmes (some of which are dismantled when it looks as if they may become successful from the point of view of people) and the shifting mediations of the financial superstructure can also be regarded as functional to the perpetuation of the social order in its existing basic configuration. Indeed, the whole pluralistic structure of politics in United States cities can be interpreted as a cooptive device designed to register when levels of discontent are such that the process has to shift to another location and to another form. In short, a moving target is much more difficult to hit, which explains why, as Engels pointed out more than a century ago, capitalism has only one way of resolving its housing problems—it moves them around.[16]

The substantive thesis which this paper has sought to document is that there is, in the United States at least, an intimate connection between the financial superstructure and the shape and form assumed by the urbanization process. Since the financial superstructure has largely been fashioned as a response to the various crises in the development of capitalism in the United States, we have to conclude that the financial superstructure provides the mediating link between the urbanization process (in all of its aspects including the building of built environments and urban social movements) and the necessities dictated by the underlying dynamic of capitalism in the United States. By the same token we have to seek for many of the technics and mechanics for the reproduction of the capitalist social order within the complex fabric of the urban process itself.

## Notes

1. The publications of the U.S. National Resources Planning Board are voluminous and it is instructive to compare them with some of the recent literature on centralized planning in the United States, such as *The Report on National Growth* in *Hearings before the Sub-committee on Housing and National Growth Policy*, House of Representatives Committee on Banking and Currency (92nd Congress, Second Session), Government Printing Office, Washington D.C., 1972.
2. These processes are largely documented in the Douglas Commission Report, *Building the American City* (Report of the National Commission on Urban Problems), Government Printing Office, Washington D.C., 1968.
3. These subsidies are documented in detail in Aaron, H. J., *Shelter and Subsidies*, Brookings Institution, Washington D.C., 1972; and *Housing in the Seventies* in *Hearings on Housing and Community Development Legislation*, House of Representatives Sub-committee on Banking and Currency (93rd Congress, First Session), Part 3, Government Printing Office, Washington D.C., 1973.

4. These matters are dealt with at greater length in Harvey, D., The political economy of urbanisation in advanced capitalist societies: the case of the United States, *Urban Affairs Annual*, No. 9, Sage Publications, Beverley Hills, California, 1975.

5. An overview of this process of financial adaption is to be found in *The Report of the President's Commission on Financial Structure and Regulation* (Hunt Commission Report), Government Printing Office, Washington D.C., 1971.

6. The details of financial structure can be gained from the Douglas Commission Report and *Housing in the Seventies*.

7. Quoted in Baltimore City Home-ownership Programme, *Home-ownership and the Baltimore Mortgage Market*, Department of Housing and Community Development, Baltimore, Maryland, 1973.

8. See the Hunt Commission Report.

9. A more detailed analysis is contained in Harvey, D., The political economy of urbanisation in advanced capitalist societies; the case of the United States, *Urban Affairs Annual*, No. 9, Sage Publications, Beverley Hills, California, 1975., and also Class-monopoly, rent, finance capital and the urban revolution, *Regional Studies*, **8**, 239–255, 1974.

10. More detailed discussions of the land-installment contract are contained in Harvey (1974, 1975), *ibid.*, and also Grigsby, W., and Rosenberg, L., *Urban Housing Policy*, Centre for Urban Policy Research, Rutgers, New Jersey, 1975.

11. See Harvey, D., *Social Justice and the City*, Arnold, London, 1973, Chap. 5.

12. Harvey, D., Class-monopoly, rent, finance capital and the urban revolution, *Regional Studies*, **8**, 239–255, 1974.

13. This case is documented in detail in Klugman, L., *The FHA and Home-ownership in the Baltimore Housing Market (1963–72)*, Ph.D. dissertation, Department of Geography, Clark University, Worcester, 1974.

14. The Baltimore City Home-ownership Programme (*op. cit.*) particularly pressed the argument that savings in a community should be reinvested in that community.

15. Certain other contradictions which attach to the urbanization process and capital accumulation are set out in Harvey, D., The political economy of urbanization in advanced capitalist societies: the case of the United States, *Urban Affairs Annual*, No. 9, Sage Publications, Beverley Hills, California, 1975.

16. Engels, F., *The Housing Question*, International Publishers, New York, 1935, pp. 74–75.

# 7

# Big Firms' Strategies, Urban Policy and Urban Social Movements*

*Jean Lojkine*

Sociological analyses referring to the notion of 'urban policy' generally make use of three divergent definitions, which in our view must be distinguished in order to avoid theoretical confusion or misunderstanding.[1]

(1) Firstly, urban policy may be defined as a rational source of urban growth, a *mechanism of state regulation* designed to resolve the *technical* problems of urban development. This implies a 'socially neutral' image of the state and state policy, cut off from the class struggle and from the contradictions between capital and labour. This first definition corresponds fairly well to the ideology shared not only by certain practitioners of urban planning but also by the state authorities, concerned to conceal all links between state policy and the social class which is its beneficiary.

(2) Secondly, urban policy may again be defined as a form of regulation, but this time as regulating *social contradictions*. On this definition the technocratic ideology is denounced, and the hiatus between the 'rationality', the 'neutrality' of planning discourse and the class orientation of the policy actually executed is clearly brought out. But the advocates of this definition persist in definition the state as a regulatory apparatus above social classes, ensuring the reproduction in perpetuity of the existing socio-economic system. Politics and policy are then defined as relating to the 'management' or 'regulation' of relations between classes, thereby limiting considerably the independence of this approach in relation to the first.

(3) Finally, a third approach is possible which likewise challenges technocratic discourse and emphasizes the relation between urban policy and social classes, but which, in my view, breaks with the first two definitions in that it defines politics not as the 'regulatory' action of an apparatus 'above' social classes but as the 'active reflection' of the class struggle, of the contradiction between capital and labour.

Thus the state, far from managing the economic and social contradiction undermining our social system, reflects it insofar as it does not diminish the contradiction by its interventions but on the contrary exacerbates it.

*Translated by C. G. Pickvance from 'Strategies des grandes entreprises, politique urbaines, et movements sociaux urbains' (slightly abbreviated by the author). (The complete original version has been published in *Sociologie du Travail*, 1, 18–40, 1975.)

A second source of confusion in the notion of 'urban policy' may be indicated, namely the two possible interpretations of 'the urban' according to whether one is referring solely to 'the social' as opposed to 'the economic' or whether on the contrary the urban is placed at the centre of the economic and social relation between the reproduction of capital and the reproduction of labour power.

The problem of defining 'urban' seems to us all the more important in that it converges, among Marxists as well as non-Marxists, with the debate over definitions (2) and (3), insofar as definition (2), in our view, tends to reduce policy simply to the 'management of the reproduction of labour power' (housing and social infrastructure) and excludes its economic dimension, a dimension which is particularly important given that within present-day capitalism the financing of so-called 'economic' urban infrastructure (main roads, major communications and telecommunication networks, zones for heavy industry, ports, etc.) takes place precisely *at the expense* of the financing of social infrastructure (or 'accompanying' infrastructure as it is modestly called).

This debate is by no means merely a quibble over words, but touches on fundamental questions insofar as its outcome in our view influences the role one gives to urban social movements. Now if our hypothesis is correct, in other words if the new relations to urban space of the big industrial and financial groups shatter the ideological boundaries within which some have attempted to confine the urban (reproduction of labour power, consumption cut off from production), the new forms of struggle against the urban environment should result in a direct confrontation with the economic agents which shape it, namely the big firms, main beneficiaries of the spatial segregation of collective infrastructure.

Having made these clarifications, we can now start to discuss the two central elements of our own problematic, the new relations to space of big firms and the role of the state in urban policy. We shall do this by confronting our hypotheses with the results of research we have carried out ourselves or which has adopted a problematic similar to our own.

## I

An analysis of the relation between the strategies of big firms and urban planning policy leads us quite naturally to define the various uses of the term 'space'. Traditionally two meanings have been distinguished: firstly, the 'use value' of space as a (natural, or natural and social) pre-condition for the utilization of human and material productive forces and, secondly, its social relation, 'the private ownership of space' and the 'monopoly of access to useful agglomeration effects' it permits. In the first sense, space is thus a means of bringing together, through the multiplication of economic agglomeration effects, factories and offices, and also wage labour, and is hence a fundamental factor in the organization of local labour markets. Conversely, in the second sense, space is defined primarily as an obstacle to the 'normal' development of our capitalist economic system and refers to the 'power' of a specific social category, land owners, to withhold the use values concealed in it.

## 1. Space as complex use value and the capitalist mode of production

We have briefly indicated the way in which capitalism uses space's agglomerative capacity in order to bring together capital and labour power. At the level of developed cooperation, i.e. in the stage of large-scale industry, space serves to agglomerate both material productive forces and human productive forces. Two contradictions—which we shall describe as 'classical' since they appear in the 'classical' (pre-monopoly) stage of capitalism—have their origin in the capitalist utilization of space's two-fold agglomerative capacity:

(*a*) A contradiction between the share of social capital (whether taken charge of or not by the state) allocated to the financing of the agglomeration of material productive forces (industrial estates, road and rail links between firms, etc.) and the share allocated to that of human productive forces (housing, public transport facilities, schools, etc.). The study of Dunkerque by Castells and Godard in my view brings out clearly this type of urban contradiction.[2]

(*b*) Finally, a contradiction between the two types of agglomeration at the level of space itself, when the reproduction of labour power is subordinated to that of capital, either directly (when the town is an appendage of the factory, e.g. as in a mining community) or indirectly (as at Dunkerque) when the firm is not involved in either the production or the management of housing developments.

These two contradictions have by no means magically disappeared today, but the structural transformation of the capitalist mode of production seems to me to have modified their content insofar as a split has occurred within the capitalist class between monopoly capital and small and medium capital as to the mode of use of space as a use value. This change is, in our view, reflected in the emergence of two main developments.

## a. A New Degree of Spatial and Temporal Mobility of Monopoly Capital

The mobility of monopoly capital results in a whole series of new contradictions among 'users' of space:

(1) A contradiction between the spatial mobility of the big firm operating on a multinational level, for which the region is only one among many possible locations, and the local firm whose very existence is subordinated to the use values of regional space (especially its communications infrastructure and labour market).

(2) A contradiction between the temporal mobility of the big firm for which

investment in a given location is short term and the virtual immobility of small and medium capital 'fixed' in its region of origin.

(3) Finally, a contradiction between the period for which public fixed investment to finance so-called 'reception' collective infrastructure for the firm is tied up and the period of operation in a locality of a given economic unit of a big firm.

The first two contradictions may appear in two different forms, according to to whether they relate to the setting up in a region of a new economic unit of a big multinational firm or to the spatial reorganization of existing economic units which have only recently become part of a new economic structure.

Examples of the latter case in France would be the reorganization currently taking place in the older industrial regions or the economic concentration, the disappearance of family-based medium capital to the benefit of international financial holding companies, which have completely upset traditional (fairly immobile) relations to space. Thus, research workers at the Centre d'Analyse du Développement have shown the effect on employers' housing policies (in particular, those of the Comité Interprofessionnel du Logement) of the reorganization of medium textile capital in Roubaix-Tourcoing:

'Groups in the textile industry, such as Agache Willot and Prouvost-Masurel (which are gradually replacing the medium-sized family firms threatened by new technological changes and Japanese products), do not operate solely in the Roubaix-Tourcoing agglomeration; they own production units in several regions within France and also abroad... their activities cover many parts of the textile industry, but also extend... to publishing and property.'[3]

Besides, these groups are currently considering means of resolving their labour problems other than by local interprofessional housing committees, e.g. *'the movement of factories out of the Roubaix-Tourcoing agglomeration* to places where there is less pressure on wages and labour recruitment is easier'.[4]

The final type of opposition is clearly illustrated by the studies of Usinor (a major steel company) at Dunkerque (by Castells and Godard, especially) or at Fos,[5] which reveal striking examples of the contrast between the rapidity of the construction of means of production and of economic reception infrastructure (ports, canals, motorways), on the one hand, and the long delays in the construction of housing and infrastructure related to the reproduction of labour power (schools, hospitals, sports and cultural facilities, etc.), on the other.

*b. New Forms of Social and Spatial Separation of the Economic Functions of Big Firms*

The new forms of separation and specialization of economic functions within big multinational firms clash in turn with the local requirements of small- and medium-sized regional firms, concerning inter-industry transactions and economics of scale. The very logic of the emerging social and spatial division of labour in the dominant economic groups leads in fact to a virtual 'privatization' of major collective economic infrastructure, especially means of communication, to the detriment of the industrial fabric of the region.

Thus, as Castells and Godard note, 'whereas the 1963 Bernard plan envisaged industrial and urban development taking place around an axis constituted by the wide-channel canal from Dunkerque to Valenciennes, thus strengthening industrial linkages within the *départment* and increasing the range of industrial users of the canal, the Usinor group has limited users of the canal solely to those connected with the industrial and port complex and the heavy raw materials processing industry.

The careful study by Boussard of the effects of the establishment of a big electronics group (A.O.I.P.) in a small industrial town in Brittany is very characteristic in this respect.[7] The author observes that the (classical) division of functions within A.O.I.P. has led it to concentrate its head office, administration and skilled manufacturing jobs in Paris, while the local assembly factory of Guingamp employs a majority of unskilled workers. Now,

'A.O.I.P. was to be a *propulsive* industry with catalytic effects on the other units with which it had transactions. *In fact, it has no multiplier effects:* none of its purchases are made within the region. It has no *polarisation effect:* no local factory does sub-contracting work for it. *It has no accelerator effect:* its presence is not bringing about investments in local firms. Finally, it has no complementation effect: *It is content with the infrastructural investment made by the local authorities.*'

Whereas, as the author observes, 'it should be possible to choose which factories are set up' according to the characteristics of the firms and working population in the region, capitalist logic reverses the order of priorities: it is the big firm which chooses where to establish itself, in terms of its own profitability, with the effect we have noted—a reinforcement of regional underdevelopment and of the overconcentration of command activities in Paris.

## 2. Space as Obstacle to Capital Accumulation; Ground Rent and Monopoly Capital

As we are solely concerned here with the role of the big firm in the structuring of urban space, we shall not dwell any further on the 'external' contradiction between capital as 'user' of space and the various categories of pre-capitalist land owner, in particular the small shopkeepers and artisans whose ownership of 'urban' property is an obstacle to the profitable production and circulation of the built environment by the big financial groups which control the real estate industry. Since we are rather concerned with what Topalov rightly calls the 'internal' (to the capitalist mode of production) contradiction between rent and capital, we may ask whether this contradiction is always reducible today to the opposition between productive capital 'fighting to keep the totality of surplus-value produced' and landed property *'stripped of all real power over the use of land,* but tending to appropriate rent in full.'[8]

This type of explanation is in our view unsatisfactory when one seeks to analyse the progress of large real estate operations, where monopoly capital intervenes directly to appropriate ground rent. Let us take, for example, the plan to renew the 65 hectacres between the Opéra, the Gare St. Lazaire (station) and La Bourse (the Stock Exchange), in the 'financial district' of Paris. Insurance companies own at least 735,000 square metres of real estate there, and the banks 410,000 square metres.[9] Can it be said that such land owners are 'stripped of all real power over the use of land'? Not at all, since, quite to the contrary, it is they who proposed the change of use, through the creation in 1968 of the 'Groupement d'Etudes pour le Maintien et le Développement d'un Centre Financier à Paris' (1) (Study Group for the Maintenance and Development of a Financial District in Paris), each bank or insurance company subsequently negotiating a new—national—spatial division of its activities with the public authorities.

The use and appropriation of space are thus intimately linked here and the classical analyses referred to above are of no help in understanding the nevertheless fundamental problems of ground rent of this type. Certainly, some 'official' explanations, mainly put forward by the banks and insurance companies, have attempted to suggest that this problem was simply a 'functional' one connected with the functioning of a financial centre. In fact it can easily be shown that, even if the idea of a functional problem is accepted, there is absolutely no need for more than one million square metres of office space to be kept in the area. On the contrary, the only explanation for the Study Group's strategy for the financial centre is a desire to increase the value of its real estate holdings. Many other examples could be given, especially in Paris and in the La Défense development, of the production of office blocks representing for the developer both a financial investment and a (private) use value as his headquarters. Still more subtle examples of concurrent uses may be found in the (very common) practice of many companies of selling their headquarters buildings in order to increase their liquidity and of simultaneously leasing back the building.[10] These practices, it may be said, are not restricted solely to banks or financial institutions, but are general among big monopoly groups, whether they are predominantly industrial or predominantly financial, and a characteristic feature of the present stage of capitalism.

As Lenin observed in connection with the railway companies, monopoly capitalism 'merges' bank capital with that of ground rent and means of communication, thus internalizing the contradiction between capital and landed property. One might even ask whether it does not substitute for it the more general contradiction between the speculative and parasitic tendency of monopoly (whether in relation to speculative monetary investment or to real estate investment) and the tendency to increase the rate of surplus value by increased investment in production. It might be objected that this 'modern' land obstacle is peculiar to France which, unlike its Anglo-Saxon or Scandinavian neighbours, has been incapable of creating land banks to prevent ground rent being a 'present-day problem'. But if one looks more closely at land-policy in these 'model' countries, e.g. Holland or West Germany, one discovers that the public land bank policy practised over a period of fifty years has never applied to the areas where ground rent is greatest, i.e. the centres of large cities. Thus, the City of Rotterdam, owner of the majority of land in the city, is currently reselling the land redeveloped in the city centre to the developers of the World Trade Centre which is to be set up there; as for Amsterdam, effective control by the city over land and land prices does not extend to the city centre, which remains in the hands of private land owners, and there the inflationary spiral is visible as in other Western countries.

## II

### 3. Regional and Urban Planning Policies; On the Role of the State in the Development of Urban Contradiction

A number of analyses, while rejecting the functionalist picture of a harmonious urban society free from social contradictions, nevertheless in our view surruptitiously reintroduce functionalist postulates by according the state a regulative function in relation to regional and urban planning, through which it neutralizes urban social contradictions to the benefit of the dominant class fraction. As 'a self-conscious social force', separate from economic agents, omniscient and omnipotent, the state 'above classes' acts as a marvellous safety valve, capable of granting the appropriate concession at the appropriate time to the dominated class—even against the judgement of individual agents of the dominant class—provided that the hegemony of the dominant class is preserved.

Now such a mechanistic and functionalist picture of the capitalist state is in our view completely contrary to reality. To take the example of the plan for a financial centre in Paris again, a 'regulator' state, if it existed, would have succeeded in forcing the banks and insurance companies to reduce their hundreds of thousands of square metres of office space to the several thousand square metres really 'functional' for their headquarters; or better still it would have convinced them to shift their headquarters to the east of Paris in order to provide a balance in the location of tertiary jobs throughout the Paris region and to shorten people's journeys to work. As we know, reality is quite different: neither the City of Paris and its Prefect nor even the Délègation a l'Aménagement du Territoire à l'Action Regionale (D.A.T.A.R.—a regional planning body), which a few years previously had been so hostile to the plan for a financial centre in Paris, laid a hand on the landed property of the banks and insurance companies or placed any serious obstacle in the way of the groups' plans to increase the value of their property holdings. No more than the City of Amsterdam laid hands on the property in the centre of Amsterdam, nor the City of Rotterdam interfered with the urban ground rent actualized by the World Trade Centre operation in the centre of that city. Conversely, the arsenal of weapons of juridical coercion (preemption, expropriation) and economic intervention (purchase of land by the public authorities) was used to the full against small private land owners, whether they were small shopkeepers, small industrial firms, or home owners; the 20,000 people expropriated in the La Defense district are sufficient witness to this.[11]

On a much larger scale, the enormous 'extension plans' for workers' housing and collective facilities, developed and realized in Holland and elsewhere, are there to indicate the limits of state 'regulation' in the urban field; the location of residential developments can be controlled by means of a systematic land-bank policy, but not the location of office developments, which the German and Dutch authorities leave to 'private initiative'—in other words, to the few financial groups which alone are capable of recovering ground rent in the city centre. The segregation of home and work, the exclusive occupation of the city centre by office blocks, are no more avoided in Rotterdam than in Paris, even taking into account that the size of the Paris agglomeration magnifies the severity of its commuting problem and lack of adequate public transport facilities.

It is clear that the same argument applies equally for other uses of territorial space, and in particular for the production units of monopoly groups. For example, Castells and Godard have shown clearly the subordination of the policy adopted by the Ministère de l'Equipement (roughly equivalent to the British Department of the Environment) to the more urgent needs of Usinor at Dunkerque.

## 4. Problems of the Alliance between the Different Fractions of Capital and their Repercussions on State Policy

While urban policy appears thus as clearly subordinated to the interests of the dominant big firms, it remains true that the perfecting of this single (juridical, ideological, economic) mechanism which links state policy and the strategies of big firms must take into account the contradictions we have identified between the purely monopolistic use of urban space and its 'regional' use by local capitalist agents, small and medium capitalists. At the risk of breaking up the political alliance linking small and medium capital and mono-poly capital, compromises and mediations have to be worked out. The study by the Rennes research team on urban policy in Rennes[12] shows clearly the nature of the political compromise made between medium and big capital in response to the planned setting up of supermarkets and hypermarkets in Rennes and the threat they represented for city centre stores.

This study brings out two basic points:

(a) The phenomenon of concentration is not simply one in which the 'big swallow up the little', but implies simultaneously a converse, and comple-mentary, process: the rise of a fraction of local medium capital to the national level, a rise which may take various forms (grouping together of family capitals, subordination to a national group) *but which implies the end of the social homogeneity of local commercial capital.*

(*b*) The role of the municipal apparatus was to *delay* the arrival of national companies in order to facilitate the adjustment of the dynamic faction of big city centre store owners, and this at the expense of the small shopkeepers left to their fate by the city a long time previously and of part of traditional commercial medium capital unable to adapt to the new forms of competition.

The same phenomenon is apparent in Lyon with the setting up of a Regional Shopping Precinct in the Left Bank centre (La Párt Dieu), which includes two big national department stores and several big Lyon-based department stores. But what are the actual results of this political compromise for the class situation of local commercial capital? The major part of the latter is inexorably exluded from new commercial development schemes. Only a small part is able to make a 'temporary' adjustment to the financial conditions imposed by the developers and planners, the large part is forced into debt and is immediately placed at the mercy of the banks. State policy thus has two effects in reality:

(*a*) An *ideological* and *political* effect, insofar as, through the intermediary of the city authorities of Rennes or Lyon or of certain local 'Defence Committees', the state attempts to maintain the illusion that a *consensus* exists among *all* store owners. But this ideology is cut off nowadays from its former social roots due to the pauperization of a large number of small shopkeepers who are now displaying a defiant attitude towards the municipal councils they traditionally supported, as witnessed by their massive abstention at the last elections.[13]

(*h*) An *economic* effect, insofar as state policy *accelerates* the splitting up of local commercial capital by its encouragement of highly selective planning operations.

As the Rennes team very pertinently notes, the role played by the city authorities of Rennes—and we could say the same for Lyon—in encouraging the 'adjustment' of locally 'regnant' medium capital to monopoly capital cannot be mechanically attributed to all local authorities as such:

'(The political-administrative system) is not simply a completely faithful reflection of the socio-economic structures of the overall interests of the dominant classes and their allies at a given moment. *The class struggle has an influence on its functioning and may even, especially in the differentiated local authority apparatus, change substantially the balance of forces contained within it. But this was not the case in Rennes* and the role of the City authorities there was indeed to secure the "co-existence" of the interests of the monopoly sector on the one hand and of those of the non-monopoly sector of production and commerce on the other.'[14]

Similarly, in Lyon the La Part Dieu scheme sets a seal on the concentration between the national policy of 'reorganization' of the centres of the big cities, to the benefit of banking and commercial groups, and the municipal policy of 'adjustment' of local medium capital. But at the same time it gives rise to the shattering of the old economic and political alliance between the different components of the local petit and moyenne bourgeoisie, on which the Lyon city authorities have traditionally relied for support. Both small shopkeepers, incapable of adjusting to the new conditions of capitalist competition, victims of planning operations (like those in La Part Dieu which are restricted to a narrow stratum of Lyon medium capital which was to 'coexist' with big national and multinational groups) and small industrial firms, ruined by the cost of moving to new industrial estates, are gradually removing their support from the city authorities in Lyon as they are in Rennes. Moreover, it is still difficult to know to what extent parts of local Lyon or Rennes medium capital can *really and in a lasting way* adjust to competition from big national and international groups, without themselves being swallowed up.

The Rennes research is unable to answer this question since the process of 'alliance' between medium and big capital was only just starting at the time of the study. Several years will be necessary before one can see the extent to which this alliance will change into dependence—or even into elimination pure and simple. At least the latter outcome is what we observed in Lyon in the case of the most dynamic firms in the building industry; after a period of rapid economic expansion, due to very considerable technological progress and the use of industrialized prefabrication methods, family firms which had succeeded in conquering the majority of the major construction markets in the region (especially the big Z.U.P.s)[15] were suddenly obliged to resort to bank credit, only to be finally absorbed into a subsidiary of the Paribas financial group.

Clearly, it remains to be seen to what extent these particular cases are representative of the general situation of local medium capital, a task which which will require further and more detailed research.

### 5. Urban Policy and Class Struggle; The Role of the Dominated Classes in the Formation of Urban Policy

The analytical framework just outlined is none the less inadequate, or even of no use at all, in relation to certain phenomena we have observed in urban and regional planning in France.

### a. First Group of Phenomena

These are political tendencies which relate neither to the interests of the monopoly fraction nor to those of alliance between the latter fraction and regional medium capital, nor to the direct manifest pressure of the dominated classes, especially of the labour movement. We shall describe this case as one of 'anticipation' by the political authorities of a predictable reaction on the part of the dominated classes, an anticipation resulting in a change in urban policy at the expense of the immediate interests of the monopoly fraction.

This, for example, is in our view the only possible interpretation of the 'delay' by the French state authorities in accepting the financial centre project in Paris; this scheme, though announced in 1968, was only adopted by the public authorities and the Council of Paris in 1974, as part of a new plan for Paris. This is much too long a delay for the majority of big companies which promoted the 1968 scheme and whose plans for reorganization could not wait six years. Certainly, it may be said, part of the 'delay' is only apparent insofar as the economic and spatial reorganization of the big banks and insurance companies could not have been started as early as 1968. This is true, but if one follows the course of the negotiations between the financial groups and representatives of the state more closely still, one sees that certain spatial choices were *imposed* on the companies against their will. This was true of the transfer of whole departments of insurance companies from Paris to provincial towns such as Reims or Bordeaux, where the reduced pressure for higher wages seems unlikely to outweigh, as far as the immediate profitability of the company is concerned, the limited supply of labour (especially skilled labour) and the poor communications with Paris where the 'head' of the company remains.

Now, there are two factors which appear to have determined the 'coercive' policy adopted by D.A.T.A.R. in this case. The first is awareness of the connection between the commuting problem in Paris and the overconcentration of offices in Paris. The first mass protest movements for better public transport facilities, especially in 1970 and 1971, may have acted—like the second factor, the underemployment problem in the provinces—as a 'warning signal' for this body (D.A.T.A.R.) responsible for maintaining the cohesion of the French social formation.

## b. Second Group of Phenomena

These are political tendencies relating directly and manifestly to pressure from the labour movement or from the most proletarianized categories among the middle classes. Thus the resumption of work on extensions of *métro* lines from Paris towards the suburban centres and the affirmation of priority for public transport are in complete contradiction with the repeated refusal by the officials in charge of transport policy in the 1960s to reverse the priority then given to extending motorways into Paris. It is undeniable that protest movements by people lacking adequate transport facilities had a direct role in influencing urban policy. This was flagrantly obvious in the cases of the voting on a law on transport taxation (which hit the big employers benefitting from the commuting of their labour force) and of the maintenance of the price of weekly season tickets in Paris in the face of the desire of the transport company (Régie Autonome des Transports Parisiens) for an increase.

One could go still further by showing how working class control of certain local authorities has led to a policy of 'social' urban renewal, without the expulsion of the most deprived, in complete contradiction with national political trends.

### 6. The State—Instrument of Class Domination or Organ of Socio-political Regulation 'Above Class'

It might be objected that in 'qualifying' and 'refining' our initial definition of the state (as instrument of the monopoly fraction of capital), we appear to have returned to a 'functionalist' definition of the state, as a 'regulatory organ', in the service of the dominant class fraction certainly, but functioning in pursuit of the long-term goal of preserving the cohesion of society as a whole at the cost of a few immediate concessions granted to the dominated classes. Does this not imply an indirect return to the functionalist definition we criticized at the outset?

Such a criticism would be justified if we had analysed this 'concessions policy' as a form of 'neutralization' of the economic and social contradictions which gave rise to it, and if we had concluded that the class struggle had been smothered, paralysed due to the ideological and political subordination of the dominated classes to the dominant class. Now, in our view, what is currently occurring in France in no way justifies such a 'fatalistic' interpretation; political concessions to the dominated classes because they remain 'secondary' have in no sense put an end to the various manifestations of urban and regional imbalance. In the Paris region, the victims of commuting and of the domitory suburbs have proved to be among the fiercest opponents of the policy of social segregation which remains—professions of faith notwithstanding—the urban policy actually in operation. So true is this that, as we have been able to demonstrate for Paris and Lyon, the economic foundations of urban policy remain unchanged:

(*a*) Subordination of real estate operations in city centres, loci of concentration of collective means of consumption, to the logic of urban ground rent, which leads to city centres becoming the preserve of offices and luxury dwellings.

(*b*) The casting further and further out from the centre of public housing and units of production.

The *métro* extensions 'conceded' to suburban dwellers remain minor measures in relation to the needs of the Paris region as a whole; official speeches in favour of suburban *métro* lines merely reinforce the protest movement on the part of all those who perceive a divergence between what is promised and the pace of actual construction. Moreover, as we have been able to note in the Paris region, these fragmentary government measures, short-term responses to the most obvious 'emergencies', prove incapable of breaking the vicious circle of urban imbalance—congestion in the centre of Paris and lack of employment opportunities in the suburbs. One might even ask whether the policy of giving priority to the building of radial roads does not have as its principal effect the reinforcement, the exacerbation, of urban imbalance. In the words of a Gaullist deputy, chairman of the committee on the recent bill on transport taxation:

'Everything happens as though the interventions of the State and the local authorities concerned ... had the objective, as far as investment is concerned, of *strengthening the imbalance* in existing structure. It is at the periphery of the Paris region that the transport problems of today and tomorrow are most severe. Now investment in roads is undeniably greater in the case of radial roads than in the case of ring roads or roads between suburbs in the periphery.

'The consequence of this was a 25 per cent *rise* in commuting between 1962 and 1968, with a proportionate increase in needed public transport infrastructure on these same roads, thus setting off a process of progressive deterioration.'[16]

Thus, far from removing the contradictions which gave rise to the current urban crisis, state policy intensifies them in that it now has to give them official reorganization, but without being able to provide a coherent and definitive way of resolving them.

One is thus all the better able to explain the fact that state policy has opened the way, in the 1970s, to urban social movements of a completely new type in France.

### III

### 7. Towards a New Type of Urban Social Movement

For complex historical reasons,[17] French urban social movements have until recently been characterized by a total separation between the economic demands fought for by the working class within the work place (higher wages and the slowing down of speeds) and the 'social' demands linked to the re-production of labour power (housing, transport, health and cultural facilities, etc.). The new feature of the 1970s is, on the contrary, a strongly expressed desire by the labour movement to make a close link between demands within the work place and those related to the 'environment'.

We shall take as an example developments within the most important component of the French labour movement: the P.C.F. (Parti Communiste Français) and, for trade unions, the C.G.T. (Confédération Générale du Travail) [Communist-backed trade union]. The analysis which follows makes no attempt either to deal with the French labour movement *as a whole* (the attitudes of the C.F.D.T. (socialist-backed trade union) or of the P.S.U. (radical socialist party) towards these problems, for example, have been quite different) or to deal exhaustively with the behaviour of the P.C.F. or C.G.T. The events we shall mention, however, do seem to us particularly symptomatic of the *general* trend of the labour movement. At least this is our hypothesis.

Three dates are significant, in this connection:

(*a*) On 13th June 1970 a 'day of study' on the transport problem in the Paris region was held, attended by leaders of all the Communist Party sections within the Paris region. This was the first time an attempt had been made to 'regionalize' urban demands. In his introductory report for this day of study, the Secretary of the Paris section of the P.C.F. stated that:

*'For the first time*, an examination of one of the major problems of living in Paris is going to be tackled *at the correct level, the regional level.*... In doing so, we shall be running counter to a *general orientation* which has repercussions on the circulation of traffic and the adequacy of transport facilities. This is why we feel the need to abandon a fragmented approach in favour of a global framework within which partial demands can be placed, and which embodies our views on all aspects of the problem.'[18]

(*b*) In February 1974 for the first time a meeting was held by the P.C.F. to discuss the problems of the Paris region, a meeting attended by members of section committees, deputies, councillors at the *département* level and mayors, in the eight *départements* of the Paris region. Now from the very outset the introductory report[19] is careful to state that it is

'... increasingly at the level of the region that the problems of unemployment, wages, transport facilities, housing and collective facilities are posed for the workers. It is at this level that big monopoly firms, in increasingly rapid and varied ways, decide their investment and accumulation policies.'

It will be noted that this analysis, far from limiting the 'regional' problem to the reproduction of labour power, situates it at the same time on the level of the reproduction of capital and, especially, of monopoly capital in the Paris region.

Further, the report emphasizes that 'exploitation in the work-place is extended in a generalized way and to an unrivalled extent throughout the country by exploitation outside work'[20], and attempts to show systematically that exploitation outside work in its most obvious form (the lack of adequate transport facilities) is merely the consequence of economic trends promoted by monopoly groups—in particular, the deindustrialization of the Paris region and the concentration of offices in the centre of Paris.

The same concern is manifest in the proposals for action which have two focal points, a new employment policy and a new transport policy.

(*c*) The third stage was on 9th and 10th April 1974 at Grenoble when a conférence 'Pour un Urbanisme' [For an urban planning] was organized by the Isere section of the P.C.F. and the journal *La Nouvelle Critique*. This was the first time local councillors of the P.C.F. and Parti Socialiste, political and trade union militants and planners (architects, research workers, etc.) had gathered together at a national level.[21] Out of this confrontation between the theoretical concerns of the research workers, the political concerns of the militants and the immediate management of the local councillors, a new approach to understanding the role of urban problems in the future struggles of the labour movement emerged. At least this is our hypothesis. It remains to be seen how these concerns voiced by political and trade union leaders are shared by the militants at the base and articulated with the immediate concerns of all those who, while affected by the 'degradation of the environment', do not see it as an effect of the global economic system.

In this connection the way in which the 'Rateau' conflict has been popularized by the C.G.T. and P.C.F. may be regarded as an indicator of a new type of articulation of 'economic' and 'urban' conflicts by the labour movement. Thus, the fight against the dismantling of the Rateau factory at La Courneuve quickly went beyond a straightforward fight against dismissals and unemployment. By denouncing the policy of the multinational C.G.E. group, which controls the Rateau company, underlying the threat to dismantle the factory, the trade unions quickly came to question the very logic of specialization and separation of each economic unit of the C.G.E. group (a logic governed by the overall profitability of the group, irrespective of its consequences at the level of the economy of a particular region) or of a particular nation, which today is merely a region from the point of view of the world strategy of a multinational firm.

By placing in question the future of a Paris factory with a highly skilled labour force which was also the sole manufacturer in France of certain types of turbine used exclusively in nuclear power stations, the C.G.E. group revealed the gap which exists today between the use of regional space by multinational firms and its collective, truly social use.

This conflict went to the very root of the urban crisis in Paris, with its vicious circle of deindustrialization, overconcentration of office blocks and company headquarters, and ever greater spatial segregation between public housing on the one hand and 'reception' areas for the richest companies in the world on the other. Moreover, since the attempted dismantling of the Rateau factory appeared to be strongly encouraged by D.A.T.A.R. in the name of 'decentralization', the labour movement was able to put great stress on the connection between this economic logic and urban policy.

Certainly, this was not the first time that the dismantling of a firm of regional importance had been linked to the problem of regional imbalance. But it was the first time, to our knowledge, that such a clear connection had been made between a conflict which was at first sight 'economic' and the urban crisis, in direct accordance with the recommendations of the Paul Laurent report on the need to 'regionalize' economic struggles. However, we are fully aware that such cases are at the moment more the symptoms of future struggles than manifestations of a social movement in which there is total integration between urban demands and global economic and political demands.

Nevertheless, one need not be a prophet to foresee the multiplication of conflicts in which (monopoly) economic logic and urban and regional logic (spatial segregation, the problem of the city centre, the lack of adequate transport facilities) are closely linked together. The starting points of these conflicts may be either problems of the firm, as in the Rateau case, or the link between spatial segregation and the journey to work, as in the case of movements for better public transport in the Paris region.

## Notes

1. The analysis which follows is in complete agreement with that presented by Bleitrach, D., and Chenu, A., Aménagement: régulation ou aggravation des contradictions

sociales? Un exemple: Fos sur Mer et l'aire métropolitaine marseillaise, in *Amènage-ment du Territoire et Développement Régional*, Vol. VII, C.E.R.A.T., Institut d'Etudes Politiques, Grenoble, 1974.

2. Castells, M., and Godard, F., *Monopolville*, Mouton, Paris, 1974.

3. Cornuel, D., and Duriez, B., *Le Comité Interprofessionnel du Logement de Roubaix-Toucoing*, D.G.R.S.T. Report, May 1973, p. 207.

4. *Ibid.*, p. 209.

5. See Bleitrach, D., and Chenu, A., Aménagement: régulation ou aggravation des contradictions sociales? Un exemple: Fos sur Mer et l'aire métropolitaine marseil-laise, in *Aménagement du Territoire et Développement Régional*, Vol. VII, C.E.R.A.T., Institut d'Etudes Politiques, Grenoble, 1974.

6. Castells, M., and Godard, F., *Monopolville*, Mouton, Paris, 1974.

7. Boussard, P., Guingamp Cité industrielle, *Revue de Geographie Norois*, **78**, 237 *et seq.*, April–June 1973.

8. Topalov, C., *Capital et Propriété Foncière*, Centre de Sociologie Urbaine, Paris, 1973, p. 224.

9. See Lojkine, J., Les projects de Cité financière a Paris, *Espaces et Sociétés*, **13–14**, 111–134, 1975.

10. See Lojkine, J., *La Politique Urbaine dans la Régione Parisienne*, 1945–72, Mouton, Paris, 1972, p. 33.

11. *Ibid.*

12. Huet, A., Kaufman, J. C., Laigneau, M., Peron, R., and Sauvage, A., *Röle et Portèe Economiques, Politiques et Idéologiques de la Participation à l'Aménagement Urbain*, 1973, a study financed by the Délégation Générale à la Recherche Scientifique et Technique (D.G.R.S.T.) and l'Office Social et Culturel de Rennes.

13. We are referring here to the Rennes study as well as to our own research in Lyon; see Lojkine, J., *La Politique Urbaine dans la Région Lyonnaise*, Mouton, Paris, 1974.

14. Huet, A., Kaufman, J. C., Laigneau, M., Peron, R., and Sauvage, A., *Rôle et Partée Economiques, Politiques et Idéologiques de la Participation à l'Aménagement Urbain*, 1973, a study financed by the Délégation Générale à la Recherche Scientifique et Technique (D.G.R.S.T.) and l'Office Social and Culturel de Rennes.

15. Z.U.P. = priority residential development area *(zone à urbaniser par priorité)* consist-ing of large complexes of blocks of flats or houses.

16. Quoted in Lojkine (1972), *op. cit.*, p. 258.

17. Historical reasons linked in particular to the pattern of development of French capitalism between 1870 and 1950, but which should not lead us to forget that where urban social movements have developed to any significant degree (as, for example, in the case of the Garden City movements in the Anglo-Saxon and North European countries) they have always been circumscribed within clearly defined ideological limits, *viz.* the 'social' sphere, with the economic sphere being left to capitalist entre-preneurs. The new challenge by the big multinational firms themselves to this old 'divi-sion of labour' between the public authorities and capitalists, insofar as they demand that major 'economic' infrastructure be directly financed by the state and local authori-ties, is today putting into question the old social democratic ideology 'change the city in order to change society'.

18. See the journal *Economie et Politique*, **195**, 43 *et seq.*, October 1970. See also the dis-cussion of this problem in Lojkine, J., *La Politique Urbaine dans la Region Parisienne 1945–72*, Mouton, Paris, 1974, pp. 74–81.

19. See the journal *Cahiers du Communisme*, p. 46 ('Les Problèmes de la Région Parisienne et l'Activité des Fédérations du P.C.F.').

20. This is taken up by Georges Marchais, Secretary-General of the P.C.F., in his book *Le Défi Démocratique*, which has been the main propaganda tool of communist militants since the legislative elections of March 1973.

21. The conference was attended by over one thousand participants.

# 8
# Social Conflicts of Underurbanization

*György Konrad and Ivan Szelenyi*

## 1. Introduction

Hungarian urbanization produces social tension, not because of its excessive speed but, on the contrary, because of its relatively slow rate. This proposition may well produce numerous objections. Housing construction and communal development can barely keep up with the number of those moving to towns; those living there already, as well as those responsible for managing local government affairs in towns, tend to feel a certain hostility for the masses of villagers who settle in newly built dwellings, and overcrowd public transport, schools, shops and hospitals. For that very reason the inhabitants and officials of country towns look on the growth of their own towns with mixed feelings. They would like to keep ahead of the others but they nevertheless consider the flood of the newcomers, of 'Johnny-come-latelys' to be a dilution of their true substance, and a social danger. It is certainly true that the rate of growth of urbanization is too fast compared with that of the urban infrastructure, and to that extent Hungary also shows the symptoms of 'overurbanization' common in the developing countries—the queueing up for beds, with men living in cellars and lofts, in the woodshed and in sties, in ancient buses and circus caravans and in caves. Whole settlements of lean-tos are built on the fringes of towns, not as extensive perhaps as the *favella* in Rio but hardly offering higher standards, and the price of sub-let rooms rises faster than that of any other goods or services. Overcrowding can, however, be the result not only of overurbanization but also of underurbanization. Overurbanization in developing countries means that the growth in urban population, in urbanization, takes place at a faster rate than industrialization. The infrastructure is overburdened there because of the absence of effective demand in the economic sense, i.e. demand able to pay for the services needed, owing to unemployment. This then makes it impossible to extend these services. In Hungary, on the other hand, and as far as we know in the other Eastern European countries also (certainly in Czechoslovakia and in the G.D.R., but also in Poland and to some extent in Romania), the rate of industrialization keeps well ahead of urbanization, work places in towns increase at a much faster rate than housing and those filling them are therefore forced to choose between commuting, subtenancies, hostels and temporary shelters. Overurbanization in developing countries is produced by the low level of industrial investment and an insufficiency of employment; underurbanization in Eastern Europe, on the other hand, is the result of excessive industrialization at the expense of the infrastructure. The proportion of industrial investment was too high and that in consumption goods too low, and relatively little housing was built out of state resources. The overwhelming proportion of those finding new employment could therefore not be allotted dwellings by an administrative process. However, their income was too small to allow them to obtain their own housing from the limited market for dwellings that came into existence alongside the housing administration of the authorities.

In what follows an attempt will be made to describe the symptoms of under-urbanization, the causes of this process and the structure of the social conflicts grouped around it. We should also like to point out the ways in which under-urbanization handicaps the intensive stage of economic development which is about to get off the ground in Hungary. Limits on urban development also limit democratic processes in society in a double sense: the existing system or unequal regional distribution of goods and privileges becomes rigidified and the burdens of forced industrialization are unequally distributed among various social groups.

## 2. Problems of Economic and Urban Growth

The myth of fast urbanization in Hungary soon dissolves if we merely glance at census figures showing the increase of the urban population and that of those in non-agricultural employment. The proportion of the urban population grew relatively slowly during the past hundred years and fairly evenly, roughly at the rate of 2 per cent every ten years. The curve showing development between 1869 and 1970 only dips around 1949, surely a consequence of war damage in towns and the resulting migration of the urban population. The proportion of the urban population apparently grew at a relatively faster rate between 1949 and 1970; in fact, however, urban development was no faster than early this century and was slower even than in the concluding third of the nineteenth century. Between 1949 and 1970 the proportion of town and city dwellers increased by 6·7 per cent. but this was largely served to simply make good the losses suffered by the urban population during the war. It would therefore be more appropriate to take 1941 as a starting point, since the period between the wars can also be interpreted as one of regeneration after the First World War from the point of view of urban development. In the last three decades of the nineteenth century the proportion of the urban population increased by 7·3 per cent.; this figure was only 4·6 per cent. for the period between 1910 and 1941, and around 5 per cent. between 1941 and 1970. There was certainly no sort of boom in urban growth in recent decades. This becomes even more obvious for the past twenty years or so if the growth per decade of the urban population is calculated on the basis of the urban population as given by the previous census.

In other words the population of towns grew at a faster rate at the end of the nineteenth century than in the past quarter of a century and the impor-tance of the relative boom of the fifties is somewhat lessened by the fact that, between 1941 and 1960, i.e. in twenty years, the urban population grew by a total of only 12 per cent. These statistical data can be confirmed by anyone taking a stroll round any of the towns in Hungary who could observe that the structure of these towns and their most characteristic buildings were produced by the wave of urban growth at the end of the last century.

The rate of urbanization was therefore not speeded up; on the contrary, the rate (by decades) of urban population growth has only half that of the end of the nineteenth century, and the proportion of urban population only increased by 25 per cent. from 1949–70. National income, however, increased threefold in the same period, and the number of those employed in industry and the building industry increased 2·3 times at the same time. All this allows one to conclude that the rate of urban growth fell behind that of industrial growth to a significant and unjustified extent and that numerous social problems derive from these opening 'scissors'.

The relative backwardness of urban growth directly follows from Hungarian economic policy and the Hungarian strategy for furthering urban development. The delay in urban growth derives from insufficient investment in the urban infrastructure. In capitalist countries, and even in Hungary at the time of the Astro-Hungarian monarchy, industrialization took place parallel with the development of the infrastructure. Roughly 50 per cent. of capital accumulation at that time was devoted to the development of the infrastructure. For example, this was the great age of railway construction. Also, in the 1890s an average of 10,000 dwellings a year were constructed in Budapest, though the total population at the time was only half a million, i.e. twenty dwellings per year were built for every 1,000 inhabitants. In recent years not quite a third of total investments was devoted to the infrastructure, too little to allow a modern urban network to be constructed that would keep up with industrial growth. Housing construction in Budapest in the 1960s was no higher in absolute figures than in the 1890s and only 5·8 dwellings per 1,000 inhabitants per annum were built.

Urban housing stock in Hungary grew by 23 per cent. between 1960 and 1970; at the same time the number of those employed by industry, including the building industry, grew by 34 per cent. The great majority of these found employment in towns, but the largest part of new housing in towns was built not for them but to satisfy needs that had arisen earlier. Most of these men and women therefore, newly employed in industry, were unable to obtain accommodation in towns and as a result were forced to commute.

All these facts unambiguously indicate that, in Hungary, underdevelopment of the infrastructure, in what are called 'non-productive investments', in urban development and communal services is significantly greater than justified by the position of industry and the economy, that the share of national income of communal investments is much smaller than in the capitalist countries of Europe and that a one-sided strategy of industrial development which, between 1949 and 1970, has allotted 40 per cent. of investment to industry, necessarily found itself in conflict with the objective demands of urban development.

The fast growth in industrial employment and underdevelopment in the infrastructure, principally in housing, leads to underurbanization. In our view those who are forced to keep their village domicile while no longer employed there, because of problems of urban underdevelopment, are, in principle, at a disadvantage. The level of urbanization of different areas of Hungary is indicated by the level of qualification of the labour force in these areas.

(a) Hungarian society as a whole can be called urbanized, taking both the occupational distribution of all those in gainful employment and that of heads of families as indicators. Even in villages, in 1970 the heads of 64 per cent. of the households had their principal employment outside agriculture. Even this is an underestimate of urbanization if actual work done and not the sector of the economy in which someone is employed is considered. Manual work in agriculture (peasant's work in plain words) was the principal employment of only 21 per cent. of those in gainful employment in 1970.

This change has been extremely rapid in recent decades. Manual workers in agriculture as a proportion of those in gainful employment dropped from 36 to 18 per cent. between 1949 and 1970. The 30 per cent. overall who were working in agriculture in 1970 included those doing administrative work in producers' cooperatives, as well as those doing industrial work within agricultural enterprises. Bearing in mind that four-fifths of the population overall in 1970, and even 64 per cent. of those living in villages, did not do agricultural manual work, and that 71 per cent. of the population, 56 per cent. of those living in villages, were not involved in agriculture in any way as their principal employment, one might well ask why so many of them are tied to villages. It is true that there are industries in villages, industries of some significance, but well over half the young people in villages are employed by industry, including the service industries, elsewhere, i.e. not at their domicile. The tension between the location of the employment of a socially urbanized village population and their residential location could potentially lead to fast growth of the urban population, but it could also, thanks to supplementary activities organized by agricultural cooperatives (which have shown surprising initiative in exploiting the opportunities the market offers), lead to a peculiar and unique intermediate structure, perhaps to a new type of village, that is industrial and therefore on the road to urbanization.

We know very little about this very recent social phenomenon. There is occasional news of printing offices, the manufacture of spare parts for motorcars or devotional objects occurring, all within the producers' cooperatives. However, these appear to be somewhat exaggerated. But the high earning opportunities which exist and the labour migration from state enterprises back to enterprises of this sort which is going on certainly indicates that village society is beginning to create an interesting and elastic answer to the difficulties created by migration to towns, that they are in fact making a virtue of necessity. It is well known that there is a significant boom in housing construction in villages, the proportion of dwellings with two or more rooms is 51 per cent. in

Budapest and 55 per cent. in the villages. It is therefore possible that this new type of enterprise will provide an important impetus not only for the urbanization of the village but for urban growth as such.

(b) Available data for 1970 also suggest that there is no longer any particularly significant correlation between the administrative status of the community of domicile and the proportion of those in industrial employment; 59 and 52 per cent. of the population of Budapest and of the villages respectively were engaged in industrial manual work. The correlation was much closer with employment in the service industries; 40 per cent. of heads of households were so employed in Budapest and only 12 per cent. in the villages. It is the same with those doing clerical or professional work; 43 per cent. of these were gainfully employed in Budapest and only 14 per cent. in the villages. On the other hand, unskilled workers made up only 13 per cent. of the work force in Budapest and as much as 39 per cent. in the villages.

All this suggests the characteristic difference between the population of towns and villages is today to a lesser and lesser extent the industrial–agricultural dichotomy, and to a greater extent the division is between manual work in both industry and agriculture, and work in the service industries and of a clerical or professional nature. This means that the categories of vertical or hierarchical social stratification can be applied in order to differentiate between village and urban society. Families of a lower social status live in villages and those of a higher social status in towns; the bulk of those in villages work with their hands, while the proportion of those doing clerical or professional work in 1970 was one-third in towns and two-fifths in Budapest and the larger towns, a significant number of these being employed in the service industries.

As can be seen, the process which generally characterizes the urbanization of developed areas in the second half of this century is making rapid progress in Hungary also. White-collar workers are the most important section in towns, particularly in large towns, and towns particularly distinguished by the high proportion of those working in the service industries, particularly in scientific research, education and the upper reaches of the administration, more than by the presence of industry. If the development of services linked to the infrastructure were not relatively backward in Hungary (and this is so, as indicated by the fact that the proportion of those working in the service industries only increased from 22 to 23 per cent. in the forty years from 1930 to 1970), then the above-mentioned trend would be even more obvious.

It also follows that an urban dwelling, particularly one in a large town, i.e. the acquisition of domicile in such a town, is a considerable advantage, even a privilege, in Hungarian society and one which the higher social strata have a much better chance of acquiring. The slope of the urbanization curve in industrializing Hungarian society therefore corresponds to that of social stratification.

More than half of the village population do industrial work, roughly half do not work where they are domiciled, almost half of those doing manual work in industry live in villages, but only a quarter of those doing clerical or professional work live there. One could add that the stratification of the working class itself indicates that a larger proportion of better qualified and better paid workers live in towns, while those with lower qualifications and earnings live in villages. Once again, it is not the industrial–agricultural dichotomy that characterizes the difference between town and village these days; it can be better interpreted in terms of the hierarchy of social stratification. In this way inequalities deriving from social stratification also find expression as territorial and regional inequalities.

### 3. The Causes and Social Consequences of Delayed Urban Development

The facts described above show that Hungarian urban development has suffered delays and that the country is underurbanized. An attempt must also be made to provide a more systematic explanation of the factors which caused the underurbanization of Hungary and of the extent to which economic policy or regional planning can be held responsible.

Economic factors have played a role in the retarded rate of Hungarian urban development. As indicated earlier, in our view at least, the relatively slow rate of urban development in Hungary is largely due to an economic policy that set extensive industrial development as its principal aim.

Expensive industrialization, i.e. a growth in industrial production resulting neither from technological progress nor an increase in the productivity of labour but quantitative growth of relatively backward means of production and of the labour force, demanded huge industrial investments, and a large pool of free, and cheap, labour. This demand for labour and capital on the part of Hungarian industry growing in an extensive manner basically determined economic policy, agricultural policy and, in particular, policy relating to the infrastructure. Agricultural policy, apart from fixing agricultural prices in a manner that subsidized industrial production, was also designed to supply the labour needs of industry. This meant that, in addition to the extension of female employment, policy relating to the infrastructure had to ensure that the necessary capital was at the disposal of industrial investment. Wages policy was closely related, as the costs of the infrastructure were withdrawn from wages, making the employment of these funds independent of consumer decisions and allowing the central state organs to dispose over time. Wages were fixed at a relatively low level, below the value of labour, and this latter fact produced certain contradictions which are peculiar to the system which has been outlined. Fixing the price of labour below its value turned labour into 'an article in short supply', leading to excess demand both in agriculture and industry and necessitating administrative interference in order to ensure a relative equilibrium in the supply of labour. Early in the sixties measures had to be taken to limit the loss of labour from agriculture, and at present industry is urging acceptance of measures designed to secure a supply of labour. However, the shortage of labour that usually occurred because of the way in which the economy was run until recently must mainly be ascribed to industrial demands.

It follows from the above that the basic objectives of economic policy limited the principles and practice of regional planning and that they necessarily required regional planning to retard urban development. (Regional planning in this sense includes not only planners and research workers specifically concerned with it but all those, largely central, political, planning and administrative organs that are called on to determine or influence the location and distribution of the means of urban development, i.e. investments in general, and particularly the structure of industrial consumption, by virtue of the position they take up, the proposals they make or the decisions they are entitled to take.) Regional planning that retarded urban development cannot be considered simply as a product of hostility to either villages or towns. Hostility to towns or villages was part of the ideological background of regional planning itself, and therefore played a subordinate role only in determining objectives or the means to achieve them. Planning was dominated right from the start by hostility to the infrastructure deriving from economic policy, and planning ideology was only able to modify planning strategy within this context. Therefore a peculiar development occurred: planning based on a value system that was opposed to large cities but which did not actually do much for the progress and growth of community services of villages and hamlets. Those who determined the planning directives paid insufficient attention to the objective factors involved in the growth of the settlement network; rather than analysing certain basic processes, they were more inclined to justify what they were doing with the help of ideological directives. What often became only too obvious in this 'scientific and ideological superstructure' was the desire to cover up the social problems produced by planning (which, it ought to be emphasized, were generally necessary results of the factors referred to above) by either appealing to some general social interest or else by giving planning decisions which affected social interests in the guise of inviolable 'technical decisions'.

Equality was a frequently mentioned general social interest. In a number of earlier papers we have tried to show how this equality worked in practice in housing policy. Equality as a frame of reference was also most important in regional planning and in the areas of economic planning that directly touched on it. Policy and planning decisions related to the infrastructure were particularly important in this respect. As we saw, the aim of centralizing infrastructural investment decisions and withdrawing them from the sphere of consumer decisions was to ensure an increase of industrial investment at the expense of infrastructural investment. Planning ideology presented this as a consequence of the view that the infrastructure was so important that its goods and services had to be made available equally. Effective demand could not be allowed to be generated as a result of differential incomes. The exclusion of certain of the costs of infrastructural development from wages and their inclusion in the government budget was meant to ensure equality of provision and to neutralize the possible effects of social stratification in the distribution of these goods and services. The budget is, however, determined by the outcome of the conflict of various interests, and it was only natural that the stronger, i.e. industry (and in the first place heavy industry which is responsible for production and defence goods), should come out on top. It is important to emphasize once again that a system in which social capital is concentrated at the centre and redistributed by a decision-making structure based on authority has led to the spokesmen of industry of 'productive investments' being able to secure more resources than the spokesmen of the 'non-productive' infrastructure. At the time of the introduction of the new economic mechanism in 1968, those who criticized it because it emphasized market forces and who liked to refer to the democratic principle of equality frequently remembered illusions as if they were the truth, identifying the declared social policy principles of the fifties with the actual policy carried out.

Equality is a basic starting point for Hungarian regional planning. Regional planning must face up to the fact that there is an inherent inequality in growth which is unplanned and uncontrolled; there has never been a country however small, the economic development of which was evenly spread over its whole territory. Equal development is as impossible as an equal race where runners are not allowed either to forge ahead or to fall behind. There are always leading industries which forge ahead, spur development and indicate the direction and rate of growth with the help of investment incentives deriving from temporary disequilibrium. This process comes to the fore both under a market and an administratively regulated system, and results in the locations of leading industries becoming foci for growth. A precondition for the growth of such a focus, i.e. of an agglomeration, is in fact that there is such a group of enterprises or such an industry there, which brings others with it, and hence allow the multiplier effect to operate that particular region, which in turn leads to further growth, of course.

It is also natural that labour should migrate to the growth foci from the stagnating areas. Labour is more productive there, hence *per capita* income is higher. The development of these growth foci can, however, produce a depression in more distant areas if the multiplier effect does not spread to them. The necessarily resulting disequilibrium of growth then undoubtedly increases the social inequalities between individuals and local communities located in the different regions. However, social morality demands that these inequalities be limited.

It was therefore only natural that regional planning should expressly declare putting an end to inequalities between regions to be one of its fundamental objectives. However, one might well ask how this could be assured. Regional planning considered (as more or less given) the distribution of places of domicile within the regional structure, and took as its objectives a more equal distribution of employment opportunities and social advantages in this situation. The impact of this way of looking at things and its consequences can still be discerned today. The full consequences of such an approach are as follows. Given the goal of maintaining the present population distribution throughout the country, then a decentralization of industrial location, a limitation of the growth of great industrial agglomerations and the encouraged industrialization of small towns and of villages turning into towns, as well as limits on changes of domicile, should be aimed at because such administrative measures are required both to put a stop to migration from depressed areas and migration to metropolitan agglomerations. One would naturally welcome any lessening in the difference of the index of industrialization of the capital and the provinces, of developed and depressed areas and of towns and villages. Furthermore, one would not worry about the productiveness or try to calculate the optimum distribution of resources. The aim instead would be a sort of cartographical symmetry: a little of everything everywhere, or at least in every major area in the country. One would have to indicate in advance what one wished to achieve, i.e. a slowing down of internal migration and a considerable resistance to mobility on the part of population, predicting it as a likely trend. The principle that 'every settlement takes one step forward' would have to be given moral emphasis. Also, as the principles of regional planning would be ceaselessly confronted by the efforts of industrial planning to make an optimum use of resources, political and administrative limits would have to be put on further industrial growth in the capital, the establishment of further industrial plants in the Budapest agglomeration would be prohibited, obstacles would be put in the way of the reconstruction of certain plants and economic executives would be rewarded if they succeeded in transferring industrial plants to the provinces, whatever the cost. One assumption in this case would be that it costs less to establish an industrial work place than a dwelling unit. One would have to accept as an axiom that overcrowding in big cities is a major social calamity and one would have to accept, as if it were a law, that the building industry is unable to construct more dwellings per annum in Budapest than it did in the early part of this century. One would presume that the establishment of new plants would continue to be the main feature of industrialization and that industrial plant and equipment would continue to absorb more than half the fact that productive investment would lead to plants employing a low level of technology and demanding low standards of skill, as there were generally low standards of skill and training in the depressed areas. Alternatively, a relatively unskilled labour force would operate advanced technologies in an inefficient way. A system of central distribution of fuel and power resources would have to be maintained, with the justification (which was generally accepted in industry in the fifties) that the stronger must give to the weaker. In this way the further development of the developed areas would be handicapped, without at the same time giving rise to an effective industry and towns of urban appearance providing urban facilities in the underdeveloped areas. One would have to adopt and emphasize as principles the view that industrial concentration and metropolitan agglomerations were a distorted development—what is more a distortion of characteristics of capitalism—and one would have to forget that concentration is a spontaneous tendency shown by socialist industry as well. Living in a big city would have to be interpreted as a disadvantage in itself; more precisely, the advantage would have to be denied to those that desired to move there. One would have to emphasize disorganizational phenomena in big cities and difficulties of adjustment with dramatic emphasis. One would have to maintain, presuming some sort of mythic force, that the metropolitan environment in itself leads to a birth rate which in the long run would not allow the population to reproduce itself, and one would have to be confident that underdeveloped areas with a high birth rate would continue to maintain this despite industrialization. One would have to base all this on a normative statement, declaring it to be a basic condition of socialist development that industrial development must be proportional in all the regions of the country. One would consider it a political achievement if the leading force of the socialist society, i.e. the working class, was distributed in such a way throughout the country that it everywhere became a close neighbour of the cooperative peasantry, and one would presume that this would lead to a strengthening of the socialist social system. To sum up: the fact that the subsistence economy of feudal times and an agricultural society where productivity was low presupposed a fairly even distribution of the population, since undeveloped agriculture demanded a large labour force and would not have been able to supply food to large agglomerations, and that the primitive hygienic conditions and communal services of pre-industrial towns made it impossible for the population to grow beyond certain limits is still to be considered a desirable optimum, which ought to be maintained in a period of high level industrialization, up to the year 2000 and beyond.

This is *reductio ad absurdum* of the consequences of a point of view and the ideology that backs it. Such a strategy of regional development is wrong also because it is unrealizable, or else it can only be maintained given certain authoritarian central decisions, the political preconditions of which are of a kind that one would prefer to do without. It is true of course that such a strategy was never present in a simonpure state, excluding all compromises and rational decisions that paid some respect to reality. It can certainly no longer be found these days. It is a fact, however, that the Hungarian strategy of regional development is not sufficiently clear in its principles even today, that it hesitates between opposed values and that its inner, structural insecurity is also apparent in the fact that in this, the twenty-second year of the planned economy, there is still insufficient correspondence between industrial planning, regional planning and planning at the national administrative level. It is obvious that this fragmentation, this separation between planners and decision makers, does not derive purely from the impotence of those concerned and an absence of a readiness to cooperate on their part, but in the first place from the fact that their efforts and chosen values differ on questions of principle.

This is why the heterogeneous objectives of the strategy of regional development were continually wrecked on the rocks of the actual processes of regional development, that the tendency towards concentration in the long run got the upper hand over attempts to deconcentrate, though these were successful in many places, and that the limitations on internal migration in many ways exacerbated the problem. As a result, reports on regional development are full of complaints against spontaneous processes and postpone into the more and more distant future the time when some sort of equality will be produced. Various groups of planners are continuously accusing each other of failure and the economists, aiming at optimum growth, make shameful concessions to mistaken goals of social policy. Those who support principles of social policy, but whose idealism is getting sad and sour, complain of the conflict between their demands and reality. All this is a result of not fully thinking through the problem, of being encumbered by ideological taboos, and therefore setting up a false dilemma between optimum solutions and human ones based on human needs which take effect both in judging and regulating the structure of society. Finally, and this is even more painful to recall, it was as a result of this approach that the problem of the direction that development was to take remained the 'private concern' of the 'planners club'. Instead of setting out a rational structure of decisions that would actually regulate concentration and deconcentration and that would devolve the right to move capital resources and men on to those most competent to deal with the process of urbanization, i.e. on a great variety of organizations and on every single member of society, rational and not so rational, scientific and not so scientific alternative strategies of regional development all remained within the closed circle of the directing principles of bureaucratic planning, as if all that was involved was governing the world like either a wise or an unreasonable god. It is only a modest first step, but, in our view at least, the recent government regulations increasing the level of local enterprise taxes were more important for regional development than the methodology of regional planning and the associated directives could possibly be, however soundly based they might be based on research and surveys.

We should briefly mention at this stage that the strategies of regional and town planning are interlinked and that they form a system which serves and justifies a single economic policy. We have on a number of occasions pointed out that, in the present housing system, the upper, and in part also the middle, stratum obtain housing (which is built out of state resources and largely subsidized) on the basis of a system of distribution by the authorities. The large majority of manual workers, however, have to build or buy a small house of their own, regardless of the fact that they may or may not consider the way of life associated with living in a small house to be desirable. Furthermore, the building of such houses is limited by a whole series of regulations. Credit facilities are relatively poor, building is prohibited in belts designed to serve another purpose, or in process of being planned, inner and outer urban areas are rigidly delimited and it is forbidden or at best made difficult to build in the cities. All this is scientifically justified by the view that small houses make large demands on communal services and as communal services are provided below cost by the budgetary authorities, as a gift to the population, it is argued that one must carefully consider each case before providing those who build their own houses with such a costly present. However, providing a plot with all possible facilities costs about a tenth as much as a flat built by factory methods, and the latter is also distributed as a present. Moreover, even if one adds the cost of the building itself, the total cost of one of these self-built houses is considerably less than of a modern dwelling unit, of roughly half the size of the house which was produced by the bureaucratic planning construction institutions. The true choice is whether a flat worth 350,000 forints or facilities costing a tenth of that should be given as a present. There is an escape from making this choice: it is to ensure that workers who actually wish to move into towns finally build in their villages. This is largely achieved by the administrative restrictions which have been mentioned. So there is no way in which village workers employed by the industries in the towns can contribute to the development of the urban infrastructure out of their own income, also thereby participating in the advantages of urban life.

What we are trying to show is that, under the conditions which have been outlined, all Hungarian regional and settlement planning has been able to do is to contribute to the slowing down of the process of urbanization, despite the fact that its stated aim was to produce a modern urban network that democratically distributed all the advantages of society. One cannot expect regional or town planning to operate in opposition to the economic order, since the economic use of space is one of the subsystems of the economy, and so it necessarily follows the laws of this system of which it forms part. However, most planners neglected to point out the principles of operation of the economic system and the consequences, therefore, of the sort of development that they proposed. In other words, instead of drawing attention to the economic and social conflicts and the technical problems which derived from the policy of 'saving on' the urban infrastructure (which in fact in the long run handicapped industrial development), they made future projections based on variables which were already distorted and they accepted and stood by a planning mechanism which monopolized the responsibility for every decision and made it utterly impossible to plan the real processes which operated.

However, one cannot argue that the value system of regional planning and the ideological considerations which lay behind it had no effect on the growth of the Hungarian settlement system. As we said earlier, the pattern of growth of the settlement system cannot simply be interpreted as a result of hostility to either towns or villages. Also, though urban growth was slower than justified, this was not compensated for by a faster growth of communal facilities in villages, i.e. of the urbanization of the village. On the contrary, progress in communal facilities in villages has itself in turn been seriously handicapped by the need for capital for industrial investments. The main line of division, therefore, is not between town and country, but between industry and infrastructure. Underurbanization weighs as heavily on towns as on villages. Nevertheless, the antimetropolitan elements in Hungarian regional planning which were pointed out earlier did have their own effect on urban growth. This can be particularly observed in the slowing down of the growth of Budapest as well as in the growth of the population in the belt which surrounds the city. In this paper we are concentrating on the causes, nature and effect of underurbanization and cannot deal with the ways in which delayed urbanization influenced regional inequalities, lessening or perhaps increasing them. However, it is necessary to state that the growth of Budapest was slow compared with that of other towns and that county towns enjoyed certain advantages compared with the capital. These above-average restraints on the growth of the only large city in Hungary can hardly be explained as a result simply of the dominant interests of extensive industrialization. The reason must be the hostility to large towns shown by regional planning.

## 4. Social and Economic Consequences

A structure of social conflicts has come into being as a consequence of this pseudo-urbanization which results from the policies of extensive industrialization and of regional planning which is connected with it. This requires further investigation, but present knowledge already reveals certain significant tendencies as well as allowing certain hypotheses to be formulated. These will aid further research.

One of the peculiar consequences of delayed urbanization is that there is an unequal distribution of the burden of industrialization which weighs heavier on some sections and strata of society than others. It is a characteristic of underurbanization that the growth in industrial employment exceeds the growth in the capacity to absorb population of towns. Thus an increasing number are forced to have their domicile in villages, though they are employed in industry. There is not space here to show that not only did urban growth fall behind industrialization but the growth of urban facilities itself was even slower (especially with respect to services and communication). So standards of public transport, for example, have actually declined in recent decades. 'Saving' on infrastructural expenditure was thus carried out not only at the expense of the rural population working in towns for this purpose but also delayed the growth in the standard of living of the urban population.

The bulk of those newly employed in industry would obviously have preferred to move to town. However, they were unable to obtain a house or flat as five years' residence in the town concerned was the minimum requirement for access to such housing. Those who were not tied to their village of origin socially or who had enough money found a way of building in the urban agglomerations of the major towns. The majority, not being allotted a dwelling free of charge and not being able to purchase one given the rationalized and regulated credit conditions, were marooned outside the towns. They could bring their labour to town, but at best the only place they could stay was a bunk in a hostel dormitory. In the other socialist countries, as well as in Hungary, a dwelling in town came to be a privilege. In Warsaw, for example, people from outside town cannot be allotted a dwelling, they cannot buy one and even to be allowed to register one's domicile with the Warsaw police, the employer must certify that it is absolutely essential that the employee be accommodated locally. As even the right to registration, i.e. the right to live in lodgings as a subtenant, is contigent on bureaucratic permission, one can easily guess that those of a higher status in the organization will find such permission easier to obtain. The result is that, in a given particular factory, the majority of the executives, the technicians, the clerical staff and the skilled tradesmen live in town; the bulk of the semi-skilled and unskilled workers on the other hand have to commute. One can see how urban accommodations turns into a 'feudal' right, and categories of first and second class citizens are created, the metropolitan and the rural population respectively, the privileges of the first group becoming in time monopolies upheld by the administration. Turning urban accommodation, and more generally the infrastructure, the retail trade and the institutional network into a privilege is wholly unjustified because the infrastructure is paid for by a reduction in everybody's potential income, but everyone is not given an equal chance to make use of it. The problem of one million daily or weekly commuters long ago aroused social interest, but most peculiarly the problems generated by commuting are generally seen as things which can be solved by adult education. Newspapers report that workers purchase hard liquor from pot-distillers and that they spend their travelling time playing cards in an alcoholic haze, instead of reading novels. There is no doubt that serious problems arise for the families of weekly commuters because of their long absences from home, as well as because of the extra burden on the family budget which arises from having to feed and house the commuting member in another location from that of the rest of the household. It is certainly also true that a significant proportion of the daily commuters spend more time on crowded public transport than those who live in big cities. A particular problem here arises from the fact that transport timetables are not adjusted to working hours. A division of time comes into being in this way and has the consequence for those involved that they live a life which merely consists of reproducing their labour power.

However, workers commuting from villages do not merely lose part of their leisure; they are also partially deprived of use of the urban infrastructure, to which the surplus value of their work has contributed of course. As we have stated they do not obtain urban housing or the privileges given by access to the network of urban communal services, the retail trade and entertainment and culture. Furthermore, their children cannot attend urban schools that provide higher standards of education. So the disadvantages of commuters are passed on to their successors even while the latter are still at school. In these ways delayed urbanization has placed a significant proportion of the burden of extensive industrialization on the shoulders of commuting workers, without letting them share proportionately in the advantages. Though only a tenth of the Hungarian population are commuters, the contradiction between urban employment and rural domicile also affects members of their families; the disadvantages are thus felt by approximately a quarter of the Hungarian population.

Commuters are mainly peasants who are restratified as workers for eight hours a day. These mainly semi-skilled and unskilled workers make up the 'new working class'. This forms a homogeneous social group which can be described in terms of specific sociological characteristics.

The extent to which those at a social disadvantage are conscious of it is open to question. It may well be that a public opinion survey would justify those descriptive sociologists who, it seems to us, overvalue the esteem in which the village community and the biological advantages of a rural abode are really held. It is likely that the majority of those questioned would actually declare their position to be satisfactory and say that they would not dream of moving into town and nearer their place of employment. One frequently notices though, in the course of carrying out surveys, that people who are socially disadvantaged take a realistic and hence a pessimistic view of the low likelihood of their being able to change their situation; hence they tend to see their current situation in a favourable light when questioned and show less desire for change than their actual dissatisfaction would, in other circumstances, create. It is in fact precisely those who are privileged, in particular professional people, who tend to openly express their dissatisfaction with their actual situation, and it is they who are in fact most able to move, both within the housing and within the settlement system, and who do so. The socio-psychological preconditions for a criticism of reality are generally created by the real existence of a chance of a change.

There is no doubt that the 'new working class' has been able to turn some of its disadvantages to advantage. One can observe villages, particularly in industrial areas, where houses are new and are roomier than those in towns. We know of villages where families of unskilled workers built themselves houses with a floor-area of 150 to 180 square metres, i.e. houses of the average contemporary North American size. There are people who, looking at such houses, tend to question our analysis of the social disadvantages of the 'new working class', professional men and women whose flats, though obtained as a state favour, have a floor-area of no more than 50 square metres.

The position of workers from the village appears as less enviable if we bear in mind that their low industrial earnings and the minimum use they are able to make of the infrastructure is accompanied by a doubling of their working hours. Following eight hours work and long hours spent waiting and travelling, they are often met at the station by their wives, carrying two hoes, and they go off for another four or five hours work on land allotted to them as share-croppers by the cooperative or to their own household plots, which in the course of the years have been turned into extremely intensively cultivated small-holdings. A peculiar social class has come into being which lives in two economic systems at the same time, and which shows great sensitivity towards the movements that establish the state of equilibrium between the two. If there is a boom in industry, this group's labour power is transferred there; if in agriculture, then it limits or temporarily suspends its industrial work. This group comprise the bulk of the migrant labour force that is so often cursed by industry for its instability. However, this is not caused by any lack of discipline, but by the fact that the conflict between domicile and place of employment leads them to fight in this way for higher wages. Though 'new workers' may appear to be defenceless at first sight, they are certainly not powerless in the great struggle that goes on over the distribution of goods. In fact we are able to see that the system of economic growth can work in their favour in a kind of way and this extraordinary mobile section of society, not tied to any town, may well profit from the shortage of labour which is now becoming chronic towards the end of the period of extensive industrialization.

Executives of industrial enterprises located in agricultural areas complain that, while people in earlier years queued up outside labour recruiting offices, all the present publicity which now seeks to attract them is providing useless. They state that the booming agricultural producers' cooperatives are attracting the best of the skilled labour from the industrial enterprises, because (in the early seventies) they have been able to pay an hourly rate of 16–17 forints in their repair workshops and supplementary enterprises, while industrial enterprises are limited to paying 12–13 forints. The means which industrial executives have to close this gap are pretty limited; they can provide better working conditions, cleaner showers and better lunches, etc., and the foreman can adopt a more polite tone of voice, but all that cannot counterbalance the necessarily low wages. Some executives then enter into complex partnerships with cooperatives which have greater market freedom and so, following various book-keeping tricks, are able to pay their own workers a better rate in the interests of carrying out their productive objectives. However, they can easily find themselves in conflict with regulations that express a contradictory econo-mico-legal system or with the authorities which interpret the latter in various ways.

The growth in the economic power of the 'new worker' is largely due to the fact that agriculture was also able to turn disadvantage to advantage. A shortage of labour caused by the attraction of industry was counterbalanced by more intensive agricultural techniques, and this is already bearing fruit in the form of higher agricultural incomes. We may be at the threshold of an historical period where a stable agriculture sets the pace, and not industry. Extensive industrialization has created an industrial system whose super-structure is to be found in towns and whose lower level workers are in villages. This part of the labour force is able to melt away in the manner we have described because of the bureaucratically controlled limited access to the superstructure. Industry is now being punished for the monopoly position which it earlier enjoyed and which enabled administrative steps taken in its then current interests. Industry took away the financial resources from the infrastructure; as a result it slowed down the growth of towns, at the same time depriving itself of a town-based labour force that was tied to industrial employ-ment and an urban way of life. It was therefore defenceless in the face of an activity which is given greater market freedom by the economic system and which has been able to operate more flexibly in the labour market. A major conflict of social interests has thus been produced. This conflict will present economic policy with new choices which it must make in the immediate future.

One way of dealing with the situation could be the employment of administrative methods, involving a higher taxation of agricultural incomes and administrative limits on the mobility of labour, as well as a further putting off of investment in the infrastructure, and hence of urban development. The other possible answer would be to enlist the aid of economic measures by further developing the regulative system, particularly wages and incomes policy, as well as an insistance, especially by industrial executives, that infrastructural investments is paid for partly by local government rates and taxes and partly by a series of strategic decisions about distribution. One can see that, to an increasing extent, industrial executives and regional planners are beginning to realize that industrial development and housing construction are indivisible, and it is in the same way that has been outlined above that industry could answer the challenge of agriculture within the framework of economic competition. This approach would also produce a dynamic equilibrium in the labour market. However paradoxical this may sound, we expect a boom in urbanization and at least a partial solution of the social conflicts of delayed urban growth to occur precisely as a consequence of further intensive growth in agriculture.

# 9
# From 'Social Base' to 'Social Force': Some Analytical Issues in the Study of Urban Protest

*C. G. Pickvance*

The present paper is essentially a sequel to an earlier article[1] in which I attempted to initiate a discussion of the series of studies of 'urban social movements' undertaken in the last few years, mainly in France, by writers adopting a Marxist perspective.[2]

It was argued there that these studies overemphasized the role of protest movements (as opposed to local authorities) in obtaining changes in the 'urban system',[3] failed to adequately conceptualize local authorities and the social processes within them which affected their response to protest movements, and emphasized popular mobilization to the exclusion of other modes of protest action (such as personal approaches and 'institutional' methods) as reasons for their success (or lack of success). Finally, it was suggested that the resources available to organizations were a neglected but crucial influence on their survival and success.

These characteristic emphases reflect the specifically Marxist approach adopted. However, in my view, they are not intrinsic to that approach. For example, the exigencies of capital accumulation may, in certain conjunctures, create a predisposition at central and local government levels to respond favourably to protest movements seeking goals involving cuts in expenditure, e.g. abolition of motorway plans, housing improvement rather than demolition and rebuilding in certain cases, provided that the cancellation of schemes does not impair too greatly the functioning of the urban system. This predisposition will presumably be stronger in the case of local authorities in areas with large middle class populations and controlled by political parties ideologically committed to low levels of expenditure. Thus a greater analytical emphasis on government predispositions (provided they are explained in terms of class economic, political and ideological purposes), as opposed to protest action, is quite consistent with a Marxist approach.

Consequently, I see no incompatibility between adopting a Marxist approach to urban protest movements and complementing it with analyses which explicate some of the questions which have not received due attention in the studies so far. In the present paper I shall attempt to illustrate this argument by examining a further topic in the study of urban protest, namely the question of how a 'social base' becomes a 'social force', or how a population affected by an urban issue becomes mobilized. It will be suggested that some non-Marxist analyses enable us to go further towards answering this question than the Marxist studies mentioned.

The framework used to analyse urban protest movements in the studies referred to above was first advanced by Castells, who described it as 'a semi-theoretical, semi-descriptive classification of the components of each action'.[4] It comprises the following elements, in terms of which any protest movement is categorized: the issues at stake (or 'stakes'), the 'social base' affected or concerned, the organizations present, the 'social force' constituted, the opponent, the demands made, the mode of action adopted and the effects on the urban system and political system resulting. These elements are then related in the form of hypotheses, e.g. the lower the socio-economic level of the social base the greater the chances of implantation of a revolutionary political organization, providing it has a local base.[5]

We shall focus on the notions of social base, organization and social force in the belief that the inter-relation of these concepts deserves much more detailed analysis than it has received in the studies citied.[6] It will be argued that the link between social base and social force can be more thoroughly understood by means of concepts developed in non-Marxist sociology and that such an understanding is essentially complementary to that provided by the Marxist analyses which have appeared so far.

## 1. Social Base

To start with we shall examine the notion of *social base*. This refers to the population directly concerned or affected by the issue at stake.

The major weakness of the conceptualization of 'social base' in the Marxist studies of urban protest is, in my view, that it is almost entirely *demographic*— in other words, that, for the most part, it refers only to the class, ethnic, migrant and other characteristics of the *individuals* within the population concerned. This might be adequate if one was interested only at the most general level in the types of population in which protest groups developed. However, if one seeks a detailed understanding of how social bases are transformed into social forces a purely demographic approach is inadequate. Such an understanding requires that attention be paid to the *social structure* of the population, in the social anthropological sense of a system of social relationships, as well as its demographic structure.

The structure of social relations emerging in a given social base will be partly created by organized groups and institutions and partly by informal ties of kinship, friendship, etc., which develop outside any organized setting. If the social base is largely dependent upon the same institutions of work, education, church, etc., and if the density of organizations is very high, then 'multiplex' relations, i.e. relations which have several normative contents[7], will be common since people will encounter each other in several roles.[8] Conversely, a social base may contain a minimal number of multiplex relations, due to dependence on many and scattered institutions and low organization density. The extent of existing organizations within a local population is an important influence on its mobilization into protest movements.[9] Granovetter notes how 'weak ties' created through organizational participation can be an unexpectedly potent means for the circulation of information and hence the emergence of organization.

Clearly, then, it is not sufficient to know the demographic characteristics of the social base. Certainly social structure partly reflects demographic characteristics, but there is no simple relation between the two features, so the latter cannot be taken as an index of the former. We need to know not only, for example, the class and ethnic composition of the social base but to what extent class and ethnic divisions are reflected in the social structure. Are they important criteria of differentiation in social practices or not? Are inter-class and inter-ethnic relationships, informal groupings, organizations, etc., existent or not? Only when we know this can we determine to what extent a social base is likely to act in a united way or is likely to act in a fragmented way along class or ethnic lines.[10] In brief, the concept of social structure is at a different level of abstraction from that of population (since it refers to relations between individuals and not to individuals as such) and must be studied as a distinct characteristic of the social base.

A second aspect of the social base which passes unnoticed in most Marxist studies of urban protest[11] is what may be termed 'value-orientations'. I will use this term to refer to tendencies for action to take certain courses, which in actual situations are subject to constraints which fully or partially prevent their realization. (It is thus not possible to predict action from value-orientations since the nature of the situational constraints is unknown.) Value-orientations represent responses to social experience, *past and present* (and possibly depend on non-social factors too). If non-social factors are ignored, value-orientations may be legitimately used in explanations of present social phenomena, since they summarize the effect of past social experience. However, they must only be seen as second-best explanations since they do not allow identification of the past social experience to which they are responses.

Value-orientations, like social structure, are an analytically distinct aspect of the social base and cannot therefore be inferred from, for example, a knowledge of class structure though empirically, of course, there will be a correlation between the two aspects. The particular value-orientations likely to be of importance in the study of urban protest are those relating to motivations for participation in protest activity and protest organizations. For example, the author of a study of the Campaign against Racial Discrimination in Britain in the mid-1960s writes that 'Those involved in C.A.R.D. at the outset brought to the organization a number of models from their own experiences with the organizations'.[12] These 'models' of possible modes of activity and organization were orientations to activity within C.A.R.D. based on past experience, and, according to the author, their incompatibility gave rise to 'contradictory strains'.

The only studies of 'urban social movements' where value-orientations in the social base are described are those of squatting movements where the orientation of crucial importance is motivation to participate. According to Cherki, in the French squatting movement:

'Demands (type of rehousing demanded or accepted) and struggles are still economic in character, in the sense that squatting is seen as a means of satisfying an immediate economic need (housing) . . . . The political consciousness of the protagonists of the movement, the political aims of the movement, are not defined . . . .'[13]

To turn to a concrete case of squatting in Paris, a member of a political group which supported squatting for political reasons reports that 'In fact this fraction (immigrants) of squatters at No. 17 came to be rehoused without setting too many conditions. They didn't come to take part in a political struggle . . .'[14] And, in another case, the same writer illustrates the divergent orientations to squatting as follows:

'During a meeting a young woman who wanted to squat asked Robert: "You, why do you want to squat?". Robert: "What a question! I'm squatting because I've nowhere to live". "Me", said the young woman, "I've got somewhere to live, but I've come to support the squatting movement". Robert never came back. It is a fairly safe bet that this confusion between ideological motivations and practical motivations caused the breakup of the group.'[15]

The significance of this division in orientations to squatting is indicated in the vast gulf between the group of militants with their carefully defined political line and the squatters themselves whose political commitments are less clear and who are acidly described by the militant as being 'ready to abandon at the slightest setback those who have given them support'.[16]

In view of Cherki's judgement, quoted above, that demands and struggles in the French squatting movement are still economic, and that its political aims are undefined, it is somewhat surprising that in his final assessment he rejects an economistic interpretation on the grounds that it fails to grasp the political–ideological aspects of the movement. His evidence for the latter aspects is (a) that squatting represents an attack on private property and (b) that new relationships and levels of political consciousness emerge among groups of squatters themselves.[17] However, it would seem safer to stress the economic (practical) rather than the political (ideological) aspects of the movement since from his own evidence political orientations are of considerably more importance to the militants who support squatting than to the squatters themselves who are primarily in search of housing.[18]

In sum, we have argued that before we can use 'social base' as an element in sociological analysis of urban protest we must pay due attention to the social structure and value-orientations of the social base and not merely to its demographic characteristics. So far Marxist studies have failed to do this.

## 2. Social Force

We may now proceed to the second aspect of the question of how a social base is transformed into a social force. For Castells this transformation depends on the nature of issues at stake and the implantation of an organization with either reformist or revolutionary aims and which may or may not be explicitly political.[19] (The type of organization, type of protest action and type of demands made are said to be interlinked.)

In most of the studies of urban social movements so far very little attention has been paid to the process of mobilization.[20] The issues at stake and social base affected are said to be determined by structural contradictions, and the social force appears from the social base at a wave of the magic v and of organization. This appears to me to ignore what is not only a major theoretical problem but also a major problem for political practice, namely how, in Marxian terms, does a class in itself become a class for itself? To answer by the implantation of a revolutionary political group simply moves the question one step further back: under what conditions is this possible? Does one detect a certain reluctance on the part of the authors of studies of urban social movements to become involved in the analysis of consciousness? Certainly Rex's comment that 'the Marxist tradition has never adequately clarified what is involved sociologically speaking in the formation of a class-for-itself',[21] would seem to have a certain pertinence here. Rex's own work, within the Weberian tradition, is, in my opinion, one of the most valuable contributions in this field, and this is precisely because he recognizes the importance of the social structure and value-orientationa as well as the demographic characteristics of the social base and its potential for political mobilization. A brief outline of his work on this subject will now be given.

In 1967 Rex and Moore published a sociological study of a zone of transition in Sparkbrook, Birmingham, which was known as an immigrant area.[22] The focus of the study was access to housing as an urban resource by coloured immigrants. In the study, Rex and Moore argued, inter alia, that 'there is a class struggle over the use of houses and that this class struggle is the central process of the city as a social unit'.[23] Class was here being used in the wider Weberian sense of groups arising with shared interests in any market, and not solely the labour market. Hence the concept of 'housing class' was developed to refer to persons whose access to housing in the public or private housing sectors was the same. Housing class and social class were seen as logically independent and the implicit question was whether immigrants and native in the same social class were nevertheless to be found in different housing classes. Rex and Moore went on to distinguish a number of housing classes present in Sparkbrook.[24]

For our purposes the theme of interest in Rex's analysis is the process by which housing classes became 'classes-for-themselves'. Rex's approach to this question is twofold: to ask whether housing class is the only form of consciousness present or whether other 'definitions of the situation' are present which obstruct its development, and to ask whether or not the organizational means exist which could serve as vehicles for housing class action.

Firstly, Rex identifies two forms of *consciousness* which compete with consciousness of housing class (and social class) interests. The first is a set of value-orientations he terms the 'urban value system'[25] which refers to a hierarchical ranking of 'ways of life' in different districts of the city and different types of housing (from private suburban owner-occupation downwards) such that oppositions between housing classes are overlaid. (The parallel is with the way in which perception of the social class structure as a ladder to which access is open to all overlays the 'objective' dichotomous class structure.) The second form of consciousness derives from the fact that Sparkbrook is an 'immigrant area'. Immigrants are seen as participating in a three-stage process of 'adjustment': a brief stage of anomie when ties to the home society are weakened and employment is the only tie to the host society; formation of 'an intimate primary sub-community'[26] with others of the same ethnic group providing help with personal problems, a meaningful social world and preventing social isolation; and finally a stage in which the immigrant develops contacts outside this group, exercises his rights as a citizen and eventually leaves the 'colony' life of the immigrant area. It is the second stage, the ethnic community or colony, which provides the alternative form of consciousness to housing interest, namely ethnic consciousness. This is likely to create links across housing class lines, e.g. between immigrant landlord and immigrant tenant who 'cannot see their relationship as based solely on the cash nexus'.[27]

Consciousness based on the 'urban value system' and ethnic identity, then, provide alternatives to housing (and social) class consciousness which prevent the formation of housing classes-for-themselves. Not only may consciousness of housing class interests be absent but the *organizational means* necessary for the formation of a class-for-itself may also be lacking. Rex suggests that

'the area in which one would begin to look for a partial development of housing classes so that they become classes-for-themselves is in the study of the organisations, norms, values, beliefs and sentiments of the associations, which exist in great profusion in the city.'[28]

He argues that independent of their explicit purpose these associations help members overcome social isolation, provide meaningful social worlds for them, act as trade unions in defence of members' interests or do social work. The first and last functions are linked to the colony structure in the city, the third is linked to the development of interest groups and the second to both.[29] In other words, the organizational means to the formation of a housing class-for-itself may have been 'pre-empted by colony-like structures'.[30]

Thus, I would suggest that Rex's analysis demonstrates very clearly the need to examine closely alternative forms of *consciousness*[31] which may prevent the transformation of a social base into a social force and the availability of *organizational forms* to act as vehicles for the social force.

### 3. Participation in Organizations

To conclude our discussion of the necessary conditions for the transformation of a social base into a social force we shall examine some of the factors affecting participation in organizations. We shall refer mainly to studies of 'voluntary associations' which have started to tackle this problem.

So far it has been argued that organization around an issue takes place when competing forms of consciousness are absent and the issue is clearly identified and when the organizational means are available. To complete an account of participation in protest movements, however, we need to pay attention to (a) other influences on participation besides the salience of the issue itself and (b) the effect of the organization in which individuals join together to protest.

For most potential members of a protest organization participation will be a leisure-time activity. A categorical statement cannot be made, however, since there exists a growing body of neighbourhood workers, community workers and social workers (in addition to the traditional parish priest) for whom such participation is more or less part of their work role, i.e. who would be judged to be failing in their duties if they did not take an active part, or even lead, protest organizations.

For a large part of the membership, however, participation will be an activity which competes for resources of time, money and commitment, with other social obligations. It is banal but nevertheless true that the time people have free for protest activity depends on the time occupied by participation in work and domestic roles.[32] These roles affect the *amount of time* (e.g. due to overtime working or coping unaided with young children) and the *timing of its availability* (e.g. due to shift working).[33] Insofar as participation demands a membership fee the association will be selective in terms of ability to pay. Low fees are probably more common in organizations where extent of membership is an end in itself, e.g. to legitimate pressure group action, than in more 'expressive' associations where, on the contrary, social selectivity may be deliberately sought. The amount of commitment entailed by protest organization membership is likely to vary from very little to very much.[34] The source of this commitment is a particularly interesting question. According to one writer: 'Membership originating in individual voluntary commitment, from the community alone, is quite rare and ... most memberships can be explained as a correlate of social relations, mostly those of work.'[35] In other words, membership is usually engendered by membership of another institution such as work of church. However, this may be less true of protest organizations than organizations in general.

Given the time, money and commitment to engage in protest activity, a potential member may still not join an organization because the implicit terms of entry make it unattractive to him. By 'terms of entry' I mean the obligations a person has to accept in order to pursue the protest goal. The two crucial obligations are acceptance of the form of the organization (how formal, how informal) and acceptance of association with the other members.

It is a commonplace that 'voluntary associations' are a peculiarly middle class form of organization. This is more than a statistical observation. There seems to be an 'elective affinity' between the middle class and formal modes of organization which emphasize verbal and reasoning skills, planning activities, taking initiatives, following formal procedures, keeping records, etc. In other words, the skills such associations demand and the intermediate rewards they offer (in terms of correct execution of procedures, rather than attainment of ultimate protest goals) make them particularly attractive to the middle class who possess the required skills and have jobs where bureaucratic procedures are a daily reality. In others words, the form of an organization in pursuit of a given protest goal will deter from membership those who find it unacceptable, thereby limiting the organization's potential support.[36]

Similarly the obligation to interact with other members who share the protest goal will prevent the full mobilization of the social base (and prevent the 'whole from being equal to the sum of the parts'). This may be because of members' differing value-orientations (as we saw in the discussion of squatters where ideological and economic orientations to squatting were a source of conflict), differing social backgrounds (in terms of class or ethnic group), differing political lines, etc. The real question is not whether a variety of value-orientations, social backgrounds, etc., exists within a social base—since uniformity is impossible—but to what extent potential participants in a protest organization are willing to tolerate interaction with those of divergent views in pursuit of a given goal. In other words, to what extent built-in tendencies to fission can be held in check.

So far we have discussed the 'terms of entry' imposed by the obligation to interact with other members without mentioning the factor which is probably a pre-condition to any level of organization, namely trust. We shall conclude by briefly illustrating the relevance of trust in social interaction and formal organization.

Suttles has demonstrated that in a multiethnic area, which is publicly stigmatized as a 'slum' and its residents regarded as outsiders with suspicion and mistrust, interaction of any kind must be regarded as problematic since the necessary basis of trust is lacking.[37] For Suttles this means that in such an area the Durkheimian problem of how a moral order develops is posed with an added sharpness. His analysis demonstrates two strategies by which residents of the area respond to the public image of mistrust to develop safe relationships: the first is restriction of contacts to members of the household and kin, i.e. to relationships where trust already exists; the second is the establishment of 'personal' relations with non-kin by a large-scale exchange of information which provides mutual assurance of worth. These two strategies are limited: the first by the number of kin and the second by the time-consuming nature of the exchange of information and demands of intimate relationships. However, according to Suttles, the strategies nevertheless provide a basis for the extension of trust since knowledge of an individual, and hence trust, may be generalized to the ethnic, age, sex or territorial category to which he belongs.

Roberts has extended this analysis to the problem of formal organization (as opposed to informal interaction) in two low-income neighbourhoods.[38] He argues that formal organization is possible either when there are people who 'have the types of jobs and income that make them appear publicly trustworthy',[39] as was the case in one neighbourhood, or where there is a preexisting network of personal acquaintances within an area where mistrust is the norm, as in the second neighbourhood. However, in the latter case he found that formal organization was imposed by groups outside the neighbourhood in pursuit of their own aims, rather than being a locally determined response. Such externally imposed formal organization gave rise to conflict and dissension as members attempted in vain to reconcile their personal knowledge of each other with external insistence that members should be restricted to their allotted functions.

The analyses of Suttles and Roberts are a salutory reminder that work based on middle class neighbourhoods cannot be generalized to organization in neighbourhoods where the symbols of trust are lacking. They provide a possible explanation of the prevalence of the 'respectable' working class among the leadership of working class organizations. Most of all, for present purposes, they indicate how 'mobilization of the social base' implies, in certain neighbourhoods, interaction inside organizations with others who are not relatives or personal friends and thus lie outside the limits of the trusted, thereby providing a strong disincentive to membership.

In brief, we have argued that participation in protest organizations is conditional on accepting certain 'terms of entry' as regards the form of organization and interaction with other members, which are likely to deter some part of the social base from becoming mobilized. Thus, the character of protest organization has certain effects on participation (in addition to acceptance or not of its political line) which need to be studied at the same time as the availability of time, money and commitment to join.

In conclusion, we hope to have indicated a number of aspects of urban protest movements which have been neglected or ignored in Marxist analyses on this theme so far. The social base must be seen in terms of social structure and value-orientations as well as demographic characteristics; the competing forms of consciousness obstructing awareness of issues and availability of organizations for class action must be ascertained; and, finally, the availability of potential members with time, money and commitment, and the way in which they are attracted or deterred by the available protest organizations, must be studied. Only then can the full complexity of the process by which a social base is transformed into a social force be understood.[40]

## Notes

1. Pickvance, C. G., On the study of urban social movements, *Sociological Review*, **23**, 24–49, 1975.
2. Olives, J., La lutte contre la rénovation urbaine dans le quartier de 'la cité d'Aliarte' (Paris), *Espaces et Sociétés*, **6–7**, 9–27, 1972 (English translation in *Urban Sociology: Critical Essays* (Ed. C. G. Pickvance), Methuen, London, 1976); Collectif Chili, Revendication urbaine, stratégie politique et mouvement social des pobladores au Chili, *Espaces et Sociétés*, **6–7**, 37–57, 1972; Anon., Logement et lutte de classes:

compte-rendu d'une pratique militante de quartier à Paris, *Espaces et Sociétés*, **6–7**, 59–88, 1972; Cherki, E., Le mouvement d'occupation de maisons vides en France, *Espaces et Sociétés*, **9**, 69–71, 1973; Lentin, F., Le quartier de la Mouffe en rébellion, *Espaces et Sociétés*, **9**, 93–113, 1973; Pingeot, F., and Robert, M., Environment, lutte urbaine et interêts de classe, *Espaces et Sociétés*, **9**, 133–142, 1973. (The authors of all but the third of these studies take an explicitly 'structuralist' Marxist viewpoint.) A further study, which does not take a Marxist standpoint, is by Bonnier, F., Les pratiques des associations de quartier et les processus de 'récuperation', *Espaces et Sociétés*, **6–7**, 29–35, 1972.

3. Following Castells, 'urban system' refers to 'the specific articulation of the instances of the social structure within a (spatial) unit of reproduction of labour power' (Castells, M., *La Question Urbaine*, Maspero, Paris, 1972, p. 299; note that all translations are my own). Reproduction, in this sense, refers to the provision of collective facilities of all kinds (educational, medical, recreational, housing, etc.) required to reproduce labour power. Note that the terms urban protest movement, urban social movement, etc., will be used interchangeably, and not to indicate specific types of urban effect.

4. *Ibid.*, p. 421.

5. *Ibid.*, p. 421.

6. Admittedly, deliberate and justified secrecy may be one reason for the relative neglect of this topic in published work, but if one's aim is to demonstrate a mode of analysis, rather than to fully describe a concrete case, this consideration need not always be an obstacle.

7. See Mitchell, J. C., The concept and use of social networks, in *Social Networks in Urban Situations* (Ed. J. C. Mitchell), Manchester University Press, Manchester, 1969, pp. 20–24.

8. In one of the three urban protest movements described by Castells and Godard in Dunkerque, France, such multiplexity was present since the residents concerned worked in the same factory. See Castells, M., and Godard, F., *Monopolville*, Mouton, Paris, 1974, p. 418.

9. Coleman, J. S., *Community Conflicts*, Free Press, Glencoe, 1957; Granovetter, M. S., The strength of weak ties, *American Journal of Sociology*, **78**, 1360–1380, 1973.

10. This is not to suggest that existing social divisions will necessarily persist, for example, in the face of a threat to the population as a whole, but they are a fact of life which any potential new organization must come to terms with.

11. The exceptions are the studies of squatting discussed below.

12. Heineman, B. W., *The Politics of the Powerless*, Oxford University Press, London, 1972, p. 21.

13. Cherki, E., Le mouvement d'occupation des maisons vides en France, *Espaces et Sociétés*, **9**, 69–91, 1973.

14. Anon., Logement et lutte de classes: compte-rendu d'une pratique militante de quartier à Paris, *Espaces et Sociétés*, **6–7**, 59–88, 1972.

15. *Ibid.*, p. 83.

16. *Ibid.*, p. 76. The writer states that 'the masses, especially when they are unorganised, as in the neighbourhoods, couldn't care less about the initials (of the political group): they go to whoever acts, takes concrete steps or initiatives'. See also pp. 69 and 77.

17. Cherki, E., Le mouvement d'occupation des maisons vides en France, *Espaces et Sociétés*, **9**, 69–91, 1973.

18. A similar conclusion regarding both squatting and transport users' protest movements is reached by Verdes-Leroux, J., in Les conditions de transport: object de mobilisation, *Sociologie du Travail*, **3**, 225–246 (at p. 244), 1974.

19. See Castells, N., *La Question Urbaine*, Maspero, Paris, 1972., p. 421, and Olives, J., La lutte contre la rénovation urbaine dans le quartier de 'la cité d'Aliarte' (Paris), *Espaces et Sociétiés*, **6–7**, 9–27, 1972.

20. The important exception to this is the study of Chilean 'pobladores' in which attention

is paid to the conditions facilitating the implantation of political lines (Collectif Chili, Revendication urbaine, stratégie politique et mouvement social des pobladores au Chili, *Espaces et Sociétiés* **6–7**, 37–57, 1972.

21. Rex, J., The concept of housing class and the sociology of race relations, *Race*, **12**, 293–301, 1971.
22. Rex, J., and Moore, R., *Race, Community and Conflict*, Oxford University Press, London, 1967. According to Karn, 10 per cent. of the population was West Indian, 6 per cent Pakistani and Indian, and 15 per cent Irish (Karn, V., A note on race, Community and Conflict: a Study of Sparkbrook, *Race*, **9**, 100–104, 1967).
23. Rex and Moore, *ibid.*, p. 273.
24. The present discussion makes no attempt to do justice to the complexity of the argument advanced by Rex and Moore. For a full presentation see Rex and Moore, *ibid.*, especially pp. 1–18 and 272–285; Rex, J., The concept of housing class and the sociology of race relations, *Race*, **12**, 293–301, 1971; and Rex, J., The sociology of a zone of transition, in *Readings in Urban Sociology* (Ed. R. E. Pahl), Pergamon, London, 1968. For criticisms see Karn, V., A note on Race, Community and Conflict: a Study of Sparkbrook, *Race*, **9**, 100–104, 1967. Haddon, R., A minority in a welfare state society—the location of West Indians in the London housing market, *The New Atlantis*, **1**, (80–133), 1970; Lambert, J., and Filkin, C., Race relations research: some issues of approach and application, *Race*, **12**, (329–335), 1971; Dahya, B., The nature of Pakistani ethnicity in industrial cities in Britain, in *Urban Ethnicity* (Ed. A. Cohen), A. S. A. Monographs No. 12, Tavistock, London, 1974; and Pahl, R. E., Social process and spatial structure, in *Whose City*, 2nd ed., Penguin, Harmondsworth, London, 1975.
25. Rex and Moore, *ibid.*, p. 9.
26. Rex, J., The sociology of a zone of transition, in *Readings in Urban Sociology*, (Ed. R. E. Pahl), Pergamon, London, 1968, p. 219.
27. *Ibid.*, p. 221. For another analysis of the conditions under which ethnicity is socially significant, see Hannerz, U., Ethnicity and opportunity in urban America, *in Urban Ethnicity*, (Ed. A. Cohen), A.S.A. Monographs No. 12, Tavistock, London, 1974.
28. Rex, J., The concept of housing class and the sociology of race relations, *Race*, **12**, 293–301, 1971, p. 299.
29. *Ibid.*, p. 299.
30. *Ibid.*, p. 296.
31. In addition, of course, it is likely that the issue at stake will be the object of deliberate mystification in order to prevent the emergence of a social force around them or, as Cohen and Comaroff put it, the 'management of meaning' (Cohen, A. P., and Comaroff, J. C., The management of meaning, to be published in *New Directions in Social Anthropology* (Ed. B. Kapferer), A. S. A. Monograph No. 14, Tavistock, London.

The paper presented by Lambert, J., Paris, C. and Blackaby, R. to the York Conference, 'Neighbourhood Politics and Housing Opportunities', shows clearly how the non-emergence of protest movements among council housing applicants may be partly explained by 'methods of management which obscure and mystify the class base of issues' (p. 7 of mimeo version). Thus the queue, which is presented by local state institutions as a fair and legitimate means of access to council housing, 'by its very nature divides the interests of the urban poor' (p. 16 of mimeod version). Presumably this is so in two senses: setting those not eligible for council housing against those who are, and setting the latter against each other.) The result is that individual 'personal battles' are not linked in collective action. Thus the point is not that the dominant ideology of the queue necessarily smothers the emergence of collective action but that by its existence it makes it more difficult for alternative forms of consciousness (particularly radical value systems, to use Parkin's term in *Class Inequality and Political Order*) to emerge.

32. It is not necessarily true, however, that involvement in one leisure organization makes involvement in another less likely. In a study carried out by the author of members of a voluntary association it was found, on the contrary, that members who belonged to more other organizations participated *more* in the association than those who belonged to few other organizations ($r = 0.24$).

33. For example, Roberts, describing neighbourhood political organization in Guatamala City, writes that 'people are willing to be recruited if their jobs allow them the time flexibility to be useful in organising but without incurring prohibitive costs to themselves' (Roberts, B. R., *Organising Strangers: Poor Families in Gautamala City*, University of Texas Press, Austin, 1973, p. 292).

34. The latter category includes the small minority of the population for whom organizations are a 'way of life'. The existence of such a minority is attested by all statistical surveys of the extent of voluntary association membership. For example, Horton shows that 52 per cent of the population belong to no organizations, or do belong but spend less than one hour per month on them, but 9 per cent spend 21 hours or more per month on them. (Horton, M., *The Local Government Elector*, Management of Local Government, Vol. 3, HMSO, London, 1967, p. 116).

35. Ross, J. C., Toward a reconstruction of voluntary association theory, *British Journal of Sociology*, **23**, 20–32 (at p. 27), 1972.

36. For a discussion of the differential attractiveness of formal and informal modes of organization, see Weissman, H. H., *Community Councils and Community Control: the Workings of Democratic Mythology*, University of Pittsburgh Press, Pittsburgh, 1970.

37. Suttles, G. D., *The Social Order of the Slum*, University of Chicago Press, Chicago, 1968, especially pp. 3–9 and 223–234.

38. Roberts, B. R., *Organising Strangers: Poor Families in Guatamala City*, University of Texas Press, Austin, 1973, pp. 152, 229–234.

39. *Ibid.*, p. 233.

40. This analysis abstracts from the 'political conjuncture' (balance of forces in the class struggle generally) which, as Borja and Mingione have argued, cannot be ignored. Thus Mingione distinguishes between cases where the working class is socially integrated and protest organizations short lived and isolated from each other, and cases of overt class conflict (as in Italy) where protest organizations are linked with other organizations in the working class movement. Similarly, Borja distinguishes three political conjunctures and their corresponding types of protest organization in ascending degree of working class strength: 'protest movement', 'democratic movement' and 'duality of power'. For details see Mingione, E., Theoretical Elements for a Marxist Analysis of Development, Ch. 4; Borja, J., Movimientos urbanos y estructura urbana, *Cuadernos de Analisis Urbanos*, **1**, 15–42, 1974 (Published by Departamento de Geografia, Universidad Autonoma de Barcelona). I would like to thank Celina Albano for a summary translation of the latter article.

# 10
# Urban Movements in Spain

*Jordi Borja*

## 1. The High Social Costs of Urbanization

During the last twenty years Spain has been transformed into an urban industrial society. The concentration of both economic activities and population began immediately after the end of the Civil War (1939). Increasing slowly during the forties, it gathered momentum in the early fifties. At the beginning of the century the population of urban centres of more than 50,000 inhabitants was 13 per cent. of the total and almost 70 per cent. lived in nuclei of less than 10,000 inhabitants. However, at the beginning of the seventies 45 per cent. lived in centres of more than 50,000 and only 30 per cent. in those of less than 10,000 inhabitants. At the same time the structure of the economically active population has undergone a radical transformation (see Table 1).

This evolution appears to show:

(*a*) The irreversible and incomplete transformation of the agrarian structure, and the emigration from the countryside of tenants and small proprietors which will continue during the seventies.

(*b*) The growth of the tertiary sector, a phenomenon consequent on and generally produced by industrialization. Between the fifties and seventies the typical process in which urban growth augments a parasitic and marginal tertiary sector did not occur in Spain, although there was a significant sub-employed sector in the construction industry, particularly between 1950 and 1960.

(*c*) Between 1960 and 1970 industrial growth was greater than the figures for active population (33 to 36 per cent.) would appear to show. In this period industrial productivity at least doubled.

The scale of this process of concentration becomes evident when we bear in mind that it took place principally in the three great metropolitan areas of Barcelona, Madrid and Vizcaya, which absorbed almost the total volume of

Table 1 Structure of the economically active population Spain

|      | Primary sector | Secondary sector | Tertiary sector |
|------|----------------|------------------|-----------------|
| 1950 | 40%            | 26%              | 26%             |
| 1960 | 40%            | 33%              | 27%             |
| 1970 | 26%            | 36%              | 37%             |

urban growth. With actual densities of approximately 500 inhabitants per square kilometre (national average 50 per square kilometre) these three areas account for more than 26 per cent. of the population.

In Spain, therefore, we have an urban industrial society which ranks among the first twenty countries in the world. However, the process of development has taken place under particular economic and political conditions and has produced high social costs.

Firstly, throughout the period 1939–56, urban immigration has been caused by rural poverty rather than by the attraction of urban employment. Unemployment, subemployment and casual labour are, therefore, common phenomena. This situation has been modified by the industrial development of the last fifteen years and by emigration abroad so that the marginal population, or reserve army of labour of the three great metropolitan areas, is not large, although immigration provides a cheap and mobile labour force which is obliged to take on the hardest and most precarious jobs.

Secondly, the process of urban concentration has occurred without corresponding social investment, in other words without public provision of the necessary urban facilities of housing and services. During the first phase the reality, or at least the legitimacy, of the centralization process was denied in terms of a traditional 'ruralist' concept of society and the fear that was aroused by large industrial working class concentrations:

'A few industrial centres are becoming filled with a newly-arrived population, the best instrument for all kinds of revolution from the communist to the separatist.'[1]

The result was a laissez faire urban policy turning the cities into chaotic encampments, saturated and underequipped. The city was seen by the state merely as an object of public order. Housing and planning were the responsibility of the Ministry of the Interior (Ministerio de Gobernacion) until 1956.

Business and industry of all kinds became established in the city in search of the immediate maximization of particular advantages and remained unregulated until the middle of the fifties. The urban population had to adapt itself to existing facilities: for twenty years the construction of low-rent housing was minimal and the increase in the provision of services (schools, hospitals, etc.) almost negligible. The development of the urban fringe at the beginning of the fifties, particularly in Madrid and Barcelona, gave rise to various forms of marginal housing from shacks to buildings of a minimal standard.

During the entire period the city was a source of indirect benefit to capital, which failed to take account of the urban costs (for example, the weakness of local finance) and which, furthermore, accumulated land in reserve for more profitable times. Production was located according to traditional patterns and with considerable lack of organization. The resulting saturation was worse where the decentralization of much small and medium-sized industry was difficult (in Barcelona as opposed to Madrid, for example). The middle sectors could obtain certain compensations, firstly rented blocks, then subsidized housing, participation in speculative ventures in certain cases, and second homes. But the working classes were the victims of the lack of social investment in housing and services. The reproduction of the work force at the least possible cost has, in this case, a literal meaning.

However, during the fifties, the situation became rapidly untenable. Industrial growth stimulated a rapid acceleration of urban immigration, which took place within a disordered urban fabric which was overpopulated and under-equipped. An urbanization of *control* emerged, consisting of general plans for the rigidly formal zoning of central areas, and at the same time the renewal of state apparatus, such as the creation of the Ministry of Housing and the Land Law of 1956. The city began to be a profitable investment, giving rise to land speculation, the construction of protected housing, the use of plans biased towards increased densities, etc. The accumulated deficiencies were a social scandal and led to welfarist responses and the rhetorical denunciation of the so-called 'shanty towns' and 'slums'. Thus, the city became transformed into an object of plunder and of ideology.

The sixties saw the rise of the great problems of a modern metropolis founded on the inheritance of an underdeveloped country. An ambitious planning policy (at least on paper) as much at the regional as at the metropolitan level (growth poles, proposals for the control of conurbations, etc.) failed for lack of economic resources and political will. In fact the Spanish develop-ment model is one of economic growth at any price, producing immediate social costs which are borne by the majority of the population despite the middle range disequilibrium and diseconomies which such a model implies. The authoritarian political system facilitates the application of such a model as a first stage.

In the last fifteen years two new phenomena have appeared. Firstly, a considerable increase in housing construction and the realization of important housing schemes for the middle and lower classes (the number of settlements of above 10,000 dwellings have increased). Current housing policy caters for the demand from those relatively solvent sectors of the community, able, with several years of self-sacrifice and underconsumption, to find the money for an initial deposit. From a social point of view the achievement of stability in this sector is more urgent and necessary. But housing policy also fulfils functions which are anticyclical (particularly important in the context of the rapid 'stop–go' experienced by the developing Spanish economy) and monopolistic (creating opportunities for large projects which exclusively favour the big construction companies linked to finance capital). This does not mean that problems are solved, let alone that the size of accumulated deficits is increased. The construction boom accelerates immigration and the building industry's labour force will remain excluded from access to housing (which is generally for sale) for many years. Furthermore, the new residential areas on the urban periphery lack major services because sufficient new facilities are not being created. Nor is access to existing ones possible, because of distance.

The second phenomena, characteristic of the most recent period, is that of peripheral metropolitan growth. The centre, the conventional city, is becoming ossified. This is due to land values rather than because it is totally occupied or because of restrictive legislation. The city is being lost in the greater metropolitan area, while at the same time the *barrio* or neighbourhood is reappearing as a unit of social cohesion and collective action. The neglect of urban planning and its replacement by more or less coordinated sectoral action is changing the metropolis into a conglomeration of diverse conflicts, particularly in those areas such as Barcelona and the Basque Provinces with a complex social structure and a diverse and heterogeneous physical environment.

## 2. Urban Agencies and Administration: The Crisis of the Political Model

The reality of the metropolitan system has created new and difficult administrative problems. In the first place the necessity of intervention has increased, as has the rate of activities. Such interventions require considerable financial resources; they affect established interests and expectations and their consequence is a transformation of the physical environment which often entails that of the social environment, through taxes, expropriations, transfer of population, etc. To achieve this the administration relies on considerable social consensus and the various groups involved must be able to institutionalize their interests. Without this the government is socially weak and thus oscillates between withdrawal and imposition, between corruption and repression. Secondly, the number of urban agencies has increased: the complex metropolitan system, the opportunities for accumulation generated by urban development, the complexity and multiplicity of private and general interests, the disruption of traditional territorial equilibrium and existing administrative entities, all give rise to the necessity for a new institutional framework to assure the representation of the recipients of metropolitan development and the coherent functioning of the whole. Thirdly, the urban population requires some means of participation or of control (according to one's point of view) which is more complex than those of traditional local government. Its quantitative and qualitative importance, the ideology of mass consumption, the disruption of the traditional framework of integration, rapid growth, planning processes which demand response, deficiencies requiring solution, all entail the establishment of adequate forms of representation and dialogue which are unavoidable in the long term.

None of these demands and necessities find a positive response in the Spanish political system. There is a double weakness in the case of local government:

(*a*) While it is the least repressive sector of the state and has the fewest economic functions, it is the most closely linked to the organization of daily life and to the control and participation of the population. Thus it necessarily requires a strong representative element, which it does not have under the present Spanish system. (It is no accident that the timid attempts at democratization are beginning at a local level.)

(*b*) Since 1939 the centralizing ideology of the Spanish state has tended to weaken local government structures, leaving them without autonomous economic resources and functionally replaced by ministerial representatives. More recently this same centralism has been a great obstacle to the creation of new bodies and management structures of a metropolitan and regional nature.

The lack of representativeness creates various distortions in the application of urban policy and has, in some cases, produced almost insoluble obstacles. When ambitious projects which require a substantial degree of public intervention and affect numerous private interests are involved, government is unable to raise explicit support from any active majority. General plans are paralysed or mutilated; major redevelopment schemes are abandoned or transformed into more limited, speculative operations. In the case of sectoral projects, particularly where there is direct intervention from central government, schemes are realized, but interested parties who wish to obtain contracts and concessions establish secret and corrupt relations with administration, beyond the boundaries of public control. The public, for its part, excluded from formulation and decision making in the planning process, can only attempt to resist their consequences. This is generally the case with the operations of the Ministry of Public Works (Ministerio de Obras Publicas) and sometimes in the construction of public housing by the Ministry of Housing (Obra Sindical del Hogar), for example.

The urban dynamic and the increase of urban agencies demands a complex institutionalized relationship between administration and private interests, which is both public and flexible. Local government has been the traditional means by which the dominant interests have divided the urban cake in an orderly way and the representation of the remaining interests minimized conflict and inequality. Now, however, as both urban opportunities and scarcities multiply we are faced with a local government system which does not even represent the dominant interests adequately. Thus any urban project becomes an occasion for conflict to the extent that, apart from those who are direct beneficiaries, almost all find themselves excluded or prejudiced by the operation. In the case of Barcelona and the Basque Provinces the negative attitude of central government towards the incipient regionalism of these areas has accentuated the dependency and rigidity of local government structures. Urban politics thus becomes a bilateral affair between an administrative body and an urban agency confronting the rest of the population.

But the weakness of local government is particularly apparent with regard to the mass of the population, the citizens, the users of goods and services, housing and facilities, who live their daily lives within a sub-local framework such as the *barrio* (neighbourhood) or estate. They share an urban ideology that is ambivalent in its effects, in that while it establishes a false symbolic cohesion, it implicitly recognizes similar social and political rights for the whole population. The pressing demands of a population which has been victimized for more than two decades but which has, in the last few years, increased its level of consumption and requirements focus on local government for an improvement in urban living conditions. Faced with such demands, the administration, lacking significant repressive powers of its own, finds itself without even the minimal instruments of representation and negotiation. Even when it attempts dialogue (for example, Maso, the present Mayor of Barcelona, with the working class *barrios*) the lack of institutional mechanisms and the permanence of an entrenched local political class invalidates the attempt, or limits it to the resolution of transitory situations. Under present conditions in which, as we shall see, government is obliged to pursue a more aggressive urban policy the handicap of a type of local government which transforms the tensions and contradictions of the reconstruction and development process into sharp conflicts introduces an element of political instability and an obstacle to urban policy itself. This is due to the fact that the magnitude or urban conflict generates costs which end by being greater than the advantages, represented by the uncontrolled use of the city (itself impossible above a certain level of economic development and social complexity).

At present in Spain the following urban agents can be distinguished in schematic form.

### a. Major Property Interests, Linked to Finance Capital

Finance capital acts as a land owner, as does industrial capital (particularly when the use of urban industrial location is changed). It is important to distinguish speculative tendencies, linked to the old political machine and to the traditional use of the city through corruption and immediate advantage gained from absence of control, from rationalizing tendencies, involved in specific beneficial schemes, in regulating the land market, in satisfying differential demands and in assuring the minimal coherence of the urban system.

### b. Small Ownership in the Form of Land or Property

Small owners participate in speculation and the uncontrolled use of the city; they seek integration within the dominant interest group at the urban level (an aim which is impossible owing to local government structure) and are progressively displaced by the double tendency towards monopoly and rationalization in urban policy. The case of small industry and commerce is somewhat different, being more concerned to defend their traditional locations against redevelopment policies.

### c. The Stable Residential Population of Controlled Urban Zones

These zones are regulated according to planning standards and not subject to major redevelopment schemes. They are the residential areas of the middle, upper and possibly of the traditional working classes and have relatively good economic conditions and social cohesion.

### d. The Population of the Deprived Areas

These areas are underequipped and subject to change of use or social composition through redevelopment. The working class and sections of the middle class are the groups principally affected, as much by the lack of urban policy as by its character, since their necessities and aspirations are seldom taken into account or response to them is very deficient (e.g. in redevelopment schemes or estates).

Each of these agents has a different relationship with government. In the first example the relationship is a positive one but means of representation, competition and control are lacking. In the second, the small capital of the administration of the great cities, long displaced, has been increasingly provided by the peripheral nuclei as they have become incorporated in the metropolitan area. In such cases the local political personnel (counsellors, citizens' associations, etc.) do not achieve effective representation, but can become important when open conflicts and urban movements emerge. The third case is similar. Here one must stress the importance of global demands for political participation by those sectors which are more deeply imbued with an urban ideology and do not generally have to solve urgent problems of urban deprivation. Finally, the working class population of the deprived areas, which relates little if at all to government, is also the sector which has produced the first urban movements and has also created its own original forms of communication with the administration.

In the following we shall see how the relationship between urban political/ administration and public/urban movements has functioned in the last few years, from the end of the sixties until today—a period in which politics has become much more active and urban movements more widespread.

## 3. Urban Contradictions in the Period 1969–74

During the last few years the nature of urban politics has changed. While the fifties saw the appearance of urbanization based on central control and a welfarist ideology and the sixties the tentative rheotoric of planned urban development (with little effect but that of legitimizing the existing chaos), more recently a coordinated and interventionist urban policy has become essential.

(a) The urban organization of production demands an industrial location policy in which industrial zones are far from traditional centres and sites, and above all an ambitious transport and communications policy. The Third

Development Plan (1971) gave priority to this type of investment and to the three largest metropolitan areas.

(*b*) The integration of urban property accumulation within the normal mechanisms of capitalist accumulation and the concurrent necessity to organize chaotic metropolitan development leads to a tripartite policy of

(i) The substitution of fruitless attempts to achieve overall public planning by coordinated sectoral intervention (Urgent Plans Act 1970—*Decreto Actuaciones Urgentes*).

(ii) The delimitation of areas and usage and the creation of the conditions for the contribution of capital to large schemes such as public works and large suburban residential developments.

(iii) Redevelopment of central and old suburban areas with the aim of changing their function and their social composition.

(*c*) The existence of unsatisfied social demands from the middle and working classes, the viability or the political force of such demands, the necessity of stabilizing the work force and organizing its territorial location, the advisability of securing the reproduction of the work force at a better level of education and consumption, and the increase in 'minimum urban necessities' as a result of economic and urban development, all entail a more ambitious housing and public services policy. Its ideological expression is to be found in the 'importance given to social policy from the Third Development Plan onwards'. Its practical expression is found in

(i) A housing policy based less on direct public support than on direct or indirect grants to private developers (grants to the user are also beginning to be made).

(ii) The creation of large suburban estates which are less complicated to execute than renovation or redevelopment schemes although they produce higher social costs since the existing infrastructure does not improve and underequipped areas are the inevitable result.

(iii) The setting up of a programme of provision of essential services to ensure the reproduction of the labour force at a minimal level (transport, sanitation, schools, etc.).

(iv) Progressive orientation towards a policy of stratified urban services paid for by the users (for example, urban motorways financed by tolls with priority for public transport, selectivity in education and increase in its costs, etc.).

The contradictions generated by urban development itself, and the political responses it gives rise to, are multiple:

(*a*) Industrial decentralization in the metropolitan area, the need for public resources, concessions and contracts for carrying out public works, the establishment of minimal controls or 'rules of the game' for usage and expectation, redevelopment, etc., all give rise to a multiplicity of intercapitalist conflicts.

(i) Some sectors of advanced capitalism are interested in rationalizing the use of urban space and therefore of increasing public control and can bear the costs of decentralization, benefit from it and take over public works contracts and those of the major projects. However, one must also bear in mind the importance not only of small and medium-sized capital excluded from such schemes or unable to afford them but also of significant sectors of speculative and parasitic capital responsible for the existing model of urban development. Such sectors are often connected with, if they are not the same as, sectors of advanced capitalism.

(ii) The need to increase public resources conflicts with one of the cornerstones of the concentration of capital in Spain, low taxation. At the same time 'tradition' that the immediate object of public investment is to create opportunities for private gain makes it difficult for certain kinds of public expenditure and intervention to be regarded as acceptable. To this must be added the limited prestige of government, which is held to be as little effective as it is unrepresentative of 'public interest'.

(iii) Furthermore, inconsistency in the carrying out of such policies, the insufficiency of results and the distortions in the realization of approved projects generate new conflicts. The groups involved range from interested parties who take advantage of the situation to oppose schemes which do not favour them, or in which they do not participate, to technical experts whose 'rational', 'humanistic' ideology leads them to denounce the results of an urban policy they have often helped to formulate and also to citizens' groups and associations who decry the transformation of their traditional environment, as much as their exclusion from participation.

(b) But the sharpest contradictions concern the users of urban services and it is from these that urban movements emerge.

(i) 'Aggressive' urban policies (public works, redevelopment, elimination or transformation of marginal housing settlements) generate a defensive reaction in the population, e.g. the opposition to partial plans.

(ii) In other cases living conditions deteriorate through the form taken by by urban development itself: the siting of housing in inappropriate areas, e.g. those subject to flooding, the presence of rubbish tips or incineration plants or of 'dirty' industries in residential areas and, above all, the location of new housing developments on the urban periphery, so that they are not only underequipped but lack the advantages (which the older suburbs possess) of a nearby urban environment and services.

(iii) Moreover, the needs and aspirations of the urban population increase. Access to schools and hospitals and the existence of public transport become part of the minimum level of services necessary for the reproduction of the labour force. The increase in the level of consumption and its reflection in the dominant ideology and mass communication which links social acceptability to housing quality produce definite expectations in the population as far as housing is concerned. The persistence and even aggravation of urban deficiencies and the lack of fit between available housing and the ideal generate the most typical conflicts.

(iv) The existence of a strong working class movement in the large industrial metropolitan areas stimulates and reinforces urban movements. To the extent that the population involved is one and the same, workers' movements have already demonstrated the usefulness and viability of collective action. The wage struggle has as an immediate corollary the struggle for the defence or improvement of living standards or of collective consumption (indirect wages). Furthermore, the form of action and organization of the workers' movement influences urban movements, although they are more difficult to mobilize, because of the heterogeneity and dispersal of their social base and of their interests and objectives.

(v) Lastly, it must be emphasized that a related series of 'democratic' political protests, specific to the middle classes, have been articulated around the urban problematic. These groups, which are marginal to the political system, find that the problems of the urban milieu provide them with a means of participation and the expression of demands. From this base support for urban protest emerges, as well as opposition to plans and planning schemes, the denunciation of corruption, demands for the democratization of the administration, the activities of professional bodies, the Press and citizens' associations, etc. In Catalonia and the Basque Provinces the existence of the problem of 'unrecognized nationality' adds considerable force to such demands.

Before passing to a more detailed analysis of recent urban movements we can sum up the general framework within which such conflicts take place, in the following points:

(*a*) In the most recent period the tensions and contradictions between the various protagonists in the urban system have become more acute and a modification of the balance of power between them has occurred.

(*b*) The political system, and local government in particular, is noticeably weak both as a regulator and as a protagonist in organization and change and, above all, as an arbitrator in situations of conflict.

(*c*) These conflicts are a means, albeit a distorted one, for the expression of more general political conflict, and this fact increases their scope and strength.

## II

### 4. Urban Movements 1969–74: Urban Effects

Until the end of the sixties one could not talk, strictly speaking, of 'urban movements', at least if we conceive of such movements as possessing effectiveness, continuity, institutional responsiveness, social identification, cumulative progressive and organizational development.

Until the development of the sixties, the working classes in the city had been resigned to the high social costs of urban property accumulation and concentration. The effects of the war and the authoritarian nature of the political system, emigration and the search for work as a prime objective led to a low level of social aspiration and non-existant potential for political action. Self-help was the only solution to subsistence problems, e.g. the construction of shanties, squatter settlements and the collective occupation of houses, deschooling and child labour, non-use of transport, sanitation and administrative services (because they are inaccessible), and the provision of services for the *barrio* (neighbourhood) such as lighting, street cleaning, sewerage, and even the construction of social centres, by the inhabitants themselves. Even if many of these solutions were illegal, the laissez faire tradition in city planning, which lasted until the fifties and which has not completely disappeared if one goes far enough from the centre, is essential for the provision of the minimum urban necessities for such a population. On some occasions limit-situations produced resistance, e.g. the opposition of squatters to expulsion, or even organized disturbances, such as the Barcelona tram boycott of 1951. In such cases the action can have immediate results, normally in the form of 'social assistance', but the lack of continuity of the protest, unless it actually modifies the balance of power, prevents the advantages won from being maintained.

The middle classes, for their part, depoliticized and lacking means of collective action and living in relatively privileged urban areas which are still not dynamic, are unlikely to provide either a basis for their own movements or support for popular action. An urban movement requires an equilibrium of social forces and a certain economic dynamic. This assures that demands are expressed, must be recognized and negotiated, are capable of acceptance, even if partial, are socially 'legitimated' and achieve successes and are the creation of organizations which encourage the continuity and development of the movement. None of these factors were present between 1940 and 1960.

However, when the related phenomena of economic development and workers' movements came into being at the beginning of the sixties they did not immediately give rise to urban movements. Various reasons can be suggested for this delay.

The most urgent problems are those connected with direct income and the prospect of increased consumption. Furthermore, working class pressure has the support of a homogenous base, the necessary framework and an immediate and visible antagonist. It can obtain immediate results, its objectives are unified and unequivocal and it has tradition and experience behind it as well as the opportunity and legal means of setting its protests in motion, even if in limited form, through collective agreements, meetings and tribunals. Even though control planning has increased and the administration is more exacting in the maintenance of planning standards, the quasi-legal solution of problems at an individual level has been possible for some time. Such solutions range from squatting and 'autoconstruction' on the urban periphery, although this is increasingly distant from the centre, to the use of contacts and recommendations to obtain public housing. Finally, it must not be forgotten that urban movements often begin as a defensive reaction and that offensive policies did not become evident in the urban sphere until the end of the decade. At this time conditions were produced which enabled urban demands to become generalized. An aggressive policy became necessary to prevent the deterioration of living conditions. The new needs and aspirations of the population conflicted with actual housing conditions, services and environment. The progressive consolidation of collective means of action sometimes even became formalized in legal organizations and local movements received support from wider sectors of the population and citizens' organizations. We shall now turn in greater detail to the kind of movements that appear under such conditions and the part played by these factors.

## a. Natural Movements

The first type of movement is that generated by natural disasters (e.g. flooding), by the rapid deterioration of habitable conditions (rubbish dumps, industrial pollution), by the decrease in the level of existing services (disappearance of a hospital or school) or by the isolation of the area due to redevelopment (an urban motorway cutting off communication). Such movements have been numerous and at times spectacular (Llobregat-Cornella, Santa Coloma, Evandio, etc.). They are capable of acquiring considerable force but often, due to their very nature, are not of long duration. Successes, although partial, are frequent. A positive reaction by the authorities is almost inevitable since such demands form part of the minimal social rights explicitly recognized by the dominant ideology and often even in law. They occur generally in lower class and peripheral areas, although in some cases they have still not become established there. When public reaction does not occur or is weak, the situation may persist indefinitely (as in the case of refuse tips, for example) until a catastrophe arouses collective awareness.

## b. Defensive Movements

Another characteristic movement is also defensive in origin and occurs in areas of marginal settlement which become the object of integration. A typical case is the elimination of areas of shanties and shacks. Another is that which occurs in the illegal settlements on the outskirts of the city, when they are affected by a planning operation of some kind such as public works, zoning as a service area or green belt, or creation of a residential area or industrial estate. Such settlements are sometimes of a quite reasonable standard, whether or not they are the product of 'autoconstruction'. Although it may be possible to stimulate collective mobilization in such cases, this does not always take place due to the low economic level and lack of social organization found. Demands for permanent settlement thus have little chance of success. This is dependent on various factors: centrality of the area or urgency of the project, on the one hand, or cohesion of the affected population and the impact of public opinion, on the other. These factors either facilitate or hinder the operation. In some cases the conflict may be long and give way to complex processes of organization and negotiation (e.g. Pozo de Tio Raimundo); others rapidly disintegrate with the eviction of the population, since such groups can rarely afford the new location. On some occasions, however, the defensive movement acquires force and continuity and is eventually able to ensure the rights of the inhabitants to remain on the site, the improvement and legalization of their housing and the provision of infrastructure and necessary public services (e.g. Montjuic and areas of autoconstruction in Nueve Barrios in Barcelona and Pozo in Madrid).

## c. Movements from Established areas

Some of the most characteristic movements are those occurring in deteriorating central areas or in old suburbs which are today integrated into the central area by partial plans or public works which imply both redevelopment and modification of the social composition of the area. These movements, which are also defensive in origin, generally emerge among those who are expropriated or who are afraid of being expropriated. Since the process of approval and completion of such projects is a long one and they are expressed ideologically in terms of an overall concern for public welfare, the urban movements which appear are likely to be of long duration, generate stable representative organizations and modify their original character to put forward positive and general claims for housing, services and infrastructure. Sometimes these movements manage to combine different interests such as those of working class groups in deteriorating areas, residents of 'acceptable' areas, small land owners and small or medium industrialists and businessmen (e.g. Plan de la Ribera). These are the movements which have had the most complex character so far in Spain, and have been richest in experience (e.g. Nueve Barrios). The long battle which takes place moves from organized protest to legal challenge, from negotiation with government to the elaboration of an advanced programme of demands and from the development of base organizations to collective actions involving those concerned in social reconstruction and the denunciation of existing deficiencies (e.g. 'fiestas', 'olimpiads', assemblies, etc.).

## d. Housing Movements

As far as we know there have been no significant movements of the homeless or 'occupations' such as in Latin America, Italy, France or England (though even these have had little importance, except in Chile and Italy). Nor have there been direct protests in the rented sector and the consequent rent strikes or 'self-reduction' of rent. Instead, protests of a more legal nature have occurred, generally in response to the default of a developer or the provision of housing of an inferior quality to that expected. Such movements occur above all in medium to large estates and recently completed developments. Although the inhabitants do not possess well-developed collective means of action and organization due to their recent arrival, they have in their favour social homogeneity and a shared situation *vis-a-vis* their antagonist. The most important example has probably been that which occurred on the estates of the *Obra Sindical del Hogar* (Housing Ministry) as a protest against the inadequate maintenance of the blocks and their surroundings, the rapid deterioration of the buildings, the lack of infrastructure and access that had been promised. The occupants refused to pay the monthly rent and refused to buy the flats when this was suggested by the O.S.H. Other similar movements have occurred when housing was more expensive than expected, when it deteriorated rapidly (cracks or damp, for example) or when the minimum facilities were not installed. The results of such cases are highly variable, although when the low level of demands is taken into account, they are generally recognized and negotiated, at least in part.

### e. Movements Concerned with Facilities and Services

These are of a well-known generic type covering many different situations: nurseries and schools, public transport, green belts and social centres, old people homes and youth clubs, administrative services, markets, dispensaries and clinics. The list is endless. They occur in central areas or outer areas, as the result of a scheme or development which highlights the existence of a problem or an information campaign which encourages collective awareness. Sometimes they put forward concrete proposals indicating particular zones or areas or condemning existing deficiencies, by means of petitions to public bodies, while at others demands are expressed through illegal activities which create a state of force. Such situations may occur independently or at the same time. The movement may be confined to one facility or cover a whole programme, may be specific to a *barrio* (neighbourhood) or estate, or cover several; it may even take on a city-wide character. This is another type of protest movement which has produced rich experience of conflict, negotiation and organization. In some cases such movements have stimulated or revived the collective life of *barrios* whose social heterogeneity, together with the limitations imposed by the political system, have produced an atomized and apathetic society. In other cases associative life, which had been limited to recreational activities or minority culture, has been considerably enriched. In the last few years Barcelona has seen the revitalization of many of its working and middle class districts through the upsurge of such demands (San Andres, Sants, Guivardo, Barceloneta, etc.) and the same has occurred in other localities in the metropolitan area (Sabadell, Tarrasa, Cornella, Hospitalet, Badalona, Santa Coloma, etc.).

### f. Urbanite Movements

Lastly, the movement generated by the completion of a public works scheme which affects existing urban structure sometimes results in expropriation and relocation of population, but above all substantially modifies the use and image of an area. A characteristic feature of these movements is an emphasis on the defence of the area itself or of the available planning alternative, rather than a defensive response by the affected population (which could be included in one of the previous categories). Such movements are typically 'urbanite' in that they defend not only a particular social situation (maintenance of existing population) but also a particular cultural and aesthetic conception of the city. In Barcelona the opposition aroused by the destruction of public space by urban motorway projects has acquired considerable importance (Plaza Lesseps, Plaza Salvador Anglada). The same could be said of the Prado de San Sebastian in Seville. We find here, more than in the preceding movements, a convergence between the groups most directly affected and others, such as associations from other *barrios*, other city dwellers, educated people, professionals, etc. Planning alternatives are necessary. Such protests mobilize public opinion to a marked degree. Often the exposure of corruption, existing or foreseeable, is an important element. This kind of movement has very unequal effects, producing important results in some situations and insignificant ones in others. This is largely dependent on their continuity and generality, the character of the operation they oppose, the predominant interests involved and their anachronistic or progressive objectives. In general such movements are of a more political nature than the preceding ones, although they also owe more to conciliatory measures and to the passivity of the population.

Various conclusions can be drawn from this. In the first place urban movements, as opposed to most political or vindicatory movements, usually achieve victory, although seldom completely or clearly. We have seen that the outcome of conflict depends on many factors: the economic and social costs of the operation, the agents that are involved or affected (e.g. central government is not the same as local government in this respect), the functional urgency of the project (highway infrastructure is 'more urgent' than a redevelopment project) and the global or sectoral nature of the activity (the last being the most viable, especially when it is of an organized nature). In any case, the urban effects of the movements almost always appear in a tangible form.

Secondly, the political system denies the expression of collective demands outside recognized channels, which are generally extremely limited and in this case practically non-existent, despite the fact that the 'municipality' is, with the 'family' and the 'unions', one of Spain's structures of political participation. We find, however, that within the movements demands cannot only be expressed but are received, recognized, negotiated and satisfied in many cases. Such recognition, if not the tacit or explicit acceptance of the claims, exercises a considerable influence on urban politics so that in subsequent projects, and above all in the formulation of general plans, much of the content of urban movements is accepted. The recent Barcelona Regional Plan *(Plan Comarcal de Barcelona)* is significant in this respect. In any case, demands and responses have cumulative effects and urban movements tend to put forward a progressively higher level of claims and demands for rights.

Lastly, the level of general application attained by some movements, such as that concerned with the Barcelona Regional Plan and the creation of a wide federation of Residents Associations, for example, modifies the balance of power in the urban system and also has more general political consequences, as we shall see in the following sections.

## 5. Urban Movements: Political Aspects

### a. Political Effectiveness

The political effectiveness of urban movements can be analysed from three points of view:

(1) They constitute an axis around which the working classes can organize to fight collectively for their interests. Firstly, urban movements are a means of reuniting the population and of stimulating collective action; this is important given the situation of atomization and defencelessness in which the masses find themselves. Secondly, such collective action often results in immediate victory; the acquisition of goods, services or rights; the halting of a partial plan; and compensation, improvement of facilities or recognition of a residents' association, with considerable positive effects on the consciousness of the population and their confidence in their own powers. Thirdly, urban movements often rise above their immediate local context to express generalized and stable demands; e.g. those affected by a plan may join the offensive movements of working class *barrios* affected by similar plans.

So long as it puts forward general objectives *vis-a-vis* government, the urban movement constitutes a base upon which a working class movement with a marked political character can be developed.

Lastly, these movements provide a means of organization for important sectors of the population and, while informal and often illegal in their inception, they later acquire formality and legality, thus assuring their continuity, representiveness and capacity for dialogue and negotiation.

(2) Urban movements provide an occasion for the convergence of distinct social interests, for the formation of class alliances and the establishment of social and political alternatives. We have already seen that these movements are not specific to a limited social group (e.g. immigrant workers who have settled in a squatter area), but that they include a wide spectrum of groups and situations. Workers who are also likely to take part in labour movements participate, as do other groups for whom protest is practically impossible, such as small craftsmen, the self-employed or those whose demands cannot find collective expression (technicians, middle management, professionals, etc.). In any case, the movements unify the practices and objectives of those social sectors which act disparately at other levels. It is important to stress the opportunity which such movements offer for the collective action and organization of the middle classes whose heterogeneity in relations of produc-

tion makes it very difficult for them to act collectively at the work level, and also for others to whom the political system affords little scope for action. The participation of the middle classes occurs on three distinct levels:

(*a*) As groups, affected by and involved in concrete situations, due to the fact that they are often affected negatively by the urban politics of the state and metropolis and their participation in the drawing up and completion of projects and schemes is limited.

(*b*) As citizens, active at the political-ideological level, who support concrete demands and generalize them, who expose corruption and the authoritarian management of particular organizations and who demand the democratization of local life.

(*c*) As a cultural elite, who have a wider margin of manoeuvre, can make use of certain types of recreational, cultural, professional or residential associations, can easily obtain institutional support (church, schools, professional, Press) and can mount general campaigns with much greater ease (e.g. on Development Plans, Education, etc.). The demands for autonomy and the expression of regional culture in Catalonia and the Basque Provinces, which have an important social base among these groups and whose demands are easily articulated with 'urban' demands, constitute an important broadening and sharpening element in urban movements.

Because of the level of generality that can be attained and the breadth of the social base from which the movements can draw their support, it is logical that they should put forward different alternatives for both the development model and the political model (see section 8).

(3) Urban movements become an important crisis factor in some political structures. Through them the population exercises rights, creates organizations, expresses forcible demands and finds the institutional system unable to provide adequate responses or even a framework for their reception. Since such movements are not easily suppressed (because of their broad social base, the legitimacy of demands, etc.) the consequence is an accentuation of the crisis of local government structures. Furthermore, urban movements often influence internal contradictions within dominant social groups and even within political institutions themselves. The fight against general planning schemes, deficiencies of housing and services, corruption and speculation, etc., not only accentuates these internal contradictions but highlights the incapacity of the rigid and unrepresentative political system to allow them free expression and resolution. In short, we can say that urban movements have a markedly democratic nature and represent the democratic option in Spanish society: the convergence of political objectives in the struggle for the realization of working class demands, of the necessity of middle class participation and of the advantageousness of a more open and representative political system for the dominant classes.

*b. The Political Process of the Formation of Urban Movements*
Today, urban movements are characterized above all by:

(1) The existence of widespread mobilization, which while seldom violent expresses strong social pressures.

(2) The transformation of specific, discontinuous movements of a defensive nature into stable, continuous actions, with global objectives, in many cases.

(3) The development of an important legal 'associative' life with a considerable degree of popular and even administrative representativeness.

We have already indicated the general factors which explain the emergence and development of urban movements. However, the gap between these general causes and actual mobilization and organization requires the mediation of those active and dedicated individuals who constitute the most advanced element of the population. The political process to which I refer is the conscious action of the vanguard. For a long time active and organized nuclei have existed (formal or informal, legal or illegal) which have initiated the social or political action of the *barrio*. But groups relating their praxis to urban problems and developing the corresponding movements and organizations have only recently appeared.

In such cases we can distinguish three different types:

(1) Organizations which are integrated, dependent on or connected with the state apparatus; district councils and local mayors, centres of the *Movimiento* (Falange, Womens' Section, Youth Organization, etc.), Associations of Heads of Families, etc. None of these organizations have generally been capable of encompassing or representing the population and even less of putting forward their demands and aspirations, particularly in the largest cities. In some cases there has been some kind of relationship between local government and members of the local political elite. In others various attempts, now abandoned, have been made to assure political control, of a fascist nature, over broad groups of the middle and working classes. Only on one occasion have Associations of Heads of Families achieved representativeness and effectiveness, breaking their links with government in the confrontation.

(2) Cultural, recreational, welfare and religious organizations. Here the term 'organization, is used in a wide sense. Such groups do not put forward explicit demands for improved living standards and public participation and may even sometimes contribute to the evasion or distortion of these questions (setting up other more innocuous activities or seeing only the individual aspect of problems). However, in that it unites the population, assures a minimum of collective life and concerns itself in one form or another with some aspect of living conditions, this kind of organization can encourage discontent and facilitate the germination of active groups. Parish, cultural and even sports centres have often played an important part in the inception of urban movements.

(3) Another kind of active organization, this time of an illegal nature, is that which foments political opposition in the *barrio*. In some cases there have been youth groups which have espoused the ideology of revolutionary agitation. In others there have been attempts, largely unsuccessful, to organize workers by residential areas. In yet others groups have been formed to take over the representation of different sectors and institutions and to support democratic political change. While this type of organization as such has seldom been to the forefront of urban movements, it is nevertheless certain that the raising of consciousness, the active groups that have been created, certain campaigns that have been promoted and the politicization that has been brought to various legal organizations, etc., have undoubtedly contributed to the development of a particular kind of urban movement. However, it is also certain that on other occasions they have become completely inoperative, if not negative, by isolating active groups from the rest of the population.

The active groups that have been mediators between objective conditions and urban movements have generally started from the following analysis (which has seldom been explicit):

(1) A general characteristic of the period is the reconstitution of the capacity for action and collective organization among the working classes, a process which has principally operated through conflicts over rights.

(2) The *barrios* constitute units of social life and protest in that they are the framework in which the deficiencies of collective consumption, which urban contradictions tend to accentuate, are realized (as we have already seen).

(3) The development of the movement requires the presence and initiative of a group which coordinates latent problems and necessities, informs the population, begins to pinpoint demands and instigates the first meetings and collective activities. This working group needs to be open to the population but, not possessing legal status, it must also act with caution.

The process *barrio* movements follow during their first phase has already been described on other occasions: the information of the population and the raising of consciousness by means of the exposition of problems, the identification of their immediate causes and the denunciation of those responsible, and broadly based meetings which become representative assemblies in which demands and actions capable of exercising an effective pressure are specified (from a signed petition, a denunciation or a challenge to a rent strike, a demonstration or the occupation of a site). The action taken has corresponding urban effects (as indicated above) and above all modifies the political character of the urban movement. As the population, the *barrio*, is mobilized it establishes the continuity of the course of action embarked upon or it puts forward new demands. To the extent that they have been expressed, fought for and at times satisfied, these demands acquire recognition and a certain social legitimacy which facilitates their development. Above all, collective action generates and stabilizes wider, more representative and even legal forms of organization, in which the initial active nucleus becomes assimilated or takes on the function of a global political vanguard.

## 6. Experts, Press and Professional Associations

These groups deserve separate mention because of their specific importance in urban movements. In the last few years there has been a considerable social demand for studies, projects, evaluations, critical information, etc., by planning specialists and professionals (architects, engineers, sociologists, economists, surveyors, geographers and lawyers). The new importance of urban politics, the complexity of conflicting interests, the various functions that a plan, programme or scheme has to fulfil (from the ideology of public well being to financial profitability) have all multiplied the tasks and activities that are involved in planning. The breakdown of these functions, not only because of factors also found in other capitalist countries (global plans are not completed, disequilibrium increases and social priorities are not respected) but for reasons specific to the Spanish model of politics and growth, leads to the radicalization of the specialists involved. Thus when government projects and activities provoke opposition, a number of specialists are ready to inform and advise the movement. They perform the triple function of information (about the scope and character of the project, its consequences, legal resources, etc.), of explanation (about the links between one project and others, the logic that governs urban policy) and of legitimization (their professional authority, language and image reassures the population during initial action and encourages good reception by public opinion).

In this phase the specialist, for his part, discovers the nature and respective strengths of the various urban agents involved. In the second phase, as a consultant integrated in the movement, he plays his previous role more widely, but also contributes to the evaluation of deficiencies and compensations and, above all, makes a fundamental contribution to the analysis of the reactions of the antagonists (public and private) and to the development of a programme of demands and alternative projects. In this second phase the specialist can distinguish what is rhetorical and what is real in urban planning projects, what is a priority and what is less vital, and what can be changed or blocked or can merely claim increased consumption.

On the other hand, the Press and professional associations broaden the expert's functions, particularly by contributing to the legitimacy of the movement, obtaining the support of public opinion and widening the movement to other *barrios* and social groups. They play a fundamental role in cases in which local protest develops into a city-wide movement of a more political nature.

## 7. The Fundamental Importance of the Associations Today

As we have already shown, many urban movements have recently started or revitalized their own autonomous, legal organizations, such as residents' groups, etc. In some cases these associations have managed to form a federation, as they have done in Barcelona. It is obvious, given the present political situation, that public and legal existence is precarious—so much so that in Bilbao and Valencia the most dynamic associations have been suspended by government decree. In other cases, such as in Barcelona and its province, the achievement of definitive recognition has been put back months or even years. Even when they are legalized, the associations encounter limitations, obstacles and prohibitions when trying to organize collective action.

But despite everything it is inevitable that the process of protest tends to be developed within the framework of these associations and only departs from it on a few occasions. Except in limit-situations or special circumstances only a legal or tolerated association has the power of assembly to unite the population, to be recognized in negotiation and to be able to assume responsibility at the moment of decision making. Residents' groups can meet from time to time (especially in moments of greatest tension), workers' groups are assured of the participation of an important sector of the population, but not only are they no substitute for the associations but they also make them more necessary for the preparation and coordination of their activities.

The association is an instrument of struggle, of the defence of popular interests against the administration and public and private institutions which ignore such interests. As such its strength lies in the endorsement given it by the population and the collective pressure it can exercise. Because of this the association tries to ensure the *active* participation of the residents, putting forward collective interests forcefully and not becoming limited to merely 'representing' the residents in tactful dialogue with the authorities or in joint commissions without real power. The 'self-help solution' of problems (housing cooperatives, schools, building, etc.) is neither the responsibility nor the function of the associations, although in certain exceptional cases this kind of initiative can lend prestige to the organization and cohesion to the population (e.g. the residents of Can Clos, Barcelona, built their own social centre). The association must be an autonomous organization with its own programme, but not one that is marginal to other institutions.

But the function of residents' associations cannot be reduced to that of demand making. In some *barrios* with a strong associational life, a great diversity of organizations exist (sports, folklore, cultural, youth, women, religious, heads of families, etc.). In these cases the residents' association appears to be more concerned with urban protest—trying to make the other organizations lend their support (this is the case in the older working class districts). In other cases only one or two organizations exist in the *barrio* and these tend to fulfil a multiplicity of functions: from the football club that launches a campaign for public hygiene to the residents' association that organizes swimming or sex education classes. In any case, in a situation such as the Spanish one, after thirty-five years of the most minimal collective life, it is vital for the development of an association that it knows how to combine its demands with any kind of other activity which can unite the population, help the association to take root in the *barrio* and intensify social life.

Recently, various initiatives have been developed to good effect, as far as the wider repercussion of the associations in concerned:

(a) Magazines or bulletins. Innumerable associations produce magazines or bulletins which reach a great part of the *barrio*. These publications not only analyse concrete urban problems but also discuss wider questions ranging from those of a cultural or recreational nature to statements and critiques of general problems (labour disputes, political repression, corruption, etc.).

(b) Exhibitions dealing with the *barrio* in general or some of its particular problems. From their preparation to their effects on the inhabitants, such exhibitions all contribute to the raising of consciousness.

(c) Symbolic occupations, with women and children, laying of foundation stones, *fiestas* in open spaces or other places claimed for public use, transform a primarily illegal action into something irreproachable and even sometimes acceptable to the authorities.

(d) Conventions and public dialogue with the government, the discussion of studies and programmes, the presentation of alternative projects, etc. These sorts of activity are more difficult to achieve and by following an ancient pattern have without doubt the double advantage of hastening the development of the urban movement and of sharpening the crisis of anachronistic political forms.

Lastly, it must be stressed that the life of the associations cannot be reduced merely to that of urban protest or to social and cultural activities. The associations also take up political positions of a general nature, in spite of the fact that this is not one of their specific attributes. In some cases this is because such positions correspond to their general demands (e.g. democratization of government, election of mayors and councillors). In others it is in solidarity with others movements (workers, students, etc.), emphasizing their own roles as workers, heads of households, etc. Finally, in others the association as a citizens' group takes a position towards particularly serious political action: deaths resulting from the repression of collective conflict, death sentences, fascist-type terrorist outrages, etc.

In all these cases what is important is whether or not the position corresponds to that held by the citizens whom the association represents, and whether they are aware of and prepared to support it, rather than the strict legality of such position-taking, which is always a debatable question. For it is public support which protects the association from possible government reprisal.

## 8. Conclusion: Elements of a General Programme and the Relationship of Urban Movements to Government

The urban movements of recent years have formulated general programmes which share many common elements. The principal ones are:

(*a*) The right to decent housing not costing more than 10 per cent. of the salary of the head of household per month and the right to immediate rehousing in the same zone or *barrio*, in case of expropriation caused by redevelopment or public works.

(*b*) Programme of provision of services for each zone or *barrio* according to existing deficiencies, demand for a well-equipped centre servicing the whole area, necessity for medium-sized facilities in each area rather than large-scale facilities at a distance (e.g. hospitals, colleges, etc.), and maintenance of the public or social service character of the facilities and opposition to the policy of stratification of provision and profitability of function.

(*c*) Maintenance of traditional urban networks for their cultural value and for the richness of their social life and the demand that new residential areas make collective life and interaction possible (centres and public meeting places, adequate communications), and opposition to public works which destroy these networks and isolate one area from another.

(*d*) Priority for rehabilitation schemes, rather than the creation of large isolated estates, and the demand that developments should be the responsibility of public initiative or that there should be strict public control to assure the fulfilment of public programmes and allow for public participation.

(*e*) Recognition of the right of the associations to study and control budgets and projects which affect their area or *barrio* and to regulate their subsequent execution, and freedom to form resident's associations and for them to function autonomously.

(*f*) Democratization of local government, elections to all public offices, especially those of mayor or councillors, and freedom of association, assembly and advertising to enable the exercise of these political rights.

It is obvious that such objectives clash with the character of the present government, its urban policies and its policies in general. The priority given to intensive monopolistic capitalist accumulation and investment in the service of production and exchange, urban aspects of the model of growth, are in opposition to the objectives formulated by urban movements, objectives which nevertheless eventually find support in certain rationalizing or advanced sectors of government or capital. On the other hand, political demands of a democratic kind are a response to the increasing necessity for participation which is frustrated by the current political system and which accentuates the crisis of such a system.

In this situation the practice of open and legal action followed by the movements whenever possible, in some cases occupying positions within local government (through *de facto* commission or even by putting up council candidates), seems condemned, at first sight, to oscillate between achievement and repression. In fact nothing is farther from this than those uban movements which put forward a general programme based on popular interests, with clearly formulated democratic demands, and which openly denounce corruption and an urban politics serving major capitalist interests. These movements can only maintain and reinforce their social support to the extent that they do this publicly, putting forward concrete demands and negotiating their outcome with the government. The satisfaction of demands is obtained neither by the concrete nature of the claims nor by their negotiation, but by the demoralization of the authorities concerned. With regard to the defencelessness of the associations against possible repressive measures, it is enough to record two arguments of general validity in Spain today:

(*a*) Without open and representative forms of activity and organization the potential for political demands latent in Spanish society will be unable to express itself.

(*b*) The effectiveness of repression by the most reactionary elements in the present political system would not only be very limited but would also contribute to the isolation of such elements.

The urban movement which exists in Spain today is not specifically a labour movement, although it has its principal base in the working class *barrios* and zones. Nor is it merely a protest movement with short term or, alternatively, anticapitalist or socialist objectives. All these types exist, since the movements are extraordinarily diverse and the force working within them are multiple. But to reduce urban movements to their most generic aspects and their commonest objectives they may be defined as movements whose social base is the working and middle class, with occasional support from advanced capitalist groups, arising in response to the inescapable necessity of defending living conditions in the wider sense and which above all in the present Spanish situation have a strong political element of a democratic nature.

### Note

1. Pedro Salvador Cuesta SJ, El sentido patriotico del emplazamiento de las industrias, *La Vigoracion Economica de Castille*, Madrid, 1960.

### Bibliography

Borja, J., Elementos teóricos para el analisis de los movimientos reivindicativos urbanos, *Cudernos de Arquitectura*, Barcelona, **94**, 1973.

Borja, J., Movimientos urbanos y estructura urbana, *Documentos de Analisis Urbano*, **1**, 1974.

Borja, J., Tarrago, M., and others, *La Gran Barcelona*, Libro de la Frontera, Barcelona, 1972.

Dols, J. A., and Borja, J., Cronica Urbana section of *Cuadernos de Arquitectura*.

Articles by Piere, R., Borja, J., Brau-Teixidor-Tarrago, Sola Monales, M., in El fet urbá a Barcelona, *CAU No. 20 and 22*, 1973.

Borja, J., Politica Urbana

Tarrago, M., Politica urbana en España 1939–74

Brau, L., Papel del tecnico, *Documentos del centro de Estudios Urbanos*.

Olives, J., Los costes sociales del desarrollo urbano, Banco Urquijo, 1973. "Movimento social urbano" (typescript).

See also:
Bulletins and magazines of *barrios* of Barcelona: Nueve Barrios, San Andreu, Guinardo, Carmelo, etc., and of other districts within the metropolitan area: Grama (Santa Coloma), El pensamiento (Cornella), Can Oriach (Sabadell), etc.

Documents of *Barrio* councils, especially 'Document of the assembly of 1972', Barcelona (Cuadernos del Movimiento Obrero y Popular No. 5).
The Political groups that have given most attention to urban movements are the Communist Party (several articles in *Mundo Obrero* and special numbers of *Unitat y Treball*, 1972), and Bandera Roja (Documentos Lucha Popular, 1972–74).

# Index